FACING THE FUTURE:
AMERICAN
STRATEGY
IN THE
1990s

An
Aspen Strategy Group
Report

Published by
The Aspen Strategy Group
and
University Press of America
1991

The Aspen Institute

Library of Congress Cataloging-in-Publication Data

Facing the future : American strategy in the 1990s
/ the Aspen Strategy Group.
p.   cm.
1. United States—Foreign relations—1989-
2. United States—National security—Planning.
3. World politics—1985-1995.
I. Aspen Strategy Group (U.S.)
E881.F27   1990
327.73—dc20   90–25614 CIP

ISBN 0–8191–8159–5 (cloth : alk. paper)
ISBN 0–8191–8160–9 (pbk. : alk. paper)

Co-published by arrangement with
The Aspen Institue for Humanistic Studies

The Aspen Institute for Humanistic Studies and its logo
are trademarks of The Aspen Institute for Humanistic Studies.

Cover Design: Edward Lyon

 The paper used in this publication meets the minimum requirements of
American National Standard for Information Sciences—Permanence
of Paper for Printed Library Materials, ANSI Z39.48–1984.

The Aspen Strategy Group

The Aspen Strategy Group is a bipartisan committee organized under the auspices of The Aspen Institute. The Group's primary goal is to help advance thinking and practice in the areas of international security and East–West relations. It aims to relate differing perspectives about the long-term direction of American security to current policy debates. As a standing body, the Group acts as a source of private policy advice; it contributes to the public debate through reports and other publications; and it encourages the study of broad conceptual issues that shape security but are sometimes hurried over in debates regarding immediate policy choices.

Contents

About This Report

This study is part of a series of reports prepared under the auspices of the Aspen Strategy Group, a program of The Aspen Institute. As a bipartisan standing committee, the Group aims to relate differing perspectives about the long-term direction of international security to current policy debates in the United States. Its members are drawn from the American academic, policy, and business communities.

This report was written and prepared by the directing staff: Bobby Inman and William Perry (cochairmen), Joseph Nye (director), and Roger Smith (executive director). Many of the ideas in this report were presented and discussed at two Aspen Strategy Group workshops; the first was held at The Aspen Institute's Wye Center on March 2–3, 1990 and dealt with "The New Directions and New Sources of Insecurity in Global Politics"; and the second, which looked at "New Threats, New Responses, New Choices: American Strategy for the 1990s," was held on August 12–17, 1990 in Aspen, Colorado. Participants from the Aspen Strategy Group at the week-long conference in August included Antonia Chayes, Kenneth Dam, John Deutch, Paul Doty, Sidney Drell, Leslie Gelb, Arnold Horelick, Karen House, William Hyland, Bobby Inman, David Jones, Lawrence Korb, Jan Lodal, Joseph Nye, William Perry, George Rathjens, Alice Rivlin, Roger Smith, John Steinbruner, Strobe Talbott, Albert Wheelon, and Charles Zraket.

Guests at the August workshop included Ruth Adams, John Chipman, Richard Cooper, Stanley Hoffmann, Robert Hormats, Karl Kaiser, Robert Malott, Thierry de Montbrial, Theodore Moran, Frederic Mosher, Daniel Okimoto, Thomas Pickering,

Daniel Schorr, and William Webster. We are very grateful for their participation and contributions. We are especially indebted to those who prepared major background papers and/or delivered detailed presentations for the August conference: John Chipman, Richard Cooper, Stanley Hoffmann, David Jones, Lawrence Korb, Theodore Moran, Joseph Nye, Daniel Okimoto, William Perry, Alice Rivlin, John Steinbruner, and Charles Zraket.

Generous support for this project was provided by the Carnegie Corporation of New York and the John D. and Catherine T. MacArthur Foundation. The authors of this report would also like to thank Ann Callahan for all her detailed comments, criticisms, and editorial assistance. Finally, we would like to express our appreciation to W. Daniel Wright and his colleagues at The Aspen Institute for computer services and production support.

Readers should take careful note that the contents of the report are the sole responsibility of the directing staff of the Aspen Strategy Group. Other group members and workshop participants, as well as sponsoring organizations and The Aspen Institute, are not responsible for the views or opinions expressed in this report.

Executive Summary

Throughout 1989 and into 1990 the world was treated to a succession of dramatic and far-reaching political events. In Europe the pace of change was the greatest. Coming hard upon the heels of the European Community's decision to reinvigorate itself through the creation of a single market was the largely peaceful transition to democracy in Central and Eastern Europe. Shattering any doubt that a revolution in international politics was afoot was the quick movement toward German reunification. And casting a long shadow across Europe's evolution was the growing turmoil to the east in the Soviet Union. Although the pace of change was greatest in Europe, it was by no means confined to that continent. Elections in Nicaragua, the unbanning of anti-apartheid groups in South Africa, and an invasion of one Arab state by another signaled that the status quo was anything but static.

Writing in the spring of 1776, John Adams wrote that "all great changes are irksome to the human mind, especially those which are attended with great danger and uncertain effects." While the changes of today offer as much opportunity as danger, they are still irksome to those charged with planning American strategy for the 1990s. The guiding purpose behind the workshops sponsored by the Aspen Strategy Group in the spring and summer of 1990 was to try and make those changes less irksome by making the nature, direction, and policy implications of those changes more transparent.

When one looks at the changes in global politics, one can discern three clear trends: a diffusion of power to more states and non-state actors; growth in the networks of transnational interdependence; and, as a consequence of the first two, a fragmentation of the international political system. These changes have made power less fungible, less coercive, and less tangible. The world economy has been marked by a significant increase in the mobility of business enterprises. The consequence for the nation state in the era of the global factory is reduced authority and autonomy. The advance of technology has only reinforced the economic and political trends toward increased integration and interdependence, as new discoveries make it more difficult and even counterproductive to control the distribution of information.

In regional politics the overwhelming trend has been toward a primacy of domestic politics in the determination of a state's foreign policy. Since the end of the Cold War, the superpower rivalry is no longer the ordering principle of international politics. The end of the Cold War has thrust the Soviet Union because of its weakness and Japan because of its strength to the top of policy agendas. Meanwhile, the end of the Cold War threatens the further marginalization of the Third World. The trends in regional politics indicate that three issues above all others will dominate the security agenda for the 1990s: the need to manage the decline of the Soviet Union; the need to reconstruct the bases of European security; and the need to cope with the rise of Japanese power.

Given the changes in the structure and nature of power in the international system, the United States will need to rely on a diplomatic strategy that is at once more co-optive and more flexible in terms of partners, issues, and leadership. Militarily, the United States will have to restructure its forces so as to have a smaller active force and a larger reserve force that is both highly trained and strategically mobile. Economically, the United States will have to adapt to the increased interdependence by resisting protectionist policies and working to preserve the open trading system that has evolved under its leadership since 1945. In regard to domestic politics, the United States will need to curb the federal deficit and increase incentives for greater savings, but most important and requiring presidential leadership, is to educate the American people for a very different role than the one the United States has played in the past forty-five years. For without that kind of support the United States will be unable to operate as effectively as it could/should in the international arena.

Chapter 1

NEW DIRECTIONS
IN GLOBAL POLITICS

I. INTRODUCTION

Does history unfold in a random fashion, or does it move in patterns? Long the subject of endless wrangling by historians, in the summer of 1990 this question was suddenly being debated by presidents and pundits, by people in the know and by people in the street, as they struggled to come to terms with a world in transition. No sooner had the dust begun to settle from a succession of events (the "velvet" revolutions in Eastern Europe, the crumbling of the Berlin Wall, the slow collapse of communist authority in the Soviet Union, and the steady progress toward peace in Central America and Southern Africa), events which had led some to conclude that we had reached the "end of history,"[1] than Iraq invaded Kuwait. Even without the often strident rhetoric comparing the president of Iraq with the chancellor of Nazi Germany, a retreat to analogies based on the 1930s would have been unavoidable, the parallels too close to ignore. The invasion, occupation, and annexation of the small Persian Gulf city-state by its neighbor to the north suggested that in international politics the more things change, the more they stay the same.

The danger with analogies is that they tend to obscure as much as they reveal about current conditions. While Iraq's invasion of Kuwait exposed some of the limits and opportunities for the use of force in contemporary politics, it revealed very little

1

about the sources and types of power that will be most effective in the coming decade and who will wield that power. The purpose of this chapter is to look beyond the events on the surface to the deeper political, economic, and technological currents driving those events. This chapter will be divided into three parts: an examination of the changing nature of power in the international arena, an assessment of new trends in the world economy, and a discussion of the impact of new technologies on the relations between states.

II. THE CHANGING NATURE OF POWER[2]

The debate over whether the past is prologue had been simmering long before the Berlin Wall was sold off to collectors and Iraqi armor rolled into Kuwait City. The organizing focus of this debate was the supposed "decline" of the United States. For some, the decline was symptomatic of a larger process at work. Simply put, the American decline was the harbinger of a new era, an era in which the traditional or "territorial" state is rendered obsolete by the rise of the "trading state."[3] Others saw American decline as part of a larger process as well, but one that was neither new nor revolutionary. The United States was simply following the time-worn path of previous hegemonic powers and allowing "imperial overstretch" to inexorably sap its strength.[4] Still others argued that the alleged decline was exaggerated and the historical analogies misleading.

The debate over decline has masked the real issue at stake in the coming decade: how power is changing in world politics. What discussion there has been of this crucial issue has been distorted by a historically conditioned debate over the distribution of power. The thaw in the Cold War, when joined by the relative decline of the United States and the absolute decline of the Soviet Union, seemingly presages a return to the multipolarity that characterized nineteenth century Europe, with five or six roughly equal powers employing fluid diplomacy and flexible alliances to ensure world stability. There are two principal problems with such a vision. First, as *The Economist* insists, "'multipolarity' is not only bad English, it is sloppy thinking."[5] For conditions of multipolarity to obtain in the 1990s, economic reforms must not only stem but reverse Soviet decline; Japan must develop a full-fledged nuclear and conventional military capability; and Europe must undergo a dramatic political unification. Barring such changes, the United States will remain *the* preeminent power well into the twenty-first century. As the crisis over Iraq's invasion illustrates, the combination of American military, political, and economic might puts the United States into a class all by itself. In the three weeks immediately following Iraq's invasion the United States was able to move more men and matériel to the Persian Gulf than it was able to transfer to Northeast Asia during the first three months of the Korean War. Not only did this deployment dwarf previous American interventions, but it completely overshadowed any other nation's contribution to the defense of Saudi Arabia. During those same three weeks in August 1990, the United States was able to forge a broad-based coalition against Iraq, a coalition that included the Soviet Union and China. This U.S.-led coalition was able to approve economic sanctions against Iraq, approve the use of force to uphold those sanctions, and to arrange for financial support of those nations who would suffer the most from a cutoff of trade with Iraq. It is unlikely that any other nation or collection of nations could have put together such concerted action in such a short period of time. However, by saying that the United States will remain the world's preeminent power is not the same as saying that the United States will exercise the same degree of leverage over the international system that it once did. The fact that limits exist on unilateral action brings us to the next point.

The second reason why multipolarity is an inappropriate term to describe the evolving international system is that it does not take into account, indeed ignores, some very fundamental changes in the international system. Two changes, which were first recognized in the 1970s but which are even more evident today, are the power of non-state actors, such as transnational corporations, and the pervasive condition of economic interdependence. The role of non-state actors and the extent of interdependence have grown as modernization, urbanization, and sophisticated means of communication have found their way into the developing world. The cumulative effect of these trends is to advance the diffusion of power from government to private actors. The result for global politics is a more fragmented, less hierarchical political system.

As the international political system becomes more fragmented, the nature of power will change; it will become less fungible, less coercive, and less tangible. For centuries the currency of exchange in international affairs has been military might. However, the growth of interdependence and the withering of the Cold War has meant that the conversion of military power into economic or diplomatic power is a much more problematic exercise. On different issues, different actors will have different capabilities and vulnerabilities. The fact that interdependence brings benefits to both sides means that attempts at manipulation are more costly than in the past, and problems are less susceptible to threats. Consequently, the balance between "hard" or coercive and "soft" or co-optive power is tilting in favor of the latter. The ability to frame a debate, to set an agenda, to get others to want what you want will be crucial in a more interdependent and fragmented international system. While resources, such as military might and economic wealth, will always be important in the calculus of power, the fragmentation of the political system also implies that intangible resources, such as national cohesion, universalistic culture, and international institutions, are of increasing value. Reinforcing this trend is the changing nature of issues in world politics. "National security," an expansive term even under conditions of *realpolitik*, has come to be associated with a whole set of new issues, from acid rain and global warming to health epidemics (AIDS) and the commerce in illegal drugs.

Thus, in this emerging polyarchic world, the United States will find itself in a situation unlike the one that confronted the last hegemonic power. At the twilight of the nineteenth century Britain was confronted with a growing number of challengers for hegemony. In contrast, the United States at the end of the twentieth century will be confronted with an array of new challenges posed by transnational interdependence.

III. THE WORLD ECONOMY IN 2000 AND 2015[6]

One of the principal challenges of transnational interdependence is the growing internationalization of production. For many years now businessmen have looked beyond national frontiers for markets, sources of supply, and capital. However, in the 1990s a new dimension was added. Driven by competition to get the most from their technology and capital by utilizing low-cost capital, firms have developed suppliers and production sites throughout the world. In addition, firms have tried to improve their competitive position by entering into cooperative arrangements (such as licensing agreements and joint ventures) with firms that may appear to be their rivals in other settings. For example, IBM has entered into joint ventures with Siemens and Toshiba.

This increase in international mobility has a number of policy implications, not the least of which is that changes in economic organization have outrun national political means to control them. The increased mobility of firms has blurred, almost beyond recognition, the distinction between "home" and "host" country. The fact that Japanese firms now produce their goods in America and American firms operate in Japan (albeit with some difficulty) complicates any definition of national economic interest. Even when nations can determine their national interest, it becomes more and more difficult to regulate the activities of transnational firms. Stiff environmental or other regulations will force firms to shift production to countries where there are lower costs to doing business. The high mobility of the modern business enterprise has also reduced the effectiveness of traditional nation-based taxation. Corporations, through their pricing on intra-corporate transactions, can shift profits from nations with high corporate profit rates to those with low ones, thereby reducing or at least deferring their total tax liability.

The internationalization of national economies will have repercussions beyond putting national sovereignty at bay. With greater internationalization, the uncertainty created by flexible exchange rates will be become less and less tolerable to governments, businesses, and populations. The uncertainty regarding exchange rates will drive firms to invest even more abroad in order to hedge against currency risk, which will reduce the overall efficiency of investment; this, in turn, will result in lower living standards than would otherwise be attainable. Exchange rate uncertainty will also compel firms to reduce total investment in tradeable goods and services, which may also reduce living standards. One final consequence of continued exchange rate uncertainty is that it will encourage firms to lobby their governments to reduce by one means or another "unfair" import competition.

The likely increase in calls for protectionist measures raises the question of whether the changes in economic organization have outstripped the international capabilities for managing the world economy. In particular, there is the question of whether international economic institutions, such as the General Agreement on Tariffs and Trade (GATT), can weather the sea changes in the world economy. Throughout the 1980s crucial trade bargains were struck outside the GATT; most notably, the Japanese agreed to "voluntary" trade restraints on automobile exports to the United States. More importantly, the controversy between the United States and the European Community (EC) near the conclusion of the Uruguay Round raises a larger question about the future effectiveness of current institutions. If such protracted disputes can exist between rather similar economies, how will these institutions reach cooperative solutions when their membership is diversified by states such as Mexico, the Soviet Union, and China? In short, can an international order equal to the challenges of transnational interdependence be created out of such national and economic diversity?

The list of potential problems that will complicate the management of the world economy in the future is long and includes such nettlesome issues as the external debt of the Third World, persistent trade imbalances among countries of the developed world, and the protection of intellectual property rights. However, none of these issues is more pressing than the immutable issue of population growth. By the most conservative estimates, the world's population is expected to grow by an annual rate of 1.6 percent a year, which means that by the year 2015 there will 7.7 billion souls on the planet. More people will mean demands for more food, more housing, more capital, and perhaps most importantly, more energy. The demand for energy will be important for two reasons. First, and more obviously, energy is need for warmth, food preparation, illumination, motive power, and production processes. Second, and more critically, the demand for energy is going to be quite high because the world has been "westernized" in its attitudes about living standards; it has absorbed the notion and the expectation of material progress. So in the future, there will be not only more people, but more people wanting higher standards of living. Historically, economic growth has been associated with an enormous growth in demand for commercial primary energy. For example, from 1950–1970 the demand for primary energy in the industrialized countries doubled.

As the world enters the next decade and the next century, it will have to find new or at least better ways to manage economic transactions within and between countries, and nations will have to work harder to increase their energy efficiency.

IV. THE IMPACT OF NEW TECHNOLOGIES ON THE FUTURE[7]

Science and technology do not offer any simple or immediate "solution" to such daunting problems as population growth, but they can moderate such problems. Part of the current demographic problem is due to improvements in medicine and disease prevention, which have reduced the chances for death among the very young and increased our ability to care for the elderly. But technology has not lead man to a Malthusian dead end. At the same time that science has made it possible for man to live longer and healthier, it has made it possible to feed more people than ever before through advances in farming and agriculture. Moreover, since technology is the engine of growth for much of the world's economy, it may be able to moderate population growth over the long term. A slowdown in population growth usually occurs only after per capita income reaches around

$1,000; at this point parents begin to realize that their children's chances for survival are improving and they begin to limit the size of their families. However, it should be noted that any significant change in the population growth rate because of technology should not be expected too soon; currently, one half of the world's population lives in countries where the average per capita income is under $1,000.

Recognition that science and technology can only moderate large problems, such as population growth, should not mask the fact that the world is on the brink of a major technological revolution. The first wave of this nascent revolution will come from an evolving set of strategic or enabling technologies. For much of this century, the leading edge in science was to be found in physics. Atomic physics, quantum theory, and particle physics transformed our understanding of the relationship between matter and energy; this new understanding formed the basis for much of contemporary technology. Today, physics is slowly surrendering its leading role to biology and chemistry. Instead of matter and energy, the new frontiers in science are to be found in the very processes of life. Science has led us to the point where we can not only alter existing life forms, but create brand new ones. The ability to blur the distinction between "natural" and "synthetic," to actually tinker with the machinery of life offers us the ability to create disease- and weather-resistant crops, to program bacteria to clean up pollutants, and to tailor drugs to fight specific diseases. If the biotechnologies are the front edge of this new wave of technology, then the momentum behind this wave comes from the maturing of the information technologies and the material sciences. These are strategic technologies in that they encompass a number of industrial sectors, such as electronics, computer software, and telecommunications; these same technologies are enabling because they can be used as the building block for new applications.

The most fundamental implication for this emerging revolution in technology is that it will enhance the growing condition of transnational interdependence. Most directly, the exercise of national sovereignty will be reduced by the advance of technology as it becomes more and more difficult, through advances in the information technologies, to control the distribution of information. Fiber optic communication networks, like networks of roads before them, will bring the world closer and closer; and the proliferation of sophisticated remote-sensing devices will make each country more and more transparent to its neighbors and to nations on other continents. Indeed, as joint ventures in research and development increase, it will become increasingly counterproductive for states to control the flow of information. The inability to control the flow of information will reinforce two trends: the increasing globalization of the defense technology base; and the proliferation of high-tech weapon systems, conventional and nonconventional, to the Third World.[8] While it will be difficult, and in the long run counterproductive, to control information in a technology-based society, there will be a growing need for improved policy-making machinery on technology if a state is going to retain a position of strategic competitiveness. As the FSX controversy between Japan and the United States illustrated, where advanced technology is concerned, it is no longer possible to treat defense and economic concerns as separate policy issues. Whether a ministry of science and technology is required or simply a high-level advisory panel on technology and national security, it appears increasingly evident that foreign policy decision-making must incorporate economic issues related to industry and technology. One final implication for the impact of technology on the future is that given the problems of debt, population growth, and deterioration of the environment in the Third World, there is going to be an increased need for technology transfer. To be successful, this transfer must be done with considerable care. In many cases this will require not only the transfer of physical elements of a technological infrastructure, but also the development of human resources to sustain and fully exploit the transfer.

NOTES

1.　See Francis Fukuyama, "The End of History," *National Interest* (Summer 1989).

2. This section is based in large part on the presentation and paper delivered by Joseph S. Nye, Jr. to the Aspen Strategy Group on August 13, 1990. A revised and edited version of that paper is reproduced as Appendix 1.
3. For an example of this type of argument, see Richard N. Rosecrance, *The Rise of the Trading State* (New York: Basic, 1986).
4. Perhaps the most well-known proponent of this line of reasoning is Paul Kennedy; see Kennedy, *The Rise and Fall of the Great Powers: Economic Change and Military Conflict 1500–2000* (New York: Random House, 1987).
5. "America, Asia, and Europe," *The Economist*, December 24, 1988, p. 33.
6. This section is based in large part on the presentation and paper delivered by Richard N. Cooper to the Aspen Strategy Group on August 13, 1990. A revised and edited version of that paper is reproduced as Appendix 2.
7. This section is based in large part on the presentation and paper delivered by Charles A. Zraket to the Aspen Strategy Group on August 13, 1990. A revised and edited version of that paper is reproduced as Appendix 3.
8. For more on the issue of proliferation to the Third World, see Aspen Strategy Group, *New Threats: Responding to the Proliferation of Nuclear, Chemical, and Delivery Capabilities in the Third World* (Lanham, Md.: University Press of America, 1990).

Chapter 2

NEW DIRECTIONS
IN REGIONAL POLITICS

I. INTRODUCTION

As with the debate over where the course of global politics is heading, the question of history repeating itself runs through any discussion of the recent changes in regional politics. Are most of Europe's old problems returning? Have events restored the pre–World War I setting: an unstable, chaotic Russia; an increasingly dominant Germany; tension and instability in the Balkans; and the inability of Europe's oldest nation-states—France and Britain—to act together in their own behalf? In the Far East, does the increase in Japanese investment in the region signal a new attempt to create a more benign but still exclusionary "co-prosperity" trading bloc? And in the intellectual artifact known as the Third World, has the end of the Cold War meant a return to the immediate post-colonial issues of building nationalism and democracy out of feudal tribalism? Like the previous chapter, the purpose here is to examine each of these three areas in turn in order to identify those forces that will have a determining effect on whether history is repeated or made anew.

II. EUROPE IN THE 1990s[1]

When all is said and done, it is fear that drives statecraft more than any other single variable. And over the course of the last year the most talked about fear in Europe was the fear of a reunited Germany. However, fears about a reunited Germany's return to its militaristic past are probably unjustified. The primary cause of war in 1914 and 1939 was neither the fact of a unified Germany nor solely the dynamics of rival alliances, but rather the specific preferences, goals, and policies of imperial and later Nazi Germany. The political, educational, and class systems, which gave rise to those preferences, goals, and policies, have been radically transformed by the democratization of Germany.

Nonetheless, some will argue that what matters in Europe is the distribution of power, and Germany's historic fear of encirclement will invoke the dark dynamics of the "security dilemma." So long as Germany has close relations with France, Britain, and the United States, and cordial relations with the Soviet Union, there is little chance that Germany's historic concerns about encirclement will be revisited. More importantly, so long as the rewards of economic influence are far greater than those of military might, it becomes even less likely that a reunited Germany will return to the goals and policies of the past.

This analysis of the "German question" offers an important insight into *how* politics on the European continent should be evaluated during the coming decade. For both scholars and statesmen during the Cold War, it became second nature to explain and predict political action by reference to the distribution of military and economic capabilities. The underlying assumption was that intentions followed self-evidently from capabilities and power balances. In 1989, the capabilities, in "hard power" terms, of the major actors in European politics were not significantly different than before. Yet, the policies pursued by those actors, especially West Germany and the Soviet Union, were vastly different. The transformation in European politics during the past two years highlights the importance of two factors that the structural approach to international politics has neglected. The first and most obvious is the importance of leadership. It was Mikhail Gorbachev who decided that the Soviet Union would no longer retain Eastern Europe as a security *glacis*. It was Helmut Kohl who made German unity an issue that would be decided by the Germans themselves and not by the four victors of World War II. These same two men negotiated a unified Germany's membership in NATO, the size and nature of a future German army, and the timetable for the Soviet withdrawal from what had been East Germany, albeit within a context earlier agreed upon with George Bush.

The second factor neglected by the structural approach is the role and importance of domestic politics, particularly the relationship between civil society and the state. The forces released by *glasnost* and *perestroika*, such as national and ethnic claims for autonomy and territory, have made it difficult, if not impossible, for the Soviet Union to pursue a foreign policy other than one of retrenchment. It was the revival of civil society in Eastern Europe, a revival fueled by economic deterioration and encouraged by Gorbachev's refusal to prop up the communist regimes there, which led to the revolutions of 1989.

By neglecting the role and importance of leaders and domestic politics in the formation of foreign policy, the structural approach missed a generational change in both the eastern and western halves of the continent. In the East, especially the Soviet Union, a new generation of cadres came to power with the firm conviction that the Stalinist model of economic and political development did not work. How this new generation of Soviet leaders will respond to the forces of secession and nationalism released by this conviction will be a key issue for the United States in the 1990s. In the West, a new generation of business leaders, civil servants, politicians, and journalists has arisen, which has acquired the habit of cooperation across common borders and seems capable of reconciling national and European perspectives. The integration of Europe, led by this new generation, will pose the second great problem of European politics for the United States in the 1990s.

A final element that the structural approach neglects, but of increasing importance in the last decade of this century, is the growing heterogeneity of Europe. Most discussion focuses on the future heterogeneity of the European Community, and whether the EC can/should absorb the nations of Central and Eastern Europe. However, there is an ongoing diversification of

Europe that, until quite recently, has received little attention: the migration of peoples. There are two components to this diversification. The first is the exodus of people from Eastern to Western Europe. The second is the movement of people from south to north, not east to west. The flow of economic refugees from North Africa in quest of jobs and prosperity is beginning to constitute a flood. While comparisons of the Mediterranean with the Rio Grande are now popular, there is crucial difference. The fact that most of these immigrants are Muslims poses a sharp challenge to European unity, especially with Islamic fundamentalism enjoying a resurgence. While it may be true that militant Islam, with its categorical rejection of things Western, rises and falls likes the tide, it is uncertain what effect the Gulf crisis will have on growing numbers of Muslim immigrants in Europe's cities.

III. ASIA IN THE 1990s[2]

While the plight of the "boat people" will occasionally make headlines, more often than not, it is the movement of capital, not people, which focuses attention on Asia. In particular, it is the movement of capital into the Asian perimeter that will play a large role in the international politics of the 1990s. The flow of the world's capital is drawn to the Asian perimeter, like iron to a magnet, by the lure of Asian products. The Asian perimeter accounts for the lion's share of world output in three important manufacturing sectors: consumer electronics, automobiles, and crude steel. Such dominance suggests that the old stereotype of Asian countries as low-wage, import-substituting sweatshops turning out semi-processed light industrial goods is obsolete. Another perception of the past that may be obsolete is the view of the Asian perimeter as a region suffering from almost constant conflict, turmoil, and violence. The unique geography of the Asian perimeter has cushioned, insulated the countries of the region from the tension, instability, and strategic entanglements that often accompany rapid economic growth. This same physical separateness, however, has made it difficult for the region to cultivate a common sense of regional identity, despite the ties of economic interdependence. Consequently, one thing that will probably not emerge in the 1990s is an Asian analogue to the European Community.

The engine of this economic transformation has been the Japanese economy. The speed with which the Japanese "miracle" has been accomplished is historically unprecedented. In 1952 the Japanese economy was only 5 percent of the American economy; by 1989 it was 70 percent, and by the end of the 1990s it is projected to be 80 percent. The size and dynamism have simultaneously made the United States–Japan relationship one of most important for stability in the 1990s and one of the most troubled. While U.S.–Japanese intergovernmental relations can be characterized as "good," the relations between the two societies, the perceptions each holds of the other, are more uncertain. Frustration over massive trade imbalances, controversy over savings rates, and recriminations over structural impediments to trade have soured relations to an almost dangerous point. What may bring this unhealthy situation to the pressure point in the 1990s is not more of the same, but a new variable: Soviet–Japanese détente.

The Soviet Union has a strong desire to normalize relations with Japan. Indeed, the Soviet Union may be willing to return the four northern territories it occupied at the end of World War II in exchange for the promise of Japanese financial, technological, and marketing resources necessary in order to develop Siberia. The challenge to U.S.–Japanese relations will not follow directly from a normalization of Soviet–Japanese relations, but from its consequences. One of the likely consequences of a Soviet–Japanese rapprochement is that it will call into question both Japan's role in the world and its relationship with the United States. The most immediate danger is not that the Japanese and the Soviets will become allies, but that normalization between the Soviet Union and Japan will weaken the pro-U.S. consensus in Japan. Such a turn in Japanese politics will make the retention of U.S. forces and base structure in Japan, as well as further trade concessions, difficult. The former may in some ways be the most critical consequence, for U.S. forces in Japan were not deployed to merely contain Soviet power; they were deployed as an integral part of the American ability to project force onto the Korean peninsula and throughout all of Asia. One element that will cushion the effects of any reduction in Soviet–Japanese tension on the American presence in Asia is the long-standing rivalry between Japan and China.

The development of Asia's perimeter stands in stark contrast to the usual path of development, which proceeds from the core to the periphery. Part of the reason for continental Asia's backwardness has been its adoption of communism as the preferred model of economic development. However, this is changing. In Mongolia, China, North Korea, and Vietnam there is a gradual inching away from the precepts of Marx, Lenin, and Stalin. The emerging crisis in Asia's communist societies will pose sharp policy choices for American decision-makers in the 1990s. Should the United States respond positively to these changes and actively encourage further change through a set of political and economic incentives? If these communist countries retreat from their nascent reforms or show an unwillingness to embrace change, should there be a negative response?

IV. THE THIRD WORLD IN THE 1990s[3]

In both Europe and Asia it appears that the future will be unlike the past in many significant respects. In Europe there has been not only an end to the division of the continent and one of its leading states, but a renaissance of the move toward economic integration, with a single market for the members of the European Community in 1992. In Asia, the countries along the perimeter are poised to become the first countries to pass from the "developing" stage into the ranks of "developed," and one state is poised on the brink of assuming a position of world leadership. But in the Third World, there is only an overwhelming sense of déjà vu.

The notion that the Third World is going "back to the future" stems from the fact that decolonization coincided with the onset of the Cold War. The Cold War had a chilling effect on the Third

World in that it froze the reconciliation of many of the issues that had appeared with the collapse of the European empires. Now that the Cold War has ended, all the old problems, such as nation-building, have come to the fore again. While the Third World has not been immune to a rise in the local pressures for democracy, which followed the remarkable events in Eastern Europe, those pressures have been blocked by the same obstacles that existed forty years earlier: poverty and ethnic fragmentation would be coextensive and democratization would lead to disintegration.

The ending of the Cold War has a number of other implications for the Third World. Chief among these is the danger of marginalization. The most ambitious attempt by the Third World to play a role on a global scale was through the policy of "nonalignment." This policy of equidistance has been rendered meaningless by the fact that the two rivals are no longer poles apart on every issue. The reduction in superpower tension also will mean that Third World countries will no longer be able to play one superpower off against the other in the scramble for scarce military and economic aid. Indeed, when one considers that the developed world is suffering from nearly forty years of aid fatigue and cynicism, needs to refurbish its own industries and infrastructure for the more competitive future, and wants to help Eastern Europe find its economic feet, it is hard to escape the conclusion that the Third World is facing a very competitive aid environment. It is quite likely that those nations desiring economic aid will have to offer attractive investment legislation and pass higher tests of "good" government and public accountability in order to receive that desired aid.

While the marginalization of the Third World will reduce the amount of superpower meddling in regional conflicts, it will not necessarily encourage a similar restraint by local powers. There is the very real threat that more conflicts in the Third World will become "Lebanonized," with local powers replaying conflicts in other locations. For example, the analogue to Israel, Iraq, Iran, and Syria replaying their many and various conflicts in Lebanon, can be found in the roles that India and Pakistan are playing in the conflict in Afghanistan and Israel and the Arab states are playing in the Eritrean rebellion in Ethiopia.

NOTES

1. This section is based in large part on the presentation and paper delivered by Stanley Hoffmann to the Aspen Strategy Group on August 14, 1990. A revised and edited version of that paper is reproduced as Appendix 4.
2. This section is based in large part on the presentation and paper delivered by Daniel I. Okimoto to the Aspen Strategy Group on August 14, 1990. A revised and edited version of that paper is reproduced as Appendix 5.
3. This section is based in large part on the presentation and paper delivered by John Chipman to the Aspen Strategy Group on August 15, 1990. A revised and edited version of that paper is reproduced as Appendix 6.

FACING THE FUTURE

I. INTRODUCTION

The starting point for any strategy is the recognition that if everything is important, then nothing is important. The end of the Cold War has made the world less threatening, but not less complicated. With each new fold that is added to the fabric of international politics, a dozen or more issues appear, each one no less compelling than another. However, when neither time nor treasure is as abundant as it once was there is no escape from the need to decide what is important and what is not. The nature of strategic decision-making is occasionally depicted as a choice between order and justice. As with many dichotomies, this is a false one, for it is impossible to have one without the other. While the selection of which issues will receive the most attention and the most resources should be informed by standards such as justice, they should be determined by the more practical measure of what is realizable. The art of statesmanship lies, in large part, in the art of defining problems that are manageable, if not solvable. Statesmanship also involves the identification and definition of issues that give meaning to a nation's purpose in the world.

For the United States as it enters the 1990s, there are four geostrategic issues, which over the course of the decade will dominate the top of the national security agenda. These four issues involve critical American interests and lend themselves to decisive American action. Each of these issues are intimately bound up with the future structure and stability of the international system. The purpose of this chapter is twofold: to briefly review each of the four issues and to outline the basic steps which the United States must take in order to meet these issues in the new world that the first two chapters described.

II. AN AGENDA OF STRATEGIC ISSUES

The Management of Soviet Decline

That the Soviet Union is in absolute decline should come as no surprise. Since the spring of 1990, experts have vied with one another to expose new weaknesses in the Soviet economy. By the fall of 1990, the economy had slipped even further (there were long lines for bread despite a record grain harvest; estimates of grain losses due to breakdowns in the transportation and distribution system have gone as high as forty million tons). The political situation was moving from bad to worse; thirteen out of fifteen Soviet republics had enacted some form of secessionist legislation, and the Russian republic had begun negotiating with the Soviet central government and other republics as though it were already a sovereign entity. While the United States may take some quiet satisfaction from the current discomfiture of the Soviet leadership, it should take little comfort in the prospect of economic collapse and violent political disintegration. The possibility of violence spilling over into Eastern Europe, the danger of unauthorized access to nuclear weapons, and the threat of a "counterrevolution" in the Soviet Union, which would restore a domestically repressive and externally aggressive regime, all these possibilities and more ask that this issue receive top priority from American policy-makers. While the United States has little interest, ethical or strategic, in the preservation of the Soviet Union as it is currently constituted, it has a great deal of interest and some influence in ensuring that a country with 30,000 nuclear weapons and enormous military might evolves peacefully. The record of declining multinational empires, for example Austria-Hungary at the beginning of this century, is a cause for concern.

The Reconstruction of European Stability

Closely related to the management of Soviet decline is the development of a new security architecture in Europe. While Germany took the leading role in setting the pace and the terms of its reunification, the United States will play the dominant role in reconstructing the security order in Europe because it is the one power which can simultaneously guard against the revival of a Soviet threat to Europe and provide the necessary reassurance that Germany will not disrupt the European balance now or a decade hence. The American investment, in both blood and treasure, in European peace and security this century demands that the United States remain engaged in the continuing transformation of Europe into a stable international system.

Managing the Rise of Japanese Power

As with Europe, American interests in Asia run deep and have been proven by the commitment of U.S. military and economic power to the region. As noted earlier, Japan is the economic locomotive that has pulled the Asian perimeter into one of the fastest growing regions in the world. The economic dynamism of the Asian perimeter has rerouted American trade patterns; 60 percent of American foreign trade is currently with Asia. Symbolic of this change is the fact that the port of Los Angeles has replaced New York as America's busiest point of entry. As the world desperately needs surplus savings to funnel into such capital starved regions as Eastern Europe, the world will need a more active Japan. As Japan's largest trading partner and security guarantor, the United States is uniquely positioned to help the Japanese develop a global role for themselves, which befits their power without raising fears.

The Diffusion of Military Power

It is more than a bit ironic that at the very moment when the Cold War is ending, an unparalleled intensification in the military competition in the Third World is occurring. Projects once thought to be without promise or danger are now seen to possess both. The steady diffusion of scientific knowledge, technological innovation, and engineering/manufacturing skills have engendered a situation in which a growing number of countries are on the threshold of acquiring and deploying the full panoply of the most sophisticated instruments of mass destruction. At present, approximately twenty countries can produce chemical weapons, sixteen states have the capability to produce ballistic missiles, and eight nations are at or fast approaching the nuclear threshold.[1] The world has entered the age of nuclear weapons and ballistic missiles, not because of the talents of a few men, but because of our attainment after centuries of scientific thought and endeavor of a certain level of knowledge of the physical universe. While such knowledge cannot be unlearned or forgotten, its diffusion can be slowed and better managed. The design of nuclear weapons requires not only a high level of scientific sophistication, but also a high degree of engineering and manufacturing skill; to make a ballistic missile such as the *Pershing* II fly over 600 miles to its assigned target one hundred thousand precision-crafted parts must operate perfectly. For developed as well as for developing countries the design and manufacture of nuclear weapons or telemetry systems is a technologically daunting and financially costly venture. Through unilateral action, such as strict export controls, and through multilateral action, such as the creation of international regimes on the spread of dangerous technologies, this diffusion can be slowed significantly. While the United States is not a hegemonic power, its leadership is of critical importance in creating new regimes and sustaining old ones.

As the two preceding chapters have intimated, this is by no means an exhaustive list of the strategic issues that will press American decision-makers throughout the 1990s. But it was not meant to be. Rather, these issues were chosen because they deny any easy, quick, or final solution. An observation that Plutarch made about politics in general is especially relevant to the politics that will surround these four issues: "They are wrong who think that politics is like an ocean voyage or military campaign, something to be done with some end in view, something which levels off as soon as that end is reached. It is not a public chore to be got over with; it is a way of life." For the 1990s, at least, the politics of managing Soviet decline, European security, the rise of

Japanese power, and the diffusion of military technology will be a way of life for American policymakers.

III. POLICY RECOMMENDATIONS FOR THE 1990s

Although four strategic issues can be identified as the leitmotif underpinning many of the changes in the coming decade, it is not our purpose here to prescribe specific policies for each of those issues. It would be a mistake, because each issue would require a book unto itself, and the actions required to meet each one will vary as conditions change. For example, at one point in time it may be necessary to send emergency food supplies to the Soviet Union to restore political stability; while at another moment, all that may be necessary for the United States to manage an orderly Soviet decline will be the pursuit of bilateral arms control and the occasional summit meeting.

By emphasizing objectives rather than tactics, our approach confronts the central element in the events of the past two years: continuity in change. The revolutions of 1989 did not create a strategic *tabula rasa*. While the crystallization of new configurations in world politics was both sudden and astonishing, the process had been slowly and steadily evolving over time. Thus, in order to meet the challenges of this evolving situation, the United States must craft a diplomatic, economic, military, and domestic political base, which can sustain over time a flexible set of tactical arrangements. The purpose of this chapter is to lay out the essentials of this strategy.

Diplomatic Strategy [2]

American Leadership. While the 1990s will be neither a replay of the nineteenth century nor a reprise of the 1930s, lessons can still be drawn from those two periods. The central insight which comes from the past is that if the strongest state does not lead, the prospects for instability increase. As appealing as it may seem, the United States cannot turn inward now that the Cold War has been "won." As noted in Chapter 1, the United States will be more than a first among equals; it will possess in the 1990s a unique combination of military, economic, and political power that no other state will come close to approximating. Like the huge financial reserves that the Japanese have accumulated, this influential combination of "hard" and "soft" power is an invaluable resource for international stability, a resource that should not be allowed to lie fallow. However, as Chapter 1 also pointed out, the international system is a far more complex place, especially now that the Cold War is gone. With transnational interdependence a fundamental condition of the current international system, the question arises: How should the United States continue to exercise its leadership?

Focused Partnerships. Traditionally, the principal strategy for states in the international system was one of balancing. Today, while balancing strategies are still effective in certain issue areas, more and more states will have to adopt strategies of cooperation. Since no one issue will have the same power structure, states will have to be open to more functional coalitions as they move from issue to issue. A phrase which captures this new imperative is "focused partnerships." The word "partnership" highlights the reversal in traditional thinking that sees alliances as instruments of balancing strategies. The term "focused" emphasizes that this concept is not to be construed as something akin to world government. Focused partnerships should be used as flexible instruments that can pull together the most resources in an efficient manner so that conflicts are contained and mediated within an overlapping network of multinational organizations tailored specifically to a particular region or issue. Where should the United States begin to forge focused partnerships?

Updating America's Alliances. The most obvious candidates are the existing alliances with Western Europe and Japan. However, these alliances were forged in the crucible of the Cold War and their focus must be recalibrated to meet a new era. While deterrence against an "existential" Soviet threat will continue to provide the common basis for sustaining the alliances spanning the Atlantic and the Pacific, the modernization of each alliance will follow a slightly different course.

Europe.[3] The most compelling problem for the United States and its European allies in the coming decade will not be finding appropriate replacements for "forward defense" and "flexible response" or designing new deployment and mobilization plans, though both of these difficult tasks will be critical if NATO is to survive as an institution. Rather, the most pressing problem will be how to craft a European security structure, of which NATO is only a part, that includes both American and Soviet participation. Fortunately, the elements of this new security "architecture" can be found in two existing institutions, one relatively old and one quite new. The notion that the future security of Europe should involve all those concerned has already found expression in the Conference on Security and Cooperation in Europe (CSCE). However, by itself, CSCE is insufficient. As it has in the past, the CSCE will offer an excellent political umbrella for a range of necessary activities, from confidence-building measures to conventional arms control negotiations. However, its inclusive membership, while providing an ideal mechanism for legitimizing and ratifying policy decisions, does not offer much in the way of effective policy coordination. A possible complement to the CSCE might be the extension of the "2 plus 4" talks, which were convened to manage the unification of Germany. Restructured after German unification into a five power forum, this body could provide the necessary policy coordination. Such an arrangement would not only provide an external impetus for NATO's internal changes, but would provide a context for NATO's continued existence as a tangible hedge against future aggression. Whatever the merits of particular proposals, the main point is that the United States will need to be flexible in its institutional choices as it continues to play a role in Europe.

Asia. In the Pacific, the central issue is less one of creating new institutions to augment the old, than nurturing the development of new roles, which complement the old. The key change will not be to encourage more spending on defense by Japan, but rather to encourage more spending, in monetary and diplomatic terms, on international stability. Greater Japanese participation in international institutions and economic assistance to developing countries would add far more to international security than any increase in the size of the Japanese Self Defense Forces. Although there is little reason to encourage any further growth in the size of the Japanese military, the United States should encourage Japanese participation in roles other than the territorial defense of Japan; participation in international peacekeeping operations would be one way for Japan to assume a role in international security consistent with its power and responsibility.

Greater Reliance on International Institutions. The role played by the United Nations in mobilizing international action against the Iraqi invasion and annexation of Kuwait underscores the importance of international institutions in the post–Cold War world. Of particular importance in the coming decade will be the reliance on international regimes. International regimes are sets of rules and institutions that govern areas of interdependence. Regimes are useful in coping with conditions of interdependence because they facilitate burden-sharing by establishing clear obligations, reduce uncertainty by providing information, and introduce greater discipline in both foreign and domestic policy by clustering issues under sets of rules. In an uncertain and ever changing world, international regimes will offer important havens of predictability.

Military Strategy[4]

The Iraqi invasion of Kuwait clearly demonstrated that the United States cannot afford the luxury of adopting a "ten-year rule" in planning its military security over the next decade. The invasion of Kuwait clearly showed that not only can the United States not assume that there will be no war for the next ten years, but it cannot even confidently predict where a military confrontation might develop. Consequently, the watchword in force planning for the 1990s will be flexibility. The basic outline of what a new American force posture would look like is readily agreed upon. A post–Cold War military structure would differ markedly from today's forces in size, character, and composition. The most dramatic change will be the sheer reduction in the size of American forces. The Soviet withdrawal from Eastern Europe means that not only can conventional forces be reduced, but that nuclear weapons need not underwrite conventional deterrence. As the heavy demands of extended deterrence recede, the United States can safely negotiate reciprocal reductions in strategic forces to the level of 3,000–4,000 warheads for each side. On an aggregate level, the United States can safely afford at the least a 20–25 percent reduction in spending on conventional forces over the next five years. Ideally, the future conventional force will have a much smaller active duty component, but much higher levels of training, supply, and readiness. Both the smaller active duty force and the larger reserve force would be outfitted with superior strategic and tactical mobility. And finally, this new force would also have a much leaner management headquarters overhead. The organizing assumption behind this proposed restructuring of the American military is that the United States must be prepared to meet a range of minor threats quickly and effectively, while major threats are to be met with a more massive mobilization of American economic and political might. The pressing political question is how do you build such a force?

Revisit Key West. To any student of the politics of force planning, it was no surprise that there was a shortage of both sea- and air-lift for Operation "Desert Shield." It was no surprise because both the Navy and the Air Force prefer sleek, multi-role combat platforms over lumbering transports. While some recent military reform has begun to bring a little more order to the defense planning process, still more is need. Specifically the series of compromises reached at the 1948 conference in Key West need to be reviewed. The roles and missions of the various services and how they mutually support one another demand reexamination in light of the new challenges the United States will probably face in the 1990s and beyond. Related to the reexamination of roles and missions is the need for the services to rethink their traditional approaches to carrying out those roles. If the the Soviet threat continues to recede, then the Army will have to reconsider how it plans to employ and counter armored forces in contingencies outside of Central Europe the Navy will have to review its methods for securing control of the sea lanes and maintaining a presence in distant regions, and the Air Force may have to amend its tactical air requirements and rethink its need for a penetrating stealth bomber.

Multiyear Authorizations. No attempt at rationalizing the defense planning process would be complete without a change in how money is appropriated for defense. For most of the Cold War era, budgets, not strategy, have driven the structure of America's military. Particularly vexing is the uncertainty that stems from year to year authorization. With the ending of the Cold War there is, to borrow a term from that struggle, a "window of opportunity" for the United States to put its defense planning on a more rational basis by authorizing funds for weapon systems on a three-year basis. This would compel the defense establishment to put forward a real plan for defense spending, and not an opening gambit in a bidding war with Congress. James Forrestal, the first secretary of defense, once observed that the defense budget can no more be separated from politics than sex can be separated from creation. A new consensus on roles and missions and multi-year authorizations would not remove interservice rivalries or banish politics from the defense planning process, but it would dilute their effects and mitigate their distortions of national security planning.

An Economic Strategy for National Security

The recommendations for how the United States can restore and preserve its economic health are legion. This report does not presume to add to that list by discussing education reforms, changes in the tax code to encourage savings, or ways to reduce the federal deficit. Instead, this report is simply going to make three specific recommendations, one about how the United States can increase its energy independence, and two on how the United States can preserve its defense technology base during a period of intense transnational interdependence and commercial competition.

Develop a National Energy Plan. Iraq's invasion of Kuwait brought to the attention of the American public in a way that no amount of statistics, charts, or expert testimony could the fact that the United States is increasing its dependence on foreign oil, primarily oil imported from the Persian Gulf. For over a year now, energy experts have warned that American dependence on foreign sources was growing at an increasing rate; a relatively conservative estimate holds that by the beginning of the next century, absent any changes in policy, American dependence on imported oil will reach upwards of 67 percent. What makes this trend worrisome is that by the end of the 1990s, the number of major oil exporters not from the Gulf region will have shrunk; countries such as Algeria, Venezuela, and Nigeria will consume domestically much of what they produce. Compounding this problem is that while demand for electricity is growing in the United States, there is growing opposition to either coal or nuclear power, leaving only oil and natural gas as economically efficient sources. There is no one easy or quick remedy to this problem. It requires action along a broad front over a sustained period of time, from tax policies which induce conservation and research on alternative sources of energy, such as solar power, to maintaining a large strategic reserve, to economic and political support for the development of a new generation of clean, safe, and cost-effective nuclear power plants. But the United States cannot wait for the market and its "hidden hand" to begin guiding a response to this development.

Guard against Undue Globalization of the Defense Technology Base. This does not mean that the United States should refuse to have any defense components made outside of the United States. On the contrary, in order to promote efficiency and to get the best products available the United States should acknowledge the comparative advantage of some nations. However, only when there is a concentration of external suppliers of strategic products should American domestic producers be protected and or subsidized. Generally, if there are more than four companies or countries supplying more than 50 percent of the world market, there is little danger that collusion to manipulate a recipient could be possible or effective.[5]

Reapportion the Defense Spending on R&D. The second measure designed to guard America's defense technology base is to reapportion the Defense Department's research, development, test, and evaluation budget so that the categories for basic and applied research receive modest and sustained increases after inflation, while the categories for detailed engineering should be reduced. The reason for these changes is that there needs to be a vigorous technology base for militarily unique items. Increased attention to the defense technology base will provide a "reserve" capability to meet the uncertain needs of U.S. security in the future. In line with these changes, the Pentagon should increase its use of commercial technology, and as a first step toward this, it should eliminate, except where absolutely necessary (i.e., systems that must operate in a nuclear environment), the costly and wasteful system of military specifications. The National Institute of Standards and Technology should develop standards that would function in both industrial and defense applications. Moreover, the Department of Defense should develop procurement regulations that give preference to civilian products.[6]

A Strategy for Domestic Politics

Finally, in order to meet the most pressing strategic needs of the 1990s in a way that acknowledges the changing nature of power in global politics, the United States government must explain to the American public why it is important that the United States play a continuing role in the management of Soviet decline, Japanese growth, and European security. Without an understanding of why these things are important and why a policy of flexible engagement called "focused partnerships" is appropriate to changed circumstances, then the United States will be ill-equipped to meets its obligations as the world's leading power. Hans Morganthau once observed that there was a tendency for American foreign policy to swing between the extremes of an "indiscriminate isolationism and equally indiscriminate internationalism or globalism"; both extremes, he concluded, are "equally hostile to that middle ground of subtle distinctions, complex choices and precarious manipulation which is the proper sphere of foreign policy." In an age when neither American exceptionalism nor containment of Soviet power lays out a compelling course of action, and in a world of diffuse, fragmented power and inescapable challenges, the United States needs to perform steadily along that middle ground. The subtle, complex role that makes as effective use of "soft power" as it does of "hard power" is unfamiliar to many Americans. For it to work there must be constant and open dialogue with the American people on the setting of the national interest.

NOTES

1. See Aspen Strategy Group, *New Threats*, pp. 1–11.
2. This section is based in large part on the presentation and paper delivered by Alice M. Rivlin, David C. Jones, and Edward C. Meyer to the Aspen Strategy Group on August 16, 1990. A revised and edited version of that paper is reproduced as Appendix 9.
3. In addition to the Rivlin, Jones, and Meyer paper, see the section in John D. Steinbruner's paper on the transformation of NATO; Steinbruner's paper can be found in Appendix 8.
4. This section is based in large part on the presentation and paper delivered by Lawrence J. Korb to the Aspen Strategy Group on August 17, 1990. A revised and edited version of that paper is reproduced as Appendix 10.
5. This section is based in large part on the presentation and paper delivered by Theodore H. Moran to the Aspen Strategy Group on August 15, 1990. A revised and edited version of that paper is reproduced as Appendix 7.
6. This section is based in large part on the presentation delivered by William Perry to the Aspen Strategy Group on August 16, 1990.

Appendix 1

AMERICAN POWER
AND A POST–COLD WAR WORLD

Joseph S. Nye, Jr.

For forty years, the United States had a grand strategy that focused on containing the power of the Soviet Union and strengthening pluralistic market economies by maintaining an open international economic system. By 1990, the success of the strategy was clear, but success brought new problems. With the Cold War over, Americans sought to understand their place in a world without a defining Soviet threat. Polls reported that half the public believed the country was in decline, and that those who believed in decline tended to be more protectionist and to counsel withdrawal from what they saw as "overextended international commitments."

In a world of growing interdependence, such advice would be counterproductive and could bring on the condition it is supposed to avert, for if the most powerful country fails to lead, the consequences for international stability could be disastrous. Throughout history, anxiety about decline and shifting power relations has been accompanied by tension and miscalculation. Now that Soviet power is declining and Japanese power is rising, misleading theories of American decline and inappropriate analogies between the United States and Britain in the late nineteenth century divert our attention from the real issue: how power is changing in world politics.

The United States is certainly less powerful at the end of the twentieth century that it was in mid-century. Even conservative estimates show that the U.S. share of global product has declined from more than a third of the total after World War II to a little more than a fifth in the 1980s. That change, however, represents the artificial effect of World War II. Unlike the other great powers, the United States was *strengthened* by the war. But that artificial preponderance was bound to erode as other nations regained their economic health. The important fact is that the U.S. economy's share of the global product has been relatively constant for the past decade and a half. The Council on Competitiveness finds that the U.S. share of world product has held constant at 23 percent since the mid-1970s. The Central Intelligence Agency, using numbers that reflect the purchasing power of different currencies, reports that the American share of world product increased slightly from 25 percent in 1975 to 26 percent in 1988.[1]

These studies suggest that the World War II effect lasted about a quarter century and that most of the decline worked its way through the system by the mid-1970s. In fact, the big adjustment to American commitments occurred at that time with Nixon's withdrawal from Vietnam and the end of the convertibility of the dollar into gold.

Now, as the United States enters the 1990s, it faces four large geopolitical problems: attempting to ensure that the decline of the Soviet empire does not spill over into international violence; guiding the rising power of Japan into peaceful institutional channels; encouraging the continuing integration of Europe as a means of promoting stability in that continent; and responding to the diffusion of power. This last challenge is least understood.

Perceptions of Power

The dictionary tells us that power means an ability to do things and control others, to get others to do what they otherwise would not do. Because the ability to control others is often associated with the possession of certain resources, politicians and statesmen commonly define power as the possession of those resources, i.e., population, territory, natural resources, economic size, military forces, and political stability. For example, in the agrarian economies of eighteenth-century Europe, population was a critical power resource, since it provided a base for taxes and recruitment of infantry.

Traditionally the test of a great power was its strength for war. However, the definition of power is moving away from the emphasis on military force and conquest that marked earlier eras. Force remains the ultimate ratio in our anarchic world, but force has become more costly for great powers to use than in earlier centuries for four reasons. First, nuclear weaponry, the most destructive form, involves means that are disproportionate to most ends. Second, it is more costly to use force to rule over nationalistically awakened populations than in colonial times. Third, force often interferes with other objectives such as economic welfare; and fourth, there is more resistance to prolonged use of force among public opinion in advanced industrial countries.

In assessing international power, the factors of technology, education, and economic growth are becoming more important, while geography, population, and raw materials, though still relevant, are becoming less important. In short, the list of resources that produce power remains largely the same, but the mix is changing.

If so, are we entering a "Japanese period" in world politics? Japan has certainly done far better with its strategy as a trading state after 1945 than it did with its military strategy to create a Greater East Asian Co-Prosperity Sphere in the 1930s.[2] On the other hand, Japan's security vis-à-vis its large military neighbors, China and the Soviet Union, depends heavily on U.S. protection. One should not leap too quickly to the conclusion that all trends favor economic power or countries like Japan.

What can we say about changes in the distribution of power resources in the coming decades? Political leaders often use the term "multipolarity" to mean a return to a balance among a number of nations with roughly equal power resources analogous to the nineteenth century. But this is not likely to be the situation at the turn of the century, for in terms of power resources, all the potential challengers except the United States are deficient in some respect. The Soviet Union and China lag economically, Europe lacks political unity, and Japan is deficient both in military power and in global ideological appeal. If economic reforms reverse Soviet decline, if Japan develops a full-fledged nuclear and conventional military capability, or if Europe experiences a dramatic increase in unification, there may be a return to classical multipolarity in the twenty-first century. But barring such changes, the United States is likely to retain a full range of power resources—military, economic, scientific, cultural, and ideological—considerably greater than those of other countries, and the Soviet Union may lose its superpower status.

The coming century may see continued American preeminence, but the sources of power in world politics are likely to undergo major changes, which will cause all countries new difficulties in achieving their goals. Proof of power lies not in resources but in the changed behavior of nations. Thus, the critical question for the future of the United States is not whether it will start the next century as a superpower with the largest supply of resources, but to what extent it will be able to control the political environment and to get other nations to do what it wants. Some trends in world politics suggest that it will be more difficult in the future for *any* great power to control the political environment and to achieve what it wants from others. The problem for the United States will be less the rising challenge of another major power than a general diffusion of power. Whereas nineteenth-century Britain faced new challengers, the twenty-first-century United States will face new challenges.

As world politics becomes more complex, the power of all major states to achieve their purposes will be diminished. To understand what is happening to the United States today, the distinction between power over other countries and power over outcomes must be clear. Although the United States still has leverage over particular countries, it has far less leverage over the system as a whole. It is less well placed to attain unilaterally the goals it prefers, but it is not alone in this situation. All major states will have to confront the changing nature of power in world politics.

Such changes, of course, are not entirely new. For example, the rapid growth of private actors operating across international borders, whether large corporations or political groups, was widely recognized in the early 1970s. Even Henry Kissinger, with his deeply rooted belief in classical balance-of-power politics, argued in 1975 that "we are entering a new era. Old international patterns are crumbling. . . . The world has become interdependent in economics, in communications, in human aspirations."[3]

By the late 1970s, however, the American mood in politics had shifted. Iran's seizure of the American embassy and the Soviet invasion of Afghanistan in 1979 seemed to restore the role of military force and the primacy of the traditional security agenda. Ronald Reagan's election to the presidency accentuated these trends in the early 1980s. The U.S. defense budget increased in real terms for five straight years, arms control was downgraded, and nuclear forces and deterrence aroused public anxieties. Conventional military force was used successfully, albeit against the extremely weak states of Grenada and Libya. The shifting agenda of world politics discredited the 1970s' concern with interdependence and restored the traditional emphasis on military power. But interdependence continued to grow, and the world of the 1980s was not the same as that of the 1950s.

Continuity and Change

After the events in the Persian Gulf, there is some danger that the same dialectic will be repeated in the 1990s. But another debate between realists and liberals would confuse matters.

The appropriate response to the changes occurring in world politics today is not to discredit the traditional wisdom and its concern for the military balance of power, but to realize its limitations and to supplement it with insights about interdependence.

In the traditional view, states are the only significant actors in world politics and only a few large states really matter. But today other actors are becoming increasingly important. Although they lack military power, transnational corporations have enormous economic resources. Twenty corporations today have annual sales greater than the GNPs of eight states. The annual profits of IBM and Shell, for example, are each larger than the central government budgets of the Philippines, Peru, or Yugoslavia.[4] Multinational corporations are sometimes more relevant to achieving a country's goals than are other states. In terms of economic growth, the annual overseas production by such corporations exceeds the value of international trade. (See the discussion by Richard Cooper, Appendix 2.) In a regional context, a portrait of the Middle East that did not include the superpowers would be woefully inadequate, but so would a description that did not tell of transnational Jewish groups, oil companies, and terrorist organizations. Thus, the issue is not whether state or nonstate actors are more important—states usually are—but that more complex coalitions affect outcomes in modern times.

With changing actors in world politics come changing goals. In the traditional view, states give priority to military security to avoid threats to their survival. Today, however, states must consider additional dimensions of security. National security has become more complicated in regions where threats shift from military (that is, threats against territorial integrity) to economic and ecological. For example, Canadians today are not afraid that U.S. troops will burn Toronto for a second time (as in 1813); rather they fear that Toronto will be programmed into a backwater by a Texas computer. The forms of vulnerability have increased, and trade-offs among policies are designed to deal with different vulnerabilities. The United States, for instance, enhanced its energy security militarily by sending military forces to the Persian Gulf, but it could also further its goals by enlarging its strategic petroleum reserve, by imposing a gasoline tax to encourage conservation at home, and by improving cooperation in institutions like the International Energy Agency.

Traditionally, military force is the dominant instrument of power, but as explained above, although force remains the ultimate form of power in a self-help system, force has become more costly for modern great powers to use than in earlier centuries. Other instruments such as communications, organizational and institutional skills, and manipulation of interdependence have become important instruments of power. Contrary to some rhetorical flourishes, interdependence does not mean harmony. It is often an unevenly balanced mutual dependence, and the less-dependent or less-vulnerable party in an interdependent relationship may derive power from threats to manipulate that interdependence. Just as the less enamored of two lovers may manipulate the other, the less vulnerable of two states may use subtle threats to the relationship as a source of power. Further, interdependence is often balanced differently in different issues such as security, trade, and finance. Thus creating and resisting linkages between issues when a nation is either less or more vulnerable than the other becomes the art of the power game. Political leaders use international institutions to discourage or promote such linkages; they shop for the forum that best suits their interests in defining the scope of an issue.

As the instruments of power change, so do the strategies to achieve goals. Traditionalists see the goal of security and the instrument of military force linked by a strategy of balancing power. States wishing to preserve their independence from military threat follow a balancing strategy to limit the relative power of other states. Today, however, economic and ecological issues involve large elements of joint gain that can be achieved only through cooperation. These issues are often critical to the reelection of political leaders. A French president today would not interfere with Germany's increased economic growth because economic interdependence means that German growth is critical to French economic growth. The French decision to forgo an independent economic policy and remain in the European monetary system in the early 1980s is one example of such interdependence. The interaction of democratic public opinion with new regional institutions tends to be self-reinforcing, a factor ignored by realists who predict that a unified Germany will go "back to the future."[5] Where such interactions produce stable expectations, the static abstract concept of "anarchy" is altered, and state strategies are adjusted accordingly in what may become a virtuous cycle.

Traditional accounts of world politics often refer to an international system that results from the balancing strategies of states. Although to a point we can usefully speak of bipolarity and multipolarity, today different issues in world politics have different distributions of power; that is, different power structures. Military power, particularly nuclear, remains largely bipolar in its distribution. But in trade, where the European Community acts as a unit, power is multipolar. Ocean resources, money, space, shipping, and airlines each have somewhat different distributions of power. The power of states varies as well, as does the significance of nonstate actors in different issues. For example, the politics of international debt cannot be understood without considering the power of private banks.

If military power could be transferred freely across economic and ecological issues, the different structures would not matter, and the overall hierarchy determined by military strength would accurately predict outcomes in world politics. But military power is more costly and less transferable today than in earlier times. Thus, there is more diversity in the hierarchies that characterize different issues. The games of world politics are being played by different actors with different piles of chips at different tables. They can transfer winnings among tables, but often only at a considerable discount. The military game and the overall structure of the balance of power dominate when the survival of states is clearly at stake, but in much of the agenda of modern world politics, physical survival is not the most pressing issue.

To evaluate power in a post–Cold War world, it is necessary to recognize that strong elements of continuity make concern for the traditional military instruments and balance-of-power strategies a necessary condition for a successful policy. But new elements in the modern world contribute to the diffusion of power away from all the great powers. Thus, any successful strategy must incorporate both continuity and change.

POWER DIFFUSION

The great powers of today are less able to use their traditional power resources to achieve their purposes than in the past. On many issues, private actors and small states have become more powerful. At least five trends have contributed to this diffusion of power: economic interdependence, transnational actors, nationalism in weak states, the spread of technology, and changing political issues.

The changing technology of communications and transportation in recent times has had a revolutionary effect on economic interdependence. (See the discussion by Charles Zraket, Appendix 3.) A century ago, it took two weeks to cross the Atlantic; in 1927, Lindbergh did it in thirty-three hours; today the Concorde flies across in three hours. Modern telecommunications are instantaneous, and satellites and fiber-optic cables have led to a tenfold increase in overseas telephone calls in the last decade. The declining costs of transportation and communication have revolutionized global markets and accelerated the development of transnational corporations that transfer economic activity across borders. World trade has grown more rapidly than world product, becoming more important in all major economies. In the United States, trade has more than doubled its role in the economy over the past two decades. Changes in financial markets are even more dramatic. International monetary flows are some twenty-five times the world's average daily trade in goods. The rapid expansion of Eurocurrency and Eurobond markets (that is, currencies held outside their home country) has eroded the ability of national authorities to control their capital markets. In 1975, foreign exchange markets handled some $10–15 billion daily; a decade later, they handle $200 billion daily.[6]

Although governments can intervene in such markets, if they do so with a heavy hand, they will incur enormous costs in their own economic growth and risk unintended effects. For instance, efforts by the U.S. government in the 1960s to slow the export of capital by U.S-based multinational firms encouraged those firms to keep and borrow dollars outside the United States. The result was the rapid burgeoning of Eurocurrency markets outside national controls.

In addition to constraining the way states pursue their national interests, transnational actors affect the way such interests are initially defined. Transnational investment creates new interests and complicates the coalitions in world politics. For example, Honda America is steadily turning into an American car maker. It plans to export 50,000 cars annually to Japan in the early 1990s. American politicians are now pressing Europeans to allow access to the European market for Japanese automobiles produced in the United States. In other words, a transnational investment changed an American interest.

The American case is not unique. For years, France restricted Japanese automobiles to three percent of the French market (the same percentage as the French auto makers' share of the Japanese market) and restricted investment by Japanese companies in France. When Japanese auto makers began to establish plants in other European countries that could export to France, the French government dropped its restrictions on Japanese auto makers. A transnational investment changed a long-standing French policy. The diffusion of power to private transnational actors and the resulting complication of national interests is likely to continue even though it is not well recognized in many comparisons of the power resources of major states.

Modernization, urbanization, and increased communication in developing nations have also diffused power from government to private actors. Military power is more difficult to apply today than in the past because social awakening has increased nationalism in otherwise poor or weak states. This increased social mobilization makes military intervention and external rule more costly. The nineteenth-century great powers carved out and ruled colonial empires with a handful of troops. In 1953, the United States was able to restore the Shah of Iran to his throne by a minor covert action. It is hard to imagine, however, how many troops would have been needed to restore the Shah in the socially mobilized and nationalistic Iran of 1979. The United States and the Soviet Union found the costs of maintaining troops in Vietnam and Afghanistan unsupportable. In each case, the cause was less an increase in the power of a weaker state than the costliness for outsiders of ruling socially mobilized and nationalistic populations.

Another trend in the diffusion of power is the spread of modern technology, which has enhanced the capabilities of backward states. While the superpowers have kept a large lead in military technology, the forces that many Third World states can deploy in the 1990s make regional intervention more costly than in the 1950s. In addition, at least a dozen Third World states have developed significant arms exports, which have been paralleled by a widespread desire for diversification among arms recipients in order to gain leverage on the major or sole supplier. When arms are supplied from outside, the supplier often has leverage through technical assistance, spare parts, and replacements. The growth of indigenous arms industries removes that leverage.

In addition, more countries are acquiring sophisticated weapons capabilities. Today, twenty countries have the capability to make chemical weapons, and by 2000 an estimated fifteen Third World nations will be producing their own ballistic missiles.[7] Five states had the bomb when the Nuclear Nonproliferation Treaty was signed in 1968, and now India, Pakistan, Israel, and South Africa also have some nuclear capability. Brazil, Argentina, and several others might develop military nuclear capabilities within a decade. However, a small nuclear capability will not make these states contenders for global power; in fact, it may increase the risks they face if their neighbors follow suit or if the weapons fall into the hands of rebel groups. On the other hand, nuclear capability would enhance these states' regional power and increase the potential costs of regional intervention by larger powers. Technology also enhances the power of private groups. For instance, hand-held anti aircraft missiles helped guerrillas in Afghanistan, and new plastic explosives are effective tools for terrorists.

The ability of great powers with impressive traditional power resources to control their environments is also diminished by the changing nature of issues in world politics. Increasingly, the issues today do not pit one state against another; they are issues in which all states try to control non-state transnational actors. The solutions to many current issues of transnational interdependence will require collective action and cooperation among states. These include ecological changes (acid rain and global warming), health epidemics (AIDS), illicit trade in drugs, and control of terrorism. Such issues are transnational because they have domestic roots and cross international borders. As the nuclear accident at the Soviet reactor in Chernobyl showed, even a domestic issue like the safety of nuclear reactors can suddenly become a transnational issue.

Although force may sometimes play a role, traditional instruments of power are rarely sufficient to deal with the changing issues in world politics. New power resources, such as the capacity for effective communication and for developing and using multilateral institutions, may prove more relevant. Moreover, cooperation will often be required from small, weak states not fully capable of managing their own domestic drug, health, or ecological problems. For example, the United States cannot use its traditional power resources to force Peru to curtail the production of cocaine if a weak Peruvian government cannot control private gangs of drug dealers. And, if the American government cannot control the U.S. demand, a transnational market for cocaine will continue. Although the traditional power resources of economic assistance and military force can play roles in coping with terrorism, proliferation, or drugs, the ability of any great power to control its environment and to achieve what it wants is often not as great as traditional hard power indicators would suggest.

SOFT POWER

There is a second way to exercise power. A nation may get the outcomes it prefers in world politics because other nations want to follow it or have agreed to a situation that produces such effects. In this sense, it is just as important to set the agenda and structure the situations in world politics as to get others to change in particular situations.

This second aspect of power—which occurs when one nation gets other nations to *want* what it wants—might be called co-optive or *soft* power in contrast with the hard or command power of *ordering* others to do what it wants.

Parents of teenagers have long known that if they have structured their child's beliefs and preferences, their power will be greater and last longer than if they try to rely only on active control. Similarly, political leaders and philosophizers have long understood the power of attractive ideas or the ability to set the political agenda and determine the framework of debate in a way that shapes the preferences that others express. The ability to affect what other nations want tends to be associated with intangible power resources such as culture, ideology, and institutions.

Soft co-optive power is just as important as hard command power. If a state can make its power seem legitimate in the eyes of others, it will encounter less resistance to its wishes. If its culture and ideology are attractive, others will more willingly follow. If it can establish international norms consistent with its society, it will less likely have to change. If it can help support institutions that make other states wish to channel or limit their activities in ways the dominant state prefers, it may not need the costly exercise of coercive or hard power in bargaining situations.

In general, power is becoming less transferable, less coercive, and less tangible. Modern trends and changes in political issues are having significant effects on the nature of power and the resources that produce it. Co-optive power—getting others to want what you want—and soft power resources—cultural attraction, ideology, and international institutions—are not new. In the early postwar period, the Soviet Union profited greatly from such soft resources as communist ideology, the myth of inevitability, and transnational communist institutions. Various trends today are making co-optive behavior and soft power resources even more important.

Diminished Fungibility

The fragmented structure of world politics among different issues has made power resources less fungible, that is, less transferable from one issue to another. Money is fungible, in that it can be easily converted from one currency to another. Power has always been less fungible than money, but it is even less so today than in earlier periods. In the eighteenth century, a monarch with a full treasury could purchase infantry to conquer new provinces, which, in turn, could enrich the treasury. That simple process comes close to describing the situation in 1740 when Frederick II of Prussia went to war to seize Austria's province of Silesia. It may also come close to describing Iraq's attack on

Kuwait in 1990. But the Middle East remains the most traditional area in world politics, more an exception than the rule.

The direct use of force for economic gain is generally too costly and dangerous for modern great powers. Even short of aggression, the translation of economic into military power resources may be very costly. For instance, there is no economic obstacle to Japan developing a major nuclear or conventional force, but the political cost both at home and in the reaction of other countries would be considerable. Militarization might then reduce rather than increase Japan's ability to achieve its purposes.

Because power is a relationship, by definition it implies some context. Diminished fungibility means that specifying the context is increasingly important in estimating the actual power that can be derived from power resources. More than ever, one must ask the question, "Power for what?" Yet at the same time, because world politics has only partly changed and the traditional geopolitical agenda remains relevant, some fungibility of military power remains. The protective role of military force is a relevant asset in bargaining among states. This is an aspect of military power that was underdeveloped in the writing of some declinists. Paul Kennedy, for example, wrote in 1990 that "the drop in Cold War tensions has caused a reduction in the value many people put on military power . . . reducing the significance of the one measure of national power in which the United States has a clear advantage over other countries."[8] One example is the dependence of conservative oil-producing states on the United States for their security, which limited their leverage on the United States during the 1973 oil crisis and led them to accept American troops in 1990. The United States is still an ultimate guarantor of the military security of Europe and Japan, and that protection creates a power resource in the complex bargaining among its allies. In general, this need for protection makes American influence greater. Even in the new context of a reduced Soviet threat, this resource may be useful as a source of American influence. There will be uncertainty about the outcome of "the second Russian Revolution," and even Russia alone has formidable potential. In the context of the Cold War, the United States often worried about the frailty of its allies and tended to sacrifice some economic interests in the effort to contain the perceived Soviet threat. In the new context, though, if the United States worries less about the Soviet threat than its allies do, it might be able to demand more of its allies.

Reduced Coercion

Another effect of changing world politics is that power behavior is becoming less coercive, at least among the major states. The present spectrum of coerciveness in the instruments of power ranges from diplomatic notes to economic threats to military coercion. In earlier periods, the costs of coercion were relatively low. Force was acceptable and economies were less interdependent. Early in this century, the United States sent in marines and customs agents to collect debts in some Caribbean countries, but under current conditions, the use of force against small countries like Nicaragua is more costly.

Manipulation of interdependence under current conditions is also more costly. Economic interdependence usually carries benefits in both directions, and threats to disrupt the relationship, if carried out, could be very expensive. For example, Japan might want the United States to reduce its budget deficit, but threatening to refuse to buy American treasury bonds would likely disrupt financial markets and have enormously costly effects on Japan as well as on the United States. Because the more threatening coercive applications of power tend to be more costly, the less threatening types of power resources are becoming more useful.

Co-optive power is the ability of a nation to structure a situation so that other nations develop preferences or define their interests in ways consistent with its own. This power tends to arise from such resources as cultural and ideological attraction as well as the rules and institutions of international regimes. The United States has more co-optive power than other countries. Institutions governing the international economy, such as the International Monetary Fund and the General Agreement on Tariffs and Trade, tend to embody the liberal free-market principles that coincide in large measure with American society and ideology. In the security area, the American ability to use the United Nations to characterize Iraq's incursion into Kuwait as aggression (rather than postcolonial recovery of a province) was an important example of institutional soft power.

Multinational corporations are another source of co-optive power. British author Susan Strange argues that U.S. power in the world economy has increased as a result of transnational production: "Washington may have lost some of its authority over the U.S.-based transnationals, but their managers still carry U.S. passports, can be subpoenaed in U.S. courts, and in war or national emergency would obey Washington first. Meanwhile, the U.S. government has gained new authority over a great many foreign corporations operating inside the United States. All of them are acutely aware that the U.S. market is the biggest prize."[9] This power arises in part from the fact that 40 percent of the largest multinational corporations are head-quartered in the United States (compared to 16 percent in Japan) and in part from the importance of the American market in any global corporate strategy.

American culture is another relatively inexpensive and useful soft power resource. Obviously, certain aspects of American culture are unattractive to other people, and there is always danger of bias in evaluating cultural sources of power. But American popular culture embodied in products and communications has widespread appeal. Nicaraguan television played American shows even while the government fought American-backed guerrillas. Similarly, Soviet teenagers wear blue jeans and seek American recordings, and Chinese student protesters used a symbol that resembled the Statue of Liberty during the 1989 uprisings. While the Chinese government launched official protests against U.S. interference, Chinese citizens were as interested as ever in American democracy and culture. Young Japanese who have never been to the United States wear sports jackets with the names of American colleges.

Of course, there is an element of triviality and fad in popular behavior, but it is also true that a country that stands astride popular channels of communication has more opportunities to get its messages across and to affect the preferences of others. According to UNESCO studies, the United States exported seven times more television shows than the next country (Britain) and had the only global network for film distribution. Although American films account for only 6 to 7 percent of all films made, they occupy about 50 percent of world screen time. In 1981, the United States was responsible for 80 percent of worldwide transmission and processing of data.[10] Moreover, the American language has become the *lingua franca* of the global economy.

Although Japanese consumer products and cuisine have recently become more fashionable, they seem less associated with an implicit appeal to a broader set of values than in the case of American domination of popular communication. In part, they may reflect the inward orientation of Japanese culture. And while Japan has been extraordinarily successful at accepting foreign technology, it has been far more reluctant to accept foreigners. Japan's relations with China, for example, has been hampered by cultural insensitivities. Many Japanese are concerned about their lack of "internationalization" and the absence of a broader message.

While Americans can also be parochial and inward-oriented, the ethnic openness of the American culture and the political appeal of the American values of democracy and human rights are a source of international influence that European nations have to a lesser degree and Communist countries have largely lost. Compared to Japan and Europe, America's relative openness to immigrants is a source of strength. According to European scholar Ralf Dahrendorf, it is "relevant that millions of people all over the world would wish to live in the United States and that indeed people are prepared to risk their lives in order to get there."[11] Maintaining this appeal is important.

In June 1989, after President Bush criticized the Chinese government for killing student protesters in China, ordinary Chinese never seemed so supportive of the United States. Newspaper accounts noted that, unlike earlier periods, private attitudes seem to have been detached from official relations. Subsequently, by sending too high level a delegation to Beijing to seek reconciliation, he squandered some of those soft power resources. When ideals are an important source of power, the classic distinction between realpolitik and liberalism becomes blurred. The realist who focuses only on the balance of hard power resources will miss the power of transnational ideas.

Reduced Tangibility

The changing nature of international politics has also made intangible power resources more important. National cohesion, universalistic culture, and international institutions are taking on additional significance. Intangibility also characterizes important aspects of the economic power resources that underlie command power: power is passing to the "information-rich" instead of the "capital-rich."

Information is becoming more and more plentiful, but the flexibility to act first on new information is rare. Information becomes power, especially before it spreads. Thus, a capacity for timely response to new information is a critical power resource. In the context of an information-based economy, raw materials are less important and organizational skills and flexibility are more important. Product cycles are shortening and technology is moving toward totally flexible production systems, in which the craft-era tradition of custom-tailoring products will be incorporated into modern manufacturing plants. Japan has been particularly adept at such flexible manufacturing processes; the United States and Europe need to do more, and the Soviet Union and China lag seriously behind.

Timely response to information is not only important to manufacturing but also in critical services such as finance, insurance, and transportation. In the past, markets were determined by the limits of transportation and communication between buyers and sellers. Today, however, the new means of communication allow information on market trends to be immediately accessible to buyers and sellers worldwide. Satellites and fiber-optic cables instantaneously and continuously link people watching little green screens in London, Tokyo, and New York. The fact that the Soviet Union and China do not significantly participate in these transnational credit markets is a serious deficiency in their access to intangible aspects of power. In the 1980s, other governments such as Britain and Japan had to follow American trends in the deregulation of money markets and financial operations to preserve their positions in these important markets.

Intangible changes in knowledge also affect military power. Traditionally governments have invested in human espionage. Now major powers like the United States and the Soviet Union have continuous photographic and electronic surveillance from space, providing quick access to a variety of economic, political, and military information. Other nations such as France are beginning to make some low-resolution satellite information commercially available, but the United States leads in high-resolution information.

Another intangible aspect of power arises in the context of interdependence. The "power" of the debtor' has long been known: if you owe a bank $10,000, the bank has power over you. But if you owe $100 million, you have power over the bank. Thus, if a relationship is beneficial to both parties, the possibility that the weaker side might collapse under pressure limits the power of the seemingly stronger partner. The overt distribution of economic resources poorly describes the power situation in an interdependent relationship. The ability of the ostensibly stronger state may be limited by the greater organization and concentration of the smaller state. This difference helps to account for Canada's surprising success bargaining with the United States. If, however, Mexico or some Caribbean states became too weak to deal with internal poverty or domestic problems, transborder flows of migrants, drugs, or contraband might create a new foreign policy agenda for the United States. Similarly, developing countries that cannot prevent destruction of their forests will affect the global climate, yet the very weakness of those states will diminish the power to influence them. Ironically, the current neglect of weak Third World nations may reduce America's future ability to influence them on the new transnational issues. The United States will have to devote more attention to the paradoxical power that grows out of political and economic chaos and weakness in poor countries.

CONCLUSIONS

Americans are rightly concerned about an appropriate strategy for a post–Cold War world, but it is mistaken to portray the problem as American decline rather than diffusion of power. Even so, concern about decline might be good for the United States if it cut through complacency and prodded Americans to deal with some of our serious domestic problems. However, pollsters find that excessive anxiety about decline turns American opinion toward nationalistic and protectionist policies that would constrain our ability to cope with issues created by growing international interdependence. Thus there is no virtue in either overstatement or understatement of American strength. The former leads to failure to adapt; the latter to inappropriate responses such as treating Japan as the new enemy in place of the Soviet Union.

As the world's wealthiest nation, the United States should be able to pay for both its international commitments and domestic investments. America is rich but acts poor. In real terms, gross national product (GNP) is more than twice what it was in 1960, but Americans today spend much less of their GNP on international leadership. The prevailing view is "we can't afford it" despite the fact that U.S. taxes are a smaller percent of GNP than in other advanced industrial nations. This suggests a problem of domestic political leadership rather than long-term economic decline.

Without American leadership in providing a stable military balance and geopolitical framework, the processes of economic and social evolution in world politics could be disrupted. Maintaining the military balance is necessary, but not a sufficient strategy. The United States will also have to invest more heavily in resources for managing transnational interdependence and for domestic reforms to preserve the bases of its hard and soft power. In the long term of many decades, a new strategic vision may concentrate simply on managing interdependence, but its shape will depend on many unknowns as world politics evolve. The next decade is likely to be a period of transition; a successful strategy will have a dual goal of managing the geopolitical balance of power inherited from the past as well as the emerging interdependence that will increase in the future. A successful strategy for the next decade must integrate four components: (1) restoring the domestic base of economic strength; (2) maintaining a geopolitical balance of military power; (3) managing an open international economy that preserves a vision of global comparative advantage; and (4) developing a variety of multilateral regimes and institutions to organize the collective action of states for coping with the transnational agenda.

As has happened many times in the past, the mix of resources that produce international power is changing. What may be unprecedented is that the cycle of hegemonic conflict with its attendant world wars may not repeat itself. The United States today retains more traditional hard power resources than any other country. It also has the soft ideological and institutional resources to retain its leading place in the new domains of transnational interdependence. In this sense, the situation for the United States at the end of the twentieth century is quite different from that of Britain at the century's beginning. Thus, loose historical analogies and falsely deterministic political theories are worse than merely academic, for they may divert Americans from addressing the true nature of their situation. The problem for U.S. power after the Cold War will be less the new challengers for hegemony than the new challenges of transnational interdependence.

NOTES

1. Herbert Block, *The Planetary Product in 1980: A Creative Pause?* (Washington, D.C.: U.S. Department of State, Bureau of Public Affairs, 1981), pp. 74–75; Council on Competitiveness, *Competitiveness Index* (Washington, D.C.: 1988), app. II; Barry P. Bosworth and Robert Z. Lawrence, "America in the World Economy," *Brookings Review No. 7* (Winter 1988/89), p. 43; and Central Intelligence Agency, *Handbook of Economic Indicators, 1988* (Washington, D.C.: U.S. Government Printing Office, 1988), Table 7.
2. See Richard Rosecrance, *The Rise of the Trading State* (New York: Basic Books, 1986).
3. Henry Kissinger, *A New National Partnership* (Washington, D.C.: U.S. Department of State, Office of Media Services, 1975), p. 1.

4.   "The World's 50 Biggest Industrial Corporations," *Fortune*, August 1, 1988, p. D3.
5.   John Mearsheimer, "Back to the Future: Instability in Europe After the Cold War," *International Security*, Vol. 15, No. 1 (Summer 1990).
6.   Raymond Vernon and Debra L. Spar, *Beyond Globalism: Remaking American Foreign Economic Policy* (New York: Free Press, 1989), pp. 99–100.
7.   "CIA Sees a Developing World with Developed Arms," *New York Times*, February 10, 1989, p. A3.
8.   Paul Kennedy, "Fin de Siècle America," *New York Review of Books*, June 28, 1990, p. 31.
9.   Susan Strange, *States and Markets* (New York: Basil Blackwell, 1988), p. 237.
10. Hamid Mowlana, *Global Information and World Communication* (New York: Longman, 1986), pp. 48, 82, 94; and Thomas Guback, "International Circulation of U.S. Theatrical Films and Television Programming," in George Gerbner and Marsha Siefert, eds., *World Communications: A Handbook* (New York: Longman, 1984), p. 155.
11. Ralf Dahrendorf, quoted in Joseph S. Nye, Jr., *Bound to Lead: The Changing Nature of American Power* (New York: Basic Books, 1990), p. 195.

PROSPECTS FOR
THE WORLD ECONOMY

Richard N. Cooper

This paper first addresses the dominant trends in the world economy over the next quarter century. Such horizon is helpful to set the background against which developments occur in a shorter time frame. It then addresses the outlook over the next five to ten years for the elimination of major payments imbalances, for solution of the debt problem of developing countries, and for the monetary and trading systems. Finally, it touches on energy and on the possible influence on the world economy of the dramatic developments in Eastern Europe during 1989–1990.

Continuity in human events has often been falsely counterpoised to change in human events. The methodological approach adopted here can best be characterized as continuity *in* change. The world twenty-five years from now will be substantially different from what it is now, but those differences will arise mainly from tendencies and trends that have been operating in the past, and can be expected to continue to operate in the future.

DOMINANT FACTORS IN THE LONG TERM

Three features of the international economic environment will be especially important over the next twenty-five years.[1]

Population Growth

The first feature of the world economy is rapid population growth. Between 1965 and 1986 the world's population grew by 1,600 million persons, or about 1.9 percent a year. Some slowdown in population growth occurred toward the end of this period, especially in China and in a number of middle-income countries, such as South Korea, as well as in the industrialized countries. But China was the exception among low income countries. Population growth normally accelerates at first after a country begins to experience increases in per capita income, as longevity increases, as child-bearing ages are lengthened, and especially as infant mortality rates fall with better nutrition and medical care. A slowdown in population growth usually occurs only after per capita income reaches around $1,000, when modes of production change, parents realize that the probability of survival of their children has risen, and parents become better informed about family planning techniques. There are still over 3 billion persons living in countries with average per capita incomes below $1,000 (in 1986), mostly in Africa and Asia. Even if global population growth slows by a substantial 0.3 percentage points, to 1.6 percent a year, the world population would still reach 7.7 billion by the year 2015, an increase of 2.8 billion from the mid-1980s. Almost all this increase will be in relatively low income countries.[2]

More people mean more demand for energy—for warmth, food preparation, illumination, motive power, and production processes; more demand for food; more demand for fresh water; and more demand for housing and other forms of capital. It would take extraordinary efforts of a nature and magnitude not generally contemplated to alter this projection significantly, although more modest efforts now could have significant effects beyond our 25-year horizon.

Higher Per Capita Income

The second dominant feature of the world economy is the all but universal aspiration for higher standards of living in all but the richest parts of the world. In this respect the world has been westernized; it has absorbed the notion and the expectation of material progress. So in future there will not only be more people, but more people wanting higher standards of living. And we now know how, in principle, to achieve higher standards of living: install a stable social system with incentives for effort and risk-taking. Most of the world does not need to generate new technology or even savings to grow—increasingly those can be borrowed from the rest of the world. But it does require extensive investment in both physical and human capital; of the two, the latter is both more important and more difficult.

Economic growth everywhere implies economic and social change, and change almost invariably involves some losers even in an environment in which change is being generated by economic growth. For some, change involves duress. Established enterprises have extensive investment in existing ways of doing things—in their machines, their people, and their organizational hierarchy. It is much easier simply to carry on in established patterns than to change, and that is what most organizations, including business enterprises, prefer. Yet in Western societies these business enterprises are, paradoxically, the principal instruments of economic change. They change because they feel compelled to do so by competition, by fear of losing their customers to other firms. The more far-sighted ones change on their own, to stay ahead of their actual or potential competitors. But for many firms and individuals change is disagreeable. Individuals can find that once promising careers are now dead ends, that once learned skills are now obsolete. Some individuals adapt well, others do not. This is the essence of what Joseph Schumpeter called creative destruction, and it is a process that, over time, has made the average individual in Western countries unbelievably well-off when viewed from the perspective of forebears only three or four generations earlier.

Former and current communist countries will have to learn this lesson if they wish to modernize their economies, and it will not be an easy or agreeable lesson, since it runs against the strong apparent preference in many of those countries for lifelong stability. It also is being learned in many developing countries, where it carries the possibility of social upheaval, since it is not possible to modernize economic activity and norms without also altering both norms and expectations in other areas as well, as Chinese leaders have discovered but to which they have not yet become reconciled.

Historically, economic growth is associated with an enormous growth in demand for commercial primary energy. In the two strong decades following 1950 the demand for primary energy in the industrialized countries more than doubled; in the two decades following 1960 the demand for primary energy in the centrally planned economies increased by a factor of nearly 2.5; and in the two decades following 1965 the demand for primary energy in the developing countries trebled. If gross world product grows by a plausible 4 percent over the next quarter century (1.6 in population and 2.4 in per capita income), the demand for primary energy on historical relationships between energy and growth would increase by a factor of 2.6 over present energy consumption. Put another way, improvements in the energy efficiency of the world economy must exceed 4 percent a year if we are to avoid increased demand for primary energy over current levels.

Two qualifications to the above projection need to be mentioned. First, since 1975 there has been a sharp drop in the growth in energy demand traditionally associated with economic growth. This reflected a widespread response to the oil shocks of 1974 and 1979–1980, with the sharp increases in energy prices associated with those shocks. We do not know yet whether this is a new trend, or whether it represented a transitional period of conservation, which, when exhausted, will be followed by restoration of the traditional relationship of energy demand to economic growth. The experience of the past fifteen years has clearly shown that a given level of gross national product (GNP) can be sustained with considerably lower levels of energy consumption, country by country, and there is no reason to suppose that further incentives to conserve energy could not prolong that process beyond what has already been achieved. The marked improvement in economy-wide energy efficiency that has been achieved in industrial countries was due in part, but only in relatively small part, to increased imports of energy in indirect forms, such as steel from developing countries.

The second qualification is that growth of developing countries as a group (excluding China) slowed enormously in the 1980s, suggesting that a 4 percent growth in gross world product over the next twenty-five years may be too high. But there are no signs that the aspirations for higher living standards have diminished. The 1980s are thought of as a period of temporary setback that must be overcome. A best guess would be that the economic growth of developing countries will accelerate from the low levels of the 1980s. Table 1 provides some data on growth in population, output, and energy consumption after 1965.

Increased International Mobility

The third important feature of the world economy is its increased integration, in the specific sense here that business enterprises increasingly take, and are driven by competition to take, a more-than-regional or national perspective in framing their business decisions. This has been true of markets and sources of supply for a long time, and of sources of capital for the past two

Table 1   Some Important Growth Rates—Annual Average

	1965–1980	*1980–1987*	*1987–2000*[a]
Population			
Low-income countries	2.3	2.0	1.9
Middle-income countries	2.4	2.2	1.9
High-income countries	0.9	0.7	0.5
Former centrally planned economies	1.0	1.0	—
Gross Domestic Production			
Low-income countries[b]	5.5	1.7	
China and India	5.3	8.5	
Middle-income countries	6.2	2.8	
High-income countries	3.7	2.6	
Commercial Energy Consumption			
Low-income countries[b]	5.0	3.9	
China and India	8.8	4.8	
Middle-income countries	6.6	2.8	
High-income countries	3.1	0.5	
Former centrally planned economies	4.4	2.8	

[a] Projection
[b] Excludes China and India

Source: World Bank, *World Development Report 1989*, Tables 2, 5, and 26.

decades. But it will be increasingly so also for the location of production and the related issue of work force. The secular decline in transportation costs, especially in the past two decades of air freight and bulk carriage, implies they are no longer a decisive factor for location of production of many goods. Not only Persian Gulf oil but also South African coal and Liberian iron ore can be moved long distances to market. Under these circumstances many industries, in principle, become footloose, able to locate at a variety of convenient places. They seek an inexpensive labor force able to meet the required skill qualifications, social stability, and a tax and regulatory environment favorable to low production costs. These developments imply that a country, far out of line in one dimension, that is not adequately compensated in some other dimension will lose those economic activities that do not require close proximity to markets.

The influence of higher mobility should not be exaggerated. The managers of many enterprises still have strong ties of loyalty to their home society and culture, they have useful but specialized knowledge about how best to operate in a familiar political environment, and they are subject to the inertial forces that attend most human action. The trend is clear: competitive pressures are eroding these factors, and more and more firms are moving some of their activities away from their historical bases.

What are the implications of this third feature for the governmental policy? Individual countries cannot impose stiff environmental or other regulations and expect to retain the economic activities that are especially hard hit, unless for one reason or another the activities are immobile, or unless the firms in question see an offsetting benefit to themselves flowing from the stiff regulations. Over time, the activity will shift to lower cost locations. With increasingly mobile production, there will be growing conflict between each nation's exercise of its sovereign rights of regulation and its ability to retain the heavily regulated activity.

It is still possible to regulate products in the face of mobility of firms, since a country can prohibit imports as well as local production of nonconforming products, for example with respect to safety features or materials of fabrication, such as ivory.

Even here, however, when the product is used in further production, as most traded goods are, regulations on products will raise costs to local producers who use the product, relative to their offshore competitors.

An analogous problem applies to taxation, especially taxation of corporate income or of interest, dividends, and capital gains on financial investments. Through their pricing on intra-corporate transactions, corporations can shift profits from regions with high corporate profit rates to those with low ones, thereby reducing or at least deferring their total taxes. With the internationalization of two-way communication and of securities trading, individuals can hold their financial investments in many parts of the world, in many names, and thereby avoid national taxation. Indeed, many countries today do not even attempt to levy taxes on the overseas financial earnings of their residents.

High mobility of business enterprise reduces the effectiveness of traditional nation-based regulation and taxation. Of course governments are not oblivious to this trend; they attempt to cope with the increased mobility in a variety of ways: import prohibitions, extraterritorial reach, deregulation. They also increasingly recognize the need to cooperate with other like-minded governments, and even sometimes those that are not so like-minded. Cooperation is especially evident in the area of financial regulation, where principally domestic agencies, such as the Securities and Exchange Commission and the Federal Reserve, increasingly collaborate with their counterparts to preserve the effectiveness of their (now collective) actions. Tax authorities are also moving toward greater exchange of information. Increased mobility of enterprises will also lead to new patterns of cooperation among national authorities, at least at the technical level. By 2015 these practices may have become habitual.

THE NEXT DECADE

Rapid population growth, continued aspiration for and some success in achieving higher material standards of living, and increased international mobility of business enterprise are three dominant features of the world economy over the next quarter century. What about the nearer future, and the issues that have preoccupied officials concerned in recent times with foreign economic policy? These can be considered under the headings: 1) major international imbalances; 2) external debt of developing countries; 3) exchange rate arrangements and coordination of macroeconomic policies; 4) the Uruguay Round and prospects for the international trading system; and 5) energy policy.

Major International Imbalances

A dominant feature of the international economy after 1983 was the extremely large current account deficit of the United States, more or less matched by extraordinarily large surpluses in Japan and Germany plus Germany's smaller neighbors. The strong desirability of greatly reducing and preferably eliminating the large U.S. deficit has been bruited by academics, journalists, and officials for many years, some darkly forecasting the "disasters" that would occur if this were not done. That has been matched by calls for greatly reducing the large Japanese and German surpluses, although there has been less consensus with respect to those objectives in the countries concerned.

The U.S. foreign trade deficit[3] reached a peak of $162 billion (3.6 percent of GNP) in 1987, and has declined steadily since then to $86 billion (1.6 percent of GNP) at an annual rate in the first half of 1990—a dramatic reduction, but one that still leaves a very high deficit by the standards of the last seventy-five years. There are, however, two reasons for believing that further deficit reduction will be less pronounced in the early 1990s, and that it will prove impossible to eliminate the deficit by the mid-1990s. The first concerns the U.S. economy. By 1990 it had experienced an eight-year period of growth since the recession of 1982, and with exceptions here and there it was fully employed, with unemployment running at 5.2 percent of the labor force, the lowest since 1979. Further improvement in the trade balance sufficient both to eliminate the existing deficit and to cover the increased debt servicing that will be accumulated while the deficit persists during the period of decline would require mainly increased exports of manufactured goods, and that in turn would require additional investment in manufacturing capacity. To eliminate the deficit by the mid-1990s after making allowance for these points would leave very little room for increased public and private consumption during this period, something that would be politically difficult over a period as long as five years.

Drastic reductions in defense spending, particularly defense procurement, could of course relax this constraint: additional investment would be required for new capacity to produce exportable products, but the skilled labor force would be available for that task, plus a significant increase in private and public non-defense spending. So what happens to defense spending and the overall federal budget will influence the room for maneuver in the American economy over the next five years.

A major improvement in the U.S. external accounts implies a major deterioration in the external accounts of other countries. Who will it be? Many developing countries would be happy to increase their imports substantially, but their ability to do that is limited by financing, which in turn is limited for most African and Latin American countries by the continuing overhang of existing external debt. The same could be said of Eastern European countries, which have a great need for capital to restructure their economies, but little effective demand for imports in the absence of dramatically larger sources of external finance, which in the end will materialize only if it is provided directly or indirectly (via guarantees) by the governments of the rich countries.

Many other industrial countries already run substantial current account deficits—those of Britain and Spain, for instance, are much larger than those of the United States, relative to their economies—and they would not welcome further increases. That leaves Japan and Germany plus Germany's smaller neighbors, Belgium, the Netherlands, and Switzerland. Japan's surplus fell sharply after 1987, along with the U.S. deficit, but Germany's surplus actually grew (largely as a result of developments within Europe). Germany's surplus is likely to decline rapidly (but remain large) following the integration of the two German economies. The Federal Republic has taken on substantial financial obligations with respect to the East German public, and those will be defrayed through larger government spending, financed in large part by borrowing. Higher interest rates will strengthen the German mark and weaken the German trade surplus. Some further decline in their surpluses would no doubt be welcome, in both Japan and Germany, as a contribution to global equilibrium and to reduce U.S. pressures on Japanese trade policy and German macroeconomic policy.

Both Germany and Japan have thrived on export-led growth. Export performance, moreover, has become in both societies more than merely a means to greater economic prosperity; it has come to be associated with high social virtue, with international standing and even legitimacy in the community of nations, and has come to be a touchstone of relative performance in a competitive world. The rapid and large decline in their trade surpluses that would be required as the counterpart to elimination of the U.S. current account deficit (and in face of their rising earnings on foreign investments) by the mid-1990s would very likely create such high anxiety in both societies that policy measures would be introduced to stop the deterioration, as Germany in fact did in 1981 following its oil-price induced deficit of 1980. In short, public reaction abroad will probably not permit a rapid elimination of the U.S. payments deficit, even if U.S. domestic conditions permitted it. Barring a serious U.S. recession, which no one wants, only a solution to the financing constraints of developing countries and/or Eastern Europe on a scale hitherto not imagined—some additional $25 billion per year, at a minimum—will permit the United States to eliminate its deficit in the next five years.

That is perhaps not desirable from the perspective of an American, but neither is it a prescription for disaster. Foreigners willingly invest in the United States for the straightforward reason that it is a good place to invest; they do not do so as a favor to Americans. The U.S. economy remains innovative, flexible, and vibrant, and rates of return over the medium and long run are attractive. The political and the social system is stable. In a world of increasing capital mobility, in which many people around the world have been prevented from investing extensively abroad until the 1980s, the United States must appear an attractive place to put at least a small fraction of one's portfolio of assets. It takes well under five percent of the world's savings outside the United States to finance the U.S. payments deficit. So the deficit itself is a reflection in part of the desire of foreigners to invest in the United States for fundamental reasons, not exclusively related to the interest rates kept attractive to foreign investors by a continuing U.S. budget deficit.

Developing Country Debt

During the late 1980s and into the 1990s many developing countries are burdened by heavy external debt, acquired during the more buoyant 1970s and in the early 1980s, following the second major increase in oil prices. Difficulties in servicing this debt have led private and even governmental lenders around the world to hesitate to lend to many of these countries, especially those in Latin America and in Africa. As a consequence, the net flow of resources into developing countries as a group has diminished substantially from levels of a decade ago, and a few individual countries are even transferring resources to the creditor nations insofar as their actual interest payments exceed new inflows of capital.

Over the course of the next twenty-five years, this problem is likely to be solved so that from the perspective of 2015 the "debt problem" will be seen as a historical event of the 1980s and the early 1990s. For some countries, especially those in Latin America, the solution will lie largely in outgrowing the debt, thus reducing debt-to-GDP (gross domestic product) and debt service ratios to the point at which these countries will again become creditworthy and attractive places to invest. For others, mainly the very poor countries of Africa, the problem will be solved largely by effective write-offs of significant portions of the debt, which in the case of these countries is owed mainly to other governments and to international organizations.

In the next ten years, however, the debt problem is likely to continue to plague the international economy, in part by inhibiting economic growth in developing countries, in part by preventing elimination of the U.S. payments deficit, as just discussed.

The "Brady initiative" of March 1989—it can hardly be called a plan, since it was a series of unconnected and indeed partially inconsistent points—has perhaps not completely reached the end of its usefulness. But the arrangements for Mexico, Costa Rica, Venezuela, and the Philippines made under its rubric, while undoubtedly helpful, fall far short of a comprehensive solution. The main point they illustrate is how difficult it is to get private banks to make substantive concessions to debtor countries on a voluntary basis. A more comprehensive solution on a significant scale will require even larger injections of public funds (or guarantees) than those implicit in an enlarged role for the multilateral development banks, and they will require a degree of compulsion on the private banks.[4] Neither of these is being seriously contemplated in 1990.

The most significant feature of the Brady initiative was its removal of debtor-creditor agreement as a condition for disbursement by the International Monetary Fund (IMF). The arguments surrounding this issue are complex and need not be rehearsed here, but there is little doubt that this condition (which had obtained since 1983) strengthened the bargaining position of commercial banks in their "London Club" negotiations with debtor countries, and in many cases led to damaging delays in supporting an agreed economic program, in some cases actually undermining the program. So this necessary change, needless to say not welcomed by the commercial banks, was belatedly recognized by the U.S. government. The result will be to increase the instances of arrearage by debtor countries when they cannot reach satisfactory terms with their commercial bankers in time to support a serious economic program, in effect creating a line of credit out of the interest due. (This stratagem of course does not work if the country needs commercial bank funds beyond what it owes them in interest.) Partly as a result, the debt problem is receding gradually for most countries. In the aggregate, the peak difficulties (as measured by ratio of debt service to exports) was probably reached in 1986; it has declined since then, and on plausible assumptions about the evolution of the world economy in the early 1990s can be expected to recede further (see Table 2).

Table 2 Medium Term Debt Scenario, 1982–1995

	1982	*1986*	*1990*	*1995*
Indebted Countries				
Debt/Exports (%)	159.1	205.2	145.0	110.0
Interest Payments/Exports (%)	14.5	13.8	10.2	7.4
Western Hemisphere				
Debt/Exports (%)	271.0	349.6	264.4	192.3
Interest Payments/Exports (%)	32.1	29.3	24.5	16.3
Africa				
Debt/Exports (%)	154.1	239.7	227.8	191.6
Interest Payments/Exports (%)	9.4	11.5	13.5	10.6

Note:
• Interest payments on total debt plus amortization payments on long-term debt only. Excludes debt service payments to the IMF.
• Forecasts based on industrial country output growth of 3 percent per annum, 6-month LIBOR averages 8.25 percent per annum over the forecast period. The terms of trade are assumed to remain weak following the decline in 1990. Total financing flows change little in 1990–1995 compared with 1983–1989. The baseline developing country growth increases to 5 percent per annum over 1992–1995, and inflation falls to 12 percent per annum. Investment ratios are forecast to rise by 4–5 percentage points.

Source: IMF, *World Economic Outlook*, May 1990.

So while the foreign debt currently influences significantly the relation of heavily indebted countries to the international community, that influence is likely to diminish over time, and, as noted, economic growth will accelerate from the low levels of the 1980s.[5]

Macroeconomic Coordination and Exchange Rate Arrangements
The call for better coordination of macroeconomic policies among the major industrial countries has become commonplace, and equally commonplace is the disappointment when it does not occur. There is no doubt that failure to coordinate macroeconomic policies—or even to pay relevant attention to what other countries are doing—can have deleterious consequences for the world economy, as when in the early 1980s the United States pursued an expansionist fiscal policy combined with tight money, while other leading countries (except France) pursued strongly contractionary fiscal policies. The result was a heavy "torque" on the world economy, leading to

a sharp strengthening in the dollar relative to other major currencies, which in turn led to the sharp deterioration in the U.S. trade position.

On the other hand, it is exceptionally difficult to coordinate macroeconomic policies, and especially fiscal policies, if by "coordinate" we mean move them in conscious relation to one another (not necessarily always in the same direction). The determination of government expenditure and tax rates is at the heart of parliamentary prerogative, and in democratic societies these cannot be successfully negotiated among finance ministers or even heads of government on a year-in, year-out basis. Fortunately, there are many forms of international economic cooperation that are extremely useful even though they fall short of coordination; fortunately also, formal coordination of fiscal policies is not typically necessary, or even always desirable. Differences in fiscal policy may reflect quite legitimate differences in national preferences regarding the level, structure, and timing of government expenditures and taxation, and these different preferences should be accommodated insofar as they are not exercised largely at the expense of other countries. And they generally can be accommodated in the presence of a functioning international capital market.

One of the costs of fiscal divergences in a world of floating exchange rates will be movements in exchange rates that at best complicate, and at worst distort and discourage, investment decisions by businesses. For that reason, it would be desirable to achieve greater stability and greater predictability in exchange rates. Unfortunately, although this issue has been on the international agenda since 1985, there is as yet no consensus within either the academic or the official community on a satisfactory way to accomplish this. So the current arrangement of periodic discussion and ad hoc management of exchange rates among the finance ministers of the Group of Seven (U.S., Japan, FRG, France, UK, Italy, and Canada) is likely to continue through the 1990s.

During this period the European Community (EC) is likely to proceed toward European Monetary Union (EMU), leading to a single monetary policy for its members and ultimately to a common currency. Whether Britain will participate is still unclear, but it is increasingly likely that other European states will go ahead with or without Britain: the EMU is likely to have a juridical existence that differs from the European Community, so membership need not be identical, however desirable that might be.

One of the most pressing factors driving EMU is the common agricultural policy, whose execution is greatly complicated by movements in exchange rates among EC members. Indeed, these complications have led to a separate set of exchange rates for agricultural products, and a set of border controls to enforce them. The border controls must disappear in a Europe without borders. But more generally, Europeans feel they cannot have a true common market without having a common currency, which puts all business firms on the same footing in this regard and eliminates the capricious component (seen from a business perspective) of fluctuating exchange rates.

The same arguments that apply within Europe apply increasingly beyond Europe as well. Current monetary arrangements, with the major currencies floating against one another, are not sustainable in the long run. This observation should not be interpreted as hostility to the period of flexible exchange rates that we have had since 1973. They were a useful, probably a necessary, shock absorber during a very turbulent period, with three major movements in oil prices (up in 1974 and 1979–1980, down in 1986) and two major world recessions, both closely related to the oil price increases.

But as we look to the future and the requirements for constant renewal of the international monetary system, it is hard to imagine flexible exchanges rates combined with a liberal trading system being sustainable in the long run. The reason is a simple one. Exchange rates in the short run are determined overwhelmingly by financial transactions, by movements of capital. Exchange rates, however, are of fundamental importance to manufacturers and farmers in an open economy. The typical profit margin on manufactured goods is about five percent, perhaps a shade more, perhaps a shade less. In recent years we have seen exchange rates among major currencies move that much in a week. A business engaged in international trade, or in competition with foreigners in its home market, can find its profit margin wiped out (or doubled, but that is not so troublesome) for reasons completely beyond understanding, having to do with the arcane world of finance. It can of course hedge a particular transaction against changes in exchange rates, by using financial instruments such as futures contracts, but it cannot hedge its entire investment against such changes, except by diversifying across currency zones, i.e., by weakening the advantages of international specialization.

As national economies become more internationalized, which is an inexorable process unless broken by restrictive government actions, and as more firms are exposed to international competition, the uncertainty created by currency movements will become less and less tolerable. It will have three effects, none of them desirable. First, as noted, firms will invest increasingly abroad, which is not by itself undesirable, in order to hedge against currency risk, and that will reduce the overall efficiency of investment, hence result in living standards lower than would otherwise be attainable. Second, they will reduce total investment in tradable goods and services, with the same consequence. Third, they will appeal to their governments to reduce by one means or another what they consider "unfair" import competition, with the same consequence.

The investment decisions of the next decade, decisions made by tens of thousands of individuals with respect both to tangible and to intangible investment, such as applied research, will in their totality determine living standards twenty to thirty years from now. Exchange rate uncertainty will dampen and distort that investment. Insofar as that occurs, there is a long-run cost to a system of flexible exchange rates that we will want to avoid if we can.

That consideration leads me to the unorthodox conclusion that the industrialized democracies should adopt a single currency, which of course implies a single monetary policy, sometime early in the next century. It is a politically radical proposal, and is therefore unrealistic in the near future. But we should be thinking now about where we want the international monetary system to go in the longer run. It is not premature to think about a single currency for the industrialized democracies. The technical conditions for such a currency exist today, namely a highly developed and internationalized money and capital market. The institutional arrangements would have to be developed, but a useful starting model, which of course would require adaptation to the different circumstances of nations, would be the Federal Reserve System of the United States. It was created in 1913 around twelve regional Reserve Banks, each of which had some voice, but no one of which had a decisive voice, in determining monetary policy for the United States. The twelve Reserve Banks formally issue the currency in the United States, so there are technically twelve kinds of currency, each of which trades at par with the others under the fixed exchange rates that prevail within the United States.

It is possible to imagine an international reserve system, in which the central banks of the major market-oriented democracies continue to issue currency and perform the many routine functions of central banks, and which as a group form an open market committee that determines overall monetary policy, with all participating countries having some voice, but with no one of them having a decisive voice in that determination.

Exchange rates would be irrevocably fixed, so there would be a single currency for commercial transactions, even though banknotes labeled "dollars," "francs," "marks," or "yen" could continue to be issued.

The political conditions for such a radical step do not exist today, but it is not too early to begin thinking about such an arrangement, and comparing it with the alternatives that are likely to eventuate if we once again fail to adapt the international monetary system to new technological and economic developments. Absent greater certainty in exchange rate movements, business firms will respond in part by calling for, and succeeding in getting, greater protection against surges of imports brought about by unpredicted currency depreciations. Indeed, appeals for "anti-dumping" duties have already increased markedly in both Europe and the United States, prompted in part by exchange rate movements.

The Uruguay Round and the Future of the Trading System

In mid-1990 the nations of the world were engaged in the largest and most comprehensive set of multilateral trade negotiations ever undertaken, called the Uruguay Round, where they were formally launched in 1984. The last major multilateral trade negotiations, the Tokyo Round, concluded in 1979, and the preceding Kennedy Round in 1967. The outcome of the Uruguay Round will determine the basis for trade in goods and services for most nations of the world into the next century, since it is normal after each of these major trade negotiations to have a phase-in period of six to eight years. This Round covers international trade in services for the first time, and investment insofar as it has a bearing on international trade in goods or services. It is substantially more complex than the Tokyo Round, which itself ended up with nine separate codes covering specialized areas, such as government procurement and trade in civil aircraft, in addition to the agreed tariff reductions and new statements of principle.

Driven in part by a timetable for "fast track" action by the U.S. Congress, which must approve the results of the Round before the United States can implement them, the Uruguay Round is scheduled to finish by the end of 1990. Yet at a conference on prospects for the Uruguay Round held at Washington's Institute for International Economics in June 1990, the judgment of the paper writers was that irreconcilable differences among key trading partners continued to exist in a number of negotiating areas whose resolution is considered a *sine qua non* for successful conclusion of the Round.[6] Among these are agriculture, safeguards, and intellectual property rights. (The broad area of services was still too diffuse to tell whether there were irreconcilable differences or not.)

On agriculture, the main issue is between the United States, supported generally by other natural exporters of agricultural products (formed together as the Cairnes group, led by Australia), on the one hand, and the European Community, supported quietly by Japan, Switzerland, and other countries that protect strongly their agricultural sectors against import competition. It has finally been recognized formally that trade in agricultural products cannot be separated from domestic agricultural policies. The United States put forward the position that all agricultural subsidies, with stipulated exceptions, should be eliminated over a defined period of time, preferably by the year 2000. While agreeing that government support for farmers should be reduced, the EC cannot accept the principle of elimination of (almost) all subsidies to farmers. The negotiations remain hung up over principle, and without some principle it will be difficult to negotiate concrete changes in agricultural policy. The United States has stated that significant results in agriculture are necessary for the Round as a whole to be acceptable. In past Rounds the United States settled for relatively little in agriculture, and the EC may be waiting for the United States to come around to a minimal result. A difference in the Uruguay Round is that a number of developing countries also want significant results in agriculture, and may insist on that as a condition for agreement in other areas, such as services or intellectual property rights.

On intellectual property rights, the division runs mainly between the United States, the EC, and Japan, on the one hand, and a number of developing countries such as Brazil and India on the other. Basically, the technologically advanced countries want to receive royalties for their inventions and publications and trademarks and to control more generally who can use them, whereas the developing countries take the view that they are too poor to pay substantial royalties, and it would be socially foolish and indeed inhumane to deny them modern technology or information, particularly with respect to pharmaceuticals.

The issue of "safeguards" concerns the rules under which a country may subsequently violate one of its commitments in a previous Round and impose restrictions on imports. Under existing rules of the General Agreement on Tariffs and Trade (GATT), applicable to merchandise trade, countries experiencing injury from imports of a particular product should apply import restrictions (duties, not quantitative restrictions) to all suppliers, on a non-discriminatory basis. The spirit of this provision has been repeatedly violated with the use of so-called voluntary export restraints (VERs), whereby technically the exporting country imposes the restraint, thus avoiding a formal violation of GATT. The EC has objected to the non-discrimination provision since the time of the Tokyo Round, from which safeguards remain an unresolved issue, whereas Japan and a number of developing countries correctly see the non-discrimination provision as a safeguard against indiscriminate use of selective safeguards.

Finally, there is as yet no agreed principle for reducing tariffs in the Uruguay Round, although there is an agreed target average reduction of 33 percent.

So many issues remain not merely unresolved, but at loggerheads, that it seems difficult to believe that the Uruguay Round will be completed by its end-of-1990 deadline. But previous Rounds have also been cliff-hangers, and it is conceivable that the negotiators can overcome even their fundamental differences in a final burst of negotiating energy.

It is frequently said that the Uruguay Round must succeed, that the trading system is fragile and in danger of collapsing, and that failure would be a disaster for world trade. All of these anxieties might be justified, but they need not be. The world trading system was performing reasonably well before the inauguration of the Uruguay Round, and it could perform reasonably well without it. The main problem is that Americans somehow have the view that they are being cheated by the trading system and that everyone except Americans is being unfair. That general view unfortunately informs much congressional sentiment on trade issues, and makes Congress vulnerable to pleas for protection by what Harry Truman called the special interests. The key role of the Uruguay Round on this perspective is to provide cover for inaction, both during and following successful negotiations, in response to these self-interested pleas, on the grounds that to respond favorably would jeopardize the negotiations or violate commitments recently made. A strong president could accomplish the same result if he were willing to exert himself in that direction.

To prod other countries to successful conclusion, the United States has talked increasingly about bilateral and "pluralateral" approaches to trade, but only if the multilateral approach fails. A recent example was an altogether baffling press release from the White House in late June 1990, which states among other things, that "a comprehensive free trade agreement (FTA) for Latin America is our long-term goal. We are prepared to enter into FTAs with other markets in Latin America and the Caribbean." It is entirely unclear why it should be a prime *U.S.* goal to have a free trade area in Latin America, although the United States should not object to a genuine free trade area (as opposed to the half-hearted and selective arrangements that have dominated most Latin American arrangements since 1960); nor is it clear why the United States should want free trade areas with Latin American countries, given the suspicions that these countries have had of U.S. economic motives in the past. It will reinforce the notion that the trading world will divide into three north-south blocs by the end of the century—Europe–Africa (and possibly Middle East), Western Hemisphere, and Japan–Southeast Asia. Such arrangements would be desirable neither from an economic nor from a political point of view, and it is regrettable to see a U.S. president give even a back-handed endorsement to the idea.

Energy Policy [7]

After a decade of declining oil prices and continuing squabbling among Organization of Petroleum Exporting Countries (OPEC) ministers over nonobservance of production quotas, it may seem odd to introduce energy into a discourse on the world economy during the next five to ten years, except to those who worry about roasting 50 to 100 years from now as a result of greenhouse gas emissions. But the decline in oil (and gas) prices and the squabbling among OPEC ministers has introduced a complacency in the main consuming countries, and especially in the United States, that is wholly unjustified. As we have learned, it takes years to transform the system of energy in a modern economy. Because of that inflexibility and because of the fundamental importance of energy to the economy, disturbances in the energy sector can be profoundly disturbing to the entire national economy.

If the growth projections presented earlier come to pass, and if the previous trajectory of growth in demand for primary energy relative to growth in GNP has resumed, the current excess capacity in world oil production, all in OPEC countries, most in the Middle East, will be exhausted by the mid-1990s. From that time, another disturbance in the oil market could create again the stagflation and the economic policy dilemmas of the mid- and late-1970s. No event is likely to create greater divisions among the industrialized democracies. Given heavy concentration of oil supplies in the Middle East, some form of disturbance is all but inevitable. Whether it wreaks the havoc of the two earlier oil shocks will depend entirely on the state of economic activity in the major economies of the world at the time of the disturbance and on how well the world is prepared to cope with a disturbance under those conditions. Strategic stocks have been built in the United States, Japan, and Germany, and that will be of help, provided they will be used. Research into non-hydrocarbon sources of energy (except for fusion) was drastically cut during the 1980s, and conservation programs were often allowed to lapse. Both of these developments should be reversed, mainly in the interests of better energy security, but with the added benefit if properly handled of reducing pollutants and greenhouse gas emissions as well.

Developments in Eastern Europe

A survey of future developments in the world economy would not be complete without reference to the dramatic developments in Eastern Europe, including the Soviet Union. There is a general move toward reliance on decentralized, market-based decision-making in most of these countries, although in different ways and at different paces. There is also a tremendous need for capital to modernize their economies, agriculture as well as industry and utilities. It might be thought, therefore, that this modernization would provide a major impetus to the world economy over the next decade and a major claim on the world's savings.

An important distinction needs to be made, however, between the need for capital and the demand for capital. The need is unquestionably there, as it is (especially for human capital formation) in most developing countries, but the demand is there only if it can be financed in some way. Apart from eastern Germany, which has a wealthy patron, Eastern European imports from the rest of the world will rise only as rapidly as its exports to the rest of the world, unless there are substantial new foreign credits to or foreign investments in Eastern Europe. These are not likely from private sources in view of the already high level of debt that most Eastern European countries carry (Czechoslovakia and Romania are exceptions). As a consequence, even quite spectacular economic success in Eastern Europe, which at this time must still be judged problematic, would not make much difference for the world economy as a whole over the next decade, although it would be of great interest to particular business enterprises. We can draw on the experience of China, which increased both its growth rate and its intercourse with the rest of the world dramatically between 1978 and 1988, increasing its foreign trade by a factor of five. That left China at the end of the 1980s approaching, but not yet having reached, Switzerland in the magnitude of its foreign trade.

In 1988 the Soviet Union and communist Eastern Europe imported $36 billion and $35 billion, respectively, from the rest of the world (i.e., excluding intra-COMECON [Council of Mutual Economic Assistance] trade). This compares with China's imports in that year of $55 billion, and total world exports of $2.6 trillion. Both regions would be doing exceedingly well if they increased their share of world trade by one percentage point each over the next decade. Yet with such success they would still remain small parts of the world economy.

NOTES

1. The next few pages draw heavily on Richard N. Cooper, "The World Economic Climate," in Jessica Mathews, ed., . . . *The American Assembly*, 1990.
2. For further discussion of population growth, see Appendix 3 by Charles A. Zraket in this volume.
3. In technical terms, the foreign trade deficit as used here is the current account deficit, which covers goods, services, earnings on foreign investment, and gifts to foreigners.
4. Under U.S. domestic bankruptcy proceedings, an agreement struck between a debtor and 70 percent of its creditors can, under certain general conditions, be imposed on the remaining creditors, thus preventing the problem of holdouts that has plagued international debt negotiations with the commercial banks. Furthermore, the ultimate recourse of liquidation

generally creates a more cooperative mood among creditors so long as the firm in question is viable but for its debt.

5. Theodore H. Moran provides a more pessimistic assessment of debt prospects in Appendix 7 of this volume.

6. See Jeffrey Schott, ed., *Completing the Uruguay Round* (Washington, D.C.: Institute for International Economics, 1990).

7. This section, like the paper, was written before Iraq's invasion of Kuwait on August 2, 1990. From the perspective of the world economy, it is fortunate Iraq invaded in 1990 rather than waiting until 1995, when spare productive capacity in oil would virtually have disappeared. Even so, the damage will be significant, lowering world economic growth. This effect was unnecessarily aggravated by an unwillingness to indicate early after the embargo that the strategic petroleum reserve would be made available if necessary—a declaration that would have avoided a sharp speculative rise in the price of oil.

IMPACT OF THE NEW TECHNOLOGIES ON INDUSTRIAL ECONOMIES AND MILITARY SYSTEMS

Charles A. Zraket

INTRODUCTION

Great economic and environmental weaknesses in the Third World, the rise of economic power in the Asian perimeter led by Japan, the move to European economic integration and stability, arms control between NATO and the Warsaw Pact, and the economic decline of the Soviet Union and Eastern Europe have all led to a diffusion of power throughout the world and to multiple military, economic, and technological interdependencies. Joseph S. Nye, Jr. has described well this diffusion of power and its overall impact on the global economy and security in Appendix 1: "American Power and a Post–Cold War World."

Today's worldwide economy is characterized by the globalization of technology, production, and markets. This global economy is affected greatly by current demographic trends, education needs, energy supply, environmental degradation, food supply and agriculture, transportation, financial, and communications infrastructure. The interrelationships among all these factors affect national economic, foreign, and security policies in many ways. The changes within nations brought about by these factors are probably more important and far-reaching than those affecting their international relationships. Much emphasis by national governments must by given to these interrelationships if a nation is to become or to remain economically strong.

The complexity of government today is exemplified by the difficulty of dealing with these interrelationships, whose impacts are felt on a local, regional, and global scale and over time periods that can range from a few years to decades and more. For the United States, these issues are having a profound effect on its economic strength and on the need to encourage more investment in infrastructure systems and less in consumption in order to achieve a strong, environmentally sustainable economy.

Coupled to the economic issues raised by the globalization of technology and production have been the security issues raised by arms proliferation worldwide in high technology weapons and support systems such as aircraft, ballistic and cruise missiles, nuclear weapons, chemical weapons, submarines, sensors and communications for surveillance and intelligence, air defense systems, and space launch vehicles. This arms proliferation has brought about a new world approach to security, an approach exemplified by the role assumed by the United States and the United Nations to deal with the recent takeover of Kuwait by Iraq. For the United States, the changing and uncertain world situation indicates a need to restructure its defense forces and security assistance pacts sufficient to assure its security and those of its allies, as well as to deter the kind of military situation brought about by the Iraqi invasion of Kuwait.

Technology modulates these global trends over long time scales, and its potential impacts should be understood in formulating policies and investment choices for the economy, environment, and defense. This paper describes in the next five sections the current impact of the new technologies on the global economy and the changing demographic, energy, environmental, and the food and agriculture factors that affect it. Sections VII, VIII, and IX describe the competitiveness of U.S. high-technology industries in world trade, the impact that arms proliferation worldwide and arms control with the Soviet Union are having on the restructuring of the U.S. defense industrial and technology bases, and a summary of the effects all these changes are having on U.S. strategy in the 1990s.

THE GLOBAL ECONOMY

Market, financial, and technological globalization of industrial economies is increasing and is likely to prove irreversible. Economic interaction and interdependence are manifest in multinational corporations, their choice of which goods to make where, and their strategic relationships, which are defined by cross-licensing arrangements, joint ventures, and cooperative research and development (R&D) efforts. The generation, diffusion, and application of technology are proceeding at an increasing pace worldwide. High-technology industries have become more competitive and pluralistic. International financial transactions occur instantaneously. It is no longer possible to maintain a purely domestic industrial base or defense technology base. Trade barriers worldwide are being reduced in spite of the formation of trading blocs in Europe, North America, and the Pacific Rim. De facto integration of the U.S.–Western European economies and the U.S.–Japanese economies is occurring through what *Business Week* has termed the "stateless corporation."[1] For example, Daniel I. Okimoto notes in Appendix 5: "The Asian Perimeter, Moving Front and Center" that the Asian perimeter economies—Japan, Taiwan, South Korea, Hong Kong, and the Asian states—have a high degree of trade with the United States and with each other. The impact of restructured Soviet Union and East European economies and Third World economies on these trends is still unpredictable.

Joseph S. Nye, Jr. has noted that an open international economy contributes to global economic growth, but that "maintaining an open international economy will be difficult in a world where development states follow neo-mercantilist practices. The success of Japan in using government protection has been followed by Korea and others." Nye states further that "trade is not the only dimension of an open international economy. Current annual global trade of roughly $2 trillion is a small fraction of the annual financial flows across national borders.... In 1987, foreign in-vestment in the United States came to $1.5 trillion of stocks, bonds, and other assets, including $262 billion representing direct investment. U.S. firms have invested a fifth of their capital overseas with a book value in 1987 of $308 billion. . . . When the market share of American multinational corporations operating overseas is added to exports from the United States, the American-owned corporations' share of world markets has changed very little since the 1950s. A considerable fraction of international trade takes place among the subsidiaries of transnational corporations on the basis of corporate global planning."[2]

One can add to Nye's data that Japan, for example, places over one-third of its total investments in the United States and about 25 percent in Europe. Europe also invests heavily in the United States, with the United Kingdom and the Netherlands being the top two investors followed by Japan. These investments are in addition to industry cross-licensing and cooperative R&D arrangements. R&D expenditures of the international high-technology industries dominate those of governments. Organization for Economic Cooperation and Development (OECD) data indicate that about 50 percent of the incomes of multinational corporations come from foreign subsidiaries; this situation is more pronounced in the high-technology industries. The R&D expenditures and the exports of foreign subsidiaries sometimes exceed those of the "home parents." Both intra- and inter-industry trade is growing. Globalism is paramount from a private business perspective today. Free trade and the selective removal of technology transfer constraints remain the most desirable policies to preserve and to manage internationally, with due concern for intellectual property rights.

In the 1990s innovation from an evolving set of *strategic or enabling technologies* will continue to fuel economic growth worldwide. These encompass:

- the *information technologies* of microelectronics, software, artificial intelligence, neural networks, workstations, supercomputers, computer-aided design and computer-integrated manufacturing, robotics, space and ground-based telecommunications networks, photonics, optical storage disks, input-output sensory and display technology, digital imaging, signal and data processing, and space and other remote sensors that are revolutionizing the conduct of research, industrial automation, all the service industries, and all the media, and that are creating the age of networks and access to knowledge heretofore unknowable and to prompt knowledge at a distance;[3]

- the *biotechnologies* of recombinant DNA, monoclonal antibodies, tissue culture, fermentation, and mutagenesis that are beginning to revolutionize the fields of medical diagnostics and care, pharmaceuticals, manufacture of chemicals, agrogenetics (e.g., development of pest and drought-resistant crops), food processing, energy generation, new materials, and waste treatment;

- *specialty materials* of high strength and low weight, such as polymer composites, ceramics, metal alloys, new semiconductors, and high-temperature superconductors that will have major impacts on the performance and cost of transportation vehicles and engines, space systems, energy generation and environmental-control systems, micro-electronics and sensors, and on the use and trade of natural materials;

- *energy generation systems* such as advanced combined-cycle combustion turbines, modular and inherently safe nuclear reactors, fuel cells, and thermal and photovoltaic solar systems that will have improved safety and environmental characteristics; and

- *new manufacturing processes* that will conserve energy and materials and reduce and prevent pollution at the source.

Strategic or enabling technologies (e.g., the information technologies), sometimes termed emerging or generic technologies, are *strategic* in that they may encompass a number of industrial sectors such as electronics, software, and telecommunications for long periods of time, and *enabling* in that they may be used to create many new applications ranging from industrial manufacturing automation to automation of many kinds of services. Basic research produces new knowledge and technological processes that in turn lead to the development of enabling technologies. These technologies may be used not only in various industrial applications as noted above but also in defense systems and in large-scale research projects, such as the space station, the human genome project, and the superconducting supercollider, that in turn create new knowledge. Understanding the processes of knowledge creation and application is important in formulating policies for investment to increase economic competitiveness. Technology creates the infrastructure for science and for industry; all must be knit together by the institutions that sponsor them, including the government.

As a resource, information has become necessary to all industrial endeavors. It is a valuable commodity in itself, and it is crucially important for managing other resources. It substitutes intelligence for capital, resources, and energy by making them less necessary per unit of economic growth. The paradigm goes as follows: information as a resource provides an economic concept for sustainable growth and creation of wealth by developing more productive processes and products, by educating a more skilled work force, and by generating through innovative R&D new kinds of knowledge and activities not otherwise knowable.

The implicit societal goals of deploying these new technologies are twofold: to increase economic productivity and thereby wealth, and to use these processes and wealth to achieve, over the coming decades, an environmentally sustainable economy by helping to alleviate the problems of global warming, acid rain, toxic wastes, waste management, water resources, food distribution, deforestation, ozone depletion, soil erosion, declining agricultural and plant gene pools, and population growth. In the past, technology has fueled environmental problems. The challenges for the future are to reduce population growth through economic well-being and to mitigate environmental problems through technology and industrial processes that prevent pollution as much as possible at the source and that can recycle materials. The aim is to decouple economic growth from energy and material demands by changes in the nature of goods and services and by increased productivity, research, education, and capital investment.

It is important to note that science and technology have now become the prerequisites to economic success throughout the world. Technology and not physical resources has become the source of wealth. Continuing and timely innovation is required to compete in today's world. Knowledge, educated and trained people, and capital have become the primary economic resources.[4] The quality of R&D and the quality, costs, timeliness, and responsiveness of downstream engineering, manufacturing, marketing processes, and the delivery of services have become the determinant factors of economic success. Over the past thirty years, science has transformed engineering to the point that the computer and related technologies allow exploration of designs, materials, and processes without the need for many costly and time-consuming prototypes. These processes generate a proliferation of services and commodity goods throughout the world that are tailored to many special and local consumer markets. Such markets help to forge industrial linkages for capital, talent, and new technology through joint ventures, cooperative R&D, and cross-licensing. These linkages provide the chief protection against closed markets and large, vertically integrated conglomerates.

Nevertheless, these onrushing developments are not universally welcome. Peter F. Drucker has noted in *The New Realities* that "economic development has become a supernational bond of unity but one that has engendered more nationalism and anti-colonialism."[5] The tide of economic well-being worldwide is flowing counter to the tide of ethnocentricity. Many societies are mired 100 to 200 years in the past economically. There is a growing gap between OECD countries and the Soviet Union, Eastern Europe, and the Third World in capital, education, and technology. From the perspective of the Third World countries, developed nations are stifling them rather than emphasizing the worldwide sharing and globalization of economies and technology. Anthony Smith has noted in *The Geopolitics of Information* that "most third world countries feel threatened by a new domination of Western culture and multinationals."[6]

Much of the Third World now lacks the economic and educational base for developing and using the information technologies. These countries resent the R&D monopolies in the West, the media domination, satellite spying, international financial networks, and lack of technology transfer to them. They want the new knowledge and power that permits division of labor or specialization into productive enterprises within an industrial sector such as electronics.[7] However, technological assistance cannot simply be given; it must be appropriate to the task, assimilated, and exploited. The capacity to do so is a function of the politics, culture, capital, science, and labor skills available in the recipient nations. A concerted and cooperative effort worldwide is needed to overcome these constraints, one that recognizes the importance and motivations of private businesses in making investments and transferring technology, along with environmental, education, and health care needs.

Nevertheless, the globalization of science and engineering and the sharing of knowledge and technical information worldwide will be a highly difficult goal to achieve. There is an increasing trend toward regulating the flow of scientific and technical information, even in universities, for the following reasons: to restrict information for private gain; to use information as a stimulus for cross-licensing and cooperative R&D ventures among corporations; and to protect information as an instrument of national security and economic growth. Thus technology flow is occurring mainly through the globalization and commoditization (i.e., the transformation of technologies barely out of the laboratory into mass-produced items of international commerce) of a broad spectrum of products that work their way into the different sectors of an economy. Government-to-government technology transfer programs and the universities have not been effective channels in transferring industrial technology worldwide.

In sum, there are severe constraints to achieving an environmentally sustainable global economy through the increased output of goods and services coupled to pollution prevention and decreased energy and materials consumption per unit of gross national product (GNP) growth. First, there is the Third World's unpayable debt and the change in the balance of payments of these countries from a net inflow of capital prior to

1981 to the reverse in the 1980s. Second, an export imperative prevails worldwide, but Latin America, Africa, and South Asia, and to a lesser extent Eastern Europe and the Soviet Union, cannot compete internationally because of lack of convertible capital and technology and an undereducated and poorly trained work force. As a consequence, the Third World must now try to sell raw materials in a glutted world of fossil energy and mineral resources. Therefore, calls for environmental control measures on behalf of future generations will be ignored by a politically stronger but poorer Third World, since the nations of the West, and especially the United States, have not aggressively encouraged the use of pollution prevention and conservation processes through legislation and economic incentives and tax policy.

In the developed world, economic, environmental, and social pressures have led to local antitechnology and antigrowth movements who believe that economic growth is achieving diminishing marginal returns along with the attendant existence of nuclear weapons and power plants, acid rain, pesticides, toxic wastes, and old-age medicine, for example. Edward N. Luttwak has termed this general phenomenon of antigrowth movements *"Communitarianism,* which contains both a fundamental critique of democratic capitalism and substitute prescriptions." He notes "the anti-growth policies of a growing number of local governments throughout the industrialized world and the continued spread and intensification of environmentalist resistance to virtually all interference with nature."[8]

There are other major constraints and sources of insecurity to achieving an environmentally sustainable global economy. In addition to the problems of worldwide ethnocentrism, unavailability of capital, poor technology transfer, and the environment noted above, there are problems of worldwide demographic, energy, food, and weapons-proliferation trends that are briefly discussed from a technological perspective in the next six sections. All these issues have a significant impact on economic, environmental, and defense investment choices in a world where security must be redefined.

DEMOGRAPHIC TRENDS AND EDUCATION NEEDS

The developed world is aging, while there is a baby boom in the rest of the world—more than 2.5 billion people (one half the world's population) are less than sixteen years old. The population of the Western bloc will have fallen early in the twenty-first century to less than 10 percent of the world's population, in contrast to 30 percent prior to World War II.

Large migrations are taking place; for example, the area from Morocco to Turkey is growing rapidly in population and putting great immigration and economic pressure on Europe similar to the one that the growing Hispanic population in Latin America is putting on the United States. (Carlos Salinas de Gotari, president of Mexico, has said recently, "If we don't export products to you, we will export people.") Demographers expect population to grow to about 6 billion worldwide before 2000 and to 10 billion by the middle of the twenty-first century before it levels off, a situation that will have a profound effect on economic growth and the environment, as Richard N. Cooper notes in Appendix 2: "Prospects for the World Economy." The major growth will occur in the developing world. Education and health care are primary needs there; both can benefit greatly from the application of the new information systems and the biotechnologies on both a targeted and a mass basis.

These demographic trends increase the need for a new approach to mass education that will improve educational productivity and efficiency and that takes into account individual learning differences of different kinds of people. The information technologies that have already proved successful in industrial and military training and education of cognitive skills should be adapted and employed. Extensive use of this technology can be used worldwide for individualized learning. Electronic technology allows a wide spectrum of literacy through both oral and visual means as well as print. The application of such technology is also sorely needed in the United States to increase productivity and to broaden access in the science and technology education of a growing, unskilled work force.

ENERGY

James Schlesinger stated in September 1989 at the World Energy Conference in Montreal that "energy security and the strength of nations, or more broadly, the strength of alliances are intimately related. This is a point that is usually neglected in discussions of worldwide energy trends. Energy security in any nation cannot be taken for granted today; there is a reemergence of trends in the worldwide oil situation that had temporarily been suppressed by the oil shocks of the 1970s. . . . The better we, the West, do in the short run, the worse off we will be in the long run."

Energy use in the United States today and since 1985 is growing at about 2 percent annually. The United States is the world's largest energy consumer, accounting for 25 percent of the world total. Per capita U.S. energy consumption is more than two and one-half times Western European levels. Worldwide energy use is growing at a rate greater than 4 percent annually primarily due to population growth and increased industrialization in the developing world. Electricity use in the developed world is growing at about a 3 percent annual rate, and in the developing world at an annual rate of about 8 percent. Organization of Petroleum Exporting Countries (OPEC) oil production has been increased to over 23 million barrels per day (MBD) from about 16 MBD in the early 1980s; this production has been absorbed by the worldwide demand. U.S. and Soviet oil production is decreasing and total non-OPEC production is at best flat. The success of high-cost Western producers depends on the high-capacity producers in the Middle East limiting their production and enhancing price. Otherwise government must intervene to cover the higher costs of domestic production.

Arthur Anderson and Company, in a study done this year for the oil and gas industry, *Oil and Gas Reserve Disclosure*, states that U.S. oil production has fallen by 1.8 million barrels per day or 17 percent, since the start of 1986. U.S. production will drop by 400,000 barrels per day this year, and a further drop of up to 1 MBD per year for the next five years is expected. The report states: "The increasing disparity between supply and demand can be met only with additional imports and staggering new costs." Each incremental 1 MBD increase in imports will add about $7 billion annually (at a price of about $20 per barrel) to the U.S trade deficit.

The Anderson report also states that Soviet oil production declined by 300,000–400,000 barrels per day last year, and a similarly sized decline is expected this year. Japanese oil demand grew by 4 to 5 percent last year, and a 6 to 10 percent growth rate was recorded by South Korea, Thailand, Malaysia, and Taiwan. East Asian oil imports could increase by 2 MBD by the mid-1990s.

Low-cost producers are insisting on higher prices for oil while they are now investing to raise production capacities to meet the demands of the 1990s. Nuclear and coal use in the future is uncertain because of safety and environmental reasons. Many energy analysts expect oil price hikes up to $35 to $40 per barrel in today's dollars before 2000. By the mid-1990s the U.S. bill for imported oil could be greater than $100 billion per year unless conservation in end-use systems takes hold soon. These price trends could lead to increased use of natural gas in the OECD countries since larger supplies of gas will be available at these higher prices. This gas would be used in advanced combined-cycle combustion turbines and later in fuel cells that produce electricity with high efficiency and much reduced environmental pollution. This trend to use natural gas to generate electricity is already dominant in the United States today, where about 40 percent of new generation is by natural gas.

The worldwide oil situation as well as trends in population growth, new industrial processes and automation, increased use of appliances and lighting, and possibly increased use of electric cars will lead to greater use of electricity worldwide. Vastly increased use of electricity is overwhelming Third World economies because of the huge capital investments needed—15 percent to 30 percent of available public investment resources. Benefits of the increased use of electricity worldwide will be to mitigate environmental problems and reduce energy consumption in end-use systems (industrial, transportation, commercial, and residential) if the needed capital investments are made in new conservation technologies for these end-use systems. The challenge will also be to deploy the most environmentally compatible energy generation and transmission systems.

The most promising energy generation technology for the long term is advanced, inherently safe nuclear energy (i.e., with passive safety features for heat decay and removal). A number of technology options are currently being developed, principally advanced light-water reactors, light metal reactors, and modular gas-cooled reactors that are smaller than current plants and designed to avoid the possibility of a severe failure. Appropriate waste-storage facilities are also being developed by the Department of Energy. Nevertheless, in the United States, it will be at least fifteen to twenty years before advanced nuclear energy systems, including waste-storage facilities, are built, tested, licensed, purchased, and deployed with high reliability and at affordable cost.

Over the long term, the increased use of nuclear energy could reduce dependence on oil and gas and replace coal, an environmentally poor fuel. The deployment of advanced nuclear energy systems will require the resolution of institutional, cost, and acceptance problems that both the public and the utilities see as severe. Federal action that might help to resolve these issues is needed in the areas of streamlining licensing procedures, standardizing plants, helping to select a bank of acceptable sites, establishing waste depositories, and formulating policies and plans for relicensing of existing nuclear plants and for creating new institutional structures for the generation and distribution of electricity.

Other advanced energy technologies under development include modular and highly efficient fuel cells, which use clean fuels such as natural gas or hydrogen; clean fuels derived from biomass and the electrolysis or photolysis of water; and solar energy in the form of thermal and photovoltaic systems. Over the long term, the use of both hydrogen and electricity that are derived from solar and nuclear sources is required to reduce transportation and energy pollution and greenhouse gases. For example, large-scale use of electric cars in the United States in the next few decades can greatly reduce dapendence on oil. However, Jesse H. Ausubel has pointed out, that the large-scale use of hydrogenas a universal fuel is decades away because of technical and economic uncertainties.[9] Much more research should be supported here.

In the near to mid-term future (five to fifteen years), the most realistic options for U.S. energy supply are extensive conservation in end-use systems, additional natural gas and oil from Alaska, alternative fuels, and reliable nuclear energy systems. Given that the licences for the 102 existing nuclear power plants will start to run out in 2005, the United States has at best five to fifteen years to develop these options for deployment if massive oil import bills are to be avoided, and some degree of energy security and flexibility in U.S. foreign policy is to be achieved. Western Europe and Japan are preparing for future energy supply in terms of end-use systems and alternative sources much more aggressively than is the United States.

ENVIRONMENT

A new and more global environmental agenda is emerging in many nations. The challenges fall into three groups: atmospheric degradation, erosion of the resource base, and loss of biodiversity.[10] The current and potential effects of atmospheric degradation—greenhouse warming, acid rain, and ozone depletion—are now well publicized and are a current subject of international discussion. The United Nations' Intergovernmental Panel on Climate Change states in a recent draft report (May 2, 1990) that "the Greenhouse effect is real, even without man-made contributions; natural greenhouse gases already keep the earth warmer than it would otherwise be. Man-made emissions are substantially increasing the atmospheric concentrations of the greenhouse gases: carbon dioxide, methane, the chlorofluorocarbons, nitrous oxide, and tropospheric ozone. These increases will lead to a warming of the earth's surface."

Climate models do not now have sufficient fidelity to predict the exact effects of this warming, partly due to uncertainties in understanding the effects of cloud cover in reflecting heat into space and in understanding ocean-atmospheric interactions. The essential question, derived from research done so far and observations made during the past century, is: What happens to the frequency and intensity of extreme events (e.g., severe storms, hurricanes, droughts) as the global equilibrium temperature rises about 0.3°F per decade? Increased frequency and intensity of such extreme events may constitute the primary impact of greenhouse warming, especially in their effect on agriculture, forestry, water resources, and coastal areas.

Robert M. White calls for continued research to understand the problems of global warming and for sensible policies to remedy them, such as major investments in nonfossil energy sources, reforestation, forest preservation, and disease-resistant crops, investments that should be made anyway. Nevertheless, he says that "humanity will have to adapt to some climate changes" in energy and water use, agriculture, and land use, for example.[11]

G.J.F. MacDonald has noted the potentially severe effects that changes in the frequency of extreme weather events will bring about in the use and availability of water resources. He states that "on average, a warming will lead to increased evaporation and increased precipitation, though some regions will experience greater or lesser frequency of floods or droughts. Regional water availability can be expected to alter as precipitation and evaporation patterns change; seasonal patterns of precipitation and runoff may also shift. These changes will undoubtedly lead to international tension and political friction. . . . The combined effects of world population growth (especially in Asia and Africa), climate change, and the increase of man-made pollutants are all making water supplies more scarce and expensive. The depletion of water resources and the decline in quality of available water supplies are already affecting political calculations in the Middle East, Africa, and Eastern Europe."

Developing countries are many times more directly dependent than industrial countries on their renewable resources—soils, water, fisheries, forests, minerals, and genetic species. These resources may already be environmentally damaged for long periods of time. Greenhouse warming will exacerbate the situation. At the 43rd Session of the United Nations General Assembly in 1988, Soviet Foreign Minister Edward Shevardnadze warned that the threat to the environment constitutes "a second front fast approaching and gaining an urgency equal to that of the nuclear and space threat." Homer-Dixon has stated in *Environ-*

mental Change and Violent Conflict[14] that: "In the next decades, environmental problems may come to dominate all other factors affecting the international system. . . . This paper addresses the question, Will large-scale environmental changes produce violent national and international conflict?" He points to the example of the dams and irrigation systems that Turkey is planning to build to control the flow of the Euphrates river, a situation that will greatly reduce the flow of the river within Syria and will also add fertilizers, pesticides, and salts to the flow. He also notes that in the Philippines, civil dissent in village areas has become rampant due in large part to resource stresses and environmental degradation such as declining land productivity caused by soil erosion and deforestation. Environmental problems extend well beyond national boundaries; air and water resources must be shared regionally and globally. As energy use increases worldwide, environmental conflicts will abound.

Remote sensing from satellites to locate and help manage the care for renewable and nonrenewable sources—crops, water, minerals, forests, and land use—is necessary. NASA's planned Earth Orbiting System can help here, but Third World needs in this area will have to be subsidized by the developed countries. Present environmental trends will accelerate and may threaten the viability of the biosphere as population continues to increase. Sweeping changes in industrial production systems will be necessary, as demonstrated for example, by the deteriorating environment in Eastern Europe. Technologies exist to effect these changes, but the social, economic, and political barriers to their use are huge, especially with respect to the issue of how to distribute costs for environmental measures.

William Clark has noted that the problems are characterized by scientific ignorance, massive costs to address, and long time and space scales that transcend current institutions. He describes four underlying issues: 1) space on local, regional, and global scales; 2) time measured in decades to centuries; 3) abrupt or discontinuous change vs. evolutionary change—for example climate changes and population changes; and 4) the interaction of energy, resources, and environmental infrastructure systems coupled to urbanization, transportation, and demographic changes.[14]

Population growth reached its maximum rate between 1950–1980 but it continues. The twentieth century has seen an explosion of technology that has increased manufacturing fifty-fold and energy use and international trade 25-fold.[15] Industrial growth is now in its third revolution,[16] covering the period prior to World War II (steel making, railroads, coal and oil, and labor-intensive agriculture); the 1946–1980 period of the green revolution in agriculture, electronics, computers, light metals, jet aircraft, and nuclear fission; and the current period of the new technologies described above that have an increased range of regenerative capabilities with the potential of less impact on the physical environment and that are much less resource-depletive per unit of GNP growth. All sectors of an industrial economy are now being automated to some extent, not only in the primary and secondary sectors of resource extraction and manufacturing, but also in all the tertiary and quaternary sectors of banking, commerce, education, and health care. These population and economic trends can and will have profound effects on the environment in the coming decades. For example, even if energy use in the developed world leveled off at present values, energy use worldwide would have to increase by a factor of 5 to 10 to bring hthe rest of the world in the twent-first century up to today's minimal living standards of about $2,000 per capita.

The United States presents the archetypal case of the effects of industrial growth on the environment. In the past few years, environmental professionals have gradually recognized that current control strategies are not working.[17] We have simply been moving pollutants from one medium to another—gaseous pollutants into aqueous and solid phases, aqueous pollutants into the solid phase, and solid pollutants back into the gaseous and aqueous phases.

This end-of-pipe approach not only is not working, it is also very expensive. The United States is spending about $70 billion per year to meet environmental regulatory requirements, but only 1 percent of this $70 billion goes to pollution prevention at the source. The United States also faces a clean-up price tag of about $1 trillion for Superfund hazardous waste sites,[18] not including nuclear weapons sites. To address all these problems, some environmentalists have been advocating a switch to a pollution prevention strategy.

Pollution prevention embraces the concept of finding ways to reduce the amount of waste generated in all media by changing: 1) the nature of the product itself, and/or 2) the way in which a product is produced via control at the source of product manufacture. The first can be done by product substitution (e.g., fiber optics for copper), product conservation and composition, redesign, and recycling. Recycling, especially of materials, and conservation must be addressed in the product design and the manufacturing process. Use of recyclable materials is crucial, thereby raising the question of how recyclable such new materials as composites are compared to natural materials. The economics and technology of recycling materials (e.g., old automobiles) will have to be changed to adjust to the new products. Source control, the second technique, can be exercised through purification and substitution of input material; process modifications via use of automation in manufacturing; use of biotechnologies to improve agriculture and chemical processes; better material handling; and use of clean energy sources.

The biggest constraints to changing the nature of products or to exercising source control are the needs for economic incentives to perform the necessary research and development of new processes and to make the necessary capital investments in new process systems. This problem is akin to trying to achieve energy conservation in end-use systems. So far, the limited achievements in pollution prevention vary, but they are all startlingly positive.[19]

The new technologies offer the promise of achieving these objectives. G.J.F. MacDonald has shown that conserving materials and conserving energy go together and enhance industrial competitiveness. Current regulatory policies and laws are inadequate to achieve these objectives: economic incentives and disincentives are needed. MacDonald states that "the command and control regulatory apparatus sets fixed goals for industry and government and inhibits development and use of new process technologies. New technology is much more important in source waste reduction and energy efficiency than in end-of-pipe pollution control."[20] To achieve sustainability in economic growth, appropriate technology must be injected into each industrial sector—energy, transportation, agriculture, manufacturing, and materials.

European countries have recognized this situation and have adopted, for example, high taxes on gasoline, large grants for research (e.g., about 15 percent of West Germany's government budget for R&D goes to environmental research), and tax incentives to reduce waste generation. Western European countries are leaders in marketing waste reduction technology products and in advocating measures to control greenhouse gases. Government and industry collaborate strongly in these areas. The United States needs to increase its research budgets and to shift to economic incentives and disincentives to reduce waste and to increase energy efficiency and conservation.[21] (In this vein, some in Congress have introduced a tax on the amount of carbon released by an industrial process.) The transitional costs may be high, but a long-term perspective must be taken.

The current regulatory framework provides stability to old firms. Some environmentalists distrust technology and industry and therefore take the short-term view in favor of regulatory control. Three developments are changing these situations: 1) international competitiveness, 2) the United States running out of domestic oil, and 3) global environmental problems. These developments provide a rationale for a shift to a new framework to meet both environmental and economic goals. The ecological modernization of industry and agriculture is required.

National environmental goals should be established and communicated to the public. The efficacy of the current regulatory mechanisms should be assessed formally. The states and industry should experiment with new approaches. Industry and government should conduct cooperative R&D, and generic techniques should be developed and disseminated for widespread use. A much larger federal program in R&D and technical assistance to states should be established.

FOOD AND AGRICULTURE

With world population growing at a rate of 1.7 percent per year, about a 20 percent increase in food supply will be needed worldwide during the 1990s, not including the demands of a richer world for a better diet. The major issues involved include the availability of cropland and water, the availability of new technologies to increase productivity and to reduce energy use and environmental pollution in the agricultural process, and the availability of food storage and distribution infrastructure.

The shortage of infrastructure—roads, storage bins, process- ing plants, ports, refrigeration, and transportation—currently constrains farm output. Increased capital investment for power equipment and construction is needed, especially in the middle- income countries such as Algeria, Thailand, the Association of Southeast Asian Nations (ASEAN) bloc, Mexico, Taiwan, Korea, India, China, Brazil, and Argentina and also in the USSR.

Agricultural research has been the key factor in reducing world hunger during the past three decades; it will greatly help in pre- venting future world food shortages. At a recent conference (First Annual Conference on Global Trends in Food, Farming, and Technology, Hudson Institute, Indianapolis, April 16–17, 1990), Dr. John Campbell, President of Oklahoma State Univer- sity, stated that "bio-engineering techniques such as tissue cul- ture, micropropagation, and recombinant DNA are putting agri- cultural research into a new biorevolution. They are already al- tering plant architecture, boosting the photosynthetic efficiency of the plants." Dr. Campbell also noted that bioengineers are aggressively seeking pest control techniques that do not require chemicals, aiding farmers in both the Third World and affluent countries.[22] Expert computer systems will also allow extension agents working with illiterate small Third World farmers to adopt complex new technologies in a much shorter time period.

At the same conference, a panel of experts concluded that current farm management practices are not yet as environmen- tally safe as they could be, while farm technology cannot yet supply world food demands without chemicals. Brian Gardner, director of European Policy Analysis, reported that Western

Europe's farmers are already facing drastic new controls due to a recent backlash against agricultural pollution from fertilizers, chemicals, and animal waste. Dr. John Perek, Iowa State agronomist, faulted federal commodity programs (covering 70 percent of the nation's cropland) for discouraging alternative farming methods because base yields (for subsidy programs) are so important to the income of farmers. Many farmers manage their farms to maximize subsidies, often at the expense of environmental quality. Dr. G. W. Wallingford of the Potash and Phosphate Institute said many U.S. farmers have achieved an enormous reduction in soil erosion—and thus a major reduction in associated chemical runoff—through a little-recognized set of new management practices: conservation tillage, greater production of crop biomass, and split applications of fertilizer.

Thus, the biotechnologies, rail and road transportation, standard plant breeding, and better seeds with multiple resistance to pests and diseases (e.g., corn, rice, various trees) hold promise of meeting increasing demands for food at reduced damage to the environment. The recent high rates of increase in world agricul-tural output could continue or even increase as new knowledge continues to emerge from research laboratories that include a growing network of international agricultural research centers.[23]

COMPETITIVENESS OF THE U.S. HIGH-TECHNOLOGY INDUSTRIES IN WORLD TRADE

The strategic technologies outlined in the second section, with the exception of the information technologies and related electronics, today represent only a modest impact on the world's high-technology industries. However, their use will grow over the next ten to twenty years to dominate innovation in industrial processes in the same way that the industrial impact of the information technologies has grown over the past twenty years and will continue to grow over the next few decades.[24] The high-technology industries require not only high R&D investments but also massive capital investment in plant and facilities, thereby creating great pressure to generate profits to keep the cycle going. Many of these industries use superior process technology and flexible manufacturing systems that involve high fixed costs and a rapid innovation cycle in both process and product. With each cycle, product performance can increase by a few orders of magnitude per unit cost. Computers and microelectronics in general are outstanding examples. Each new generation of technology requires significant increases in R&D and plant investment to remain competitive.

High-technology industries are defined by those industrial sectors dedicating the highest degree of investment to research and development. The ratio between the amount of this investment and the revenues generated varies considerably depending on the sector, from about 25 percent in aerospace to 0.1 percent in textiles and shoes.[25] In some areas of the biotechnologies, the ratio is as high as 60 percent. Between these extremes are intermediate sectors, such as pharmaceuticals (6.4 percent) and chemicals (3.0 percent).[26] According to the OECD classification, six current industrial sectors qualify as high-technology: aerospace, data processing and software, electronics and telecommunications, pharmaceuticals, instruments (e.g., medical), and electrical equipment (e.g., motors and generators); all of these have ratios of R&D investment to return higher than the OECD high technology threshold of 4.5 percent. These sectors are fast growing, all are of strategic economic importance, and all have a high rate of innovation and value added. In 1988, these six industrial sectors provided 31 percent of U.S. total exports of about $400 billion annually and 27 percent of Japan's total exports of about $275 billion annually.[27] Thus, U.S. exports in absolute terms are almost double those of Japan in these six sectors.

The United States dominates in worldwide aerospace export with 57 percent of the export market in 1988 (a gain of 2 percent since 1980); in computers the United States has gone from 53 percent of the export market in 1980 to 36 percent in 1988; in telecommunications from 12 percent to 11 percent; and in microelectronics from 21 percent in 1980 to 17 percent in 1988.[28] The United States is preeminent in software development and production: U.S. firms furnish 60 percent of the software in the $200 billion per year worldwide software industry.[29] This industry is now growing at a rate greater than 10 percent per year.[30] Japan's share of world exports have gone from 15 percent in 1980 to 25 percent in 1988 in microelectronics, 6 percent to 22 percent in computers, 12 percent to 33 percent in telecommunications, and have remained at less than 1 percent of the aerospace market during the 1980s.[31] The European Community had a net global import of $33 billion worth of electronic goods, including consumer electronics in 1988, about half from the United States and half from Japan.[32] The absolute value of these various exports has probably doubled in the past decade, thereby accounting for some of the flatness in the U.S. percentages. The impact of the new technologies over the next decade will increase the growth of these six sectors, and will spawn new high-technology sectors.

West Germany, whose total annual exports are now slightly more (about 1 percent) than those of the United States, has only limited high-technology products among its major exports, except for pharmaceuticals. Its major exports are automobiles and airliner parts, specialty steels and machinery, petrochemicals and pharmaceuticals, and quick-response, custom-made equipment and components. West Germany has a strong apprenticeship program, which creates a highly skilled work force. Also, product design in its export sectors is outstanding. Nevertheless, West Germany is relatively weak in advanced information and biotechnologies and in advanced materials, as are many other European countries. These countries still have to catch up to the United States and Japan in some of these new areas, but they are now working hard at it through various well-funded government-industry R&D programs, a large and growing home market, a growing capital base, and a skilled labor base.

Although the United States is not competing well in the automobile and consumer electronic sectors, it has been and is very competitive in the high-technology sectors, both in the more mature information technologies and services (e.g., software, financial and transportation services) and in the biotechnologies, specialty metals, and other materials, especially polymers. The United States has several hundred relatively small firms in each of these latter areas that are pioneering in the research and development of new techniques and products but which are subject to purchase or investment from abroad. The recent Department of Commerce report,[33] *Emerging Technologies*, stated that the United States is ahead or even in R&D with Japan and the European Community in all twelve such technologies analyzed (six ahead and six even for the United States). The report stated that in product introduction the United States is behind Japan in six technologies and behind Europe in two, a situation that is still repairable for the United States given that these products have many cycles. Nevertheless, unless major steps are taken to improve U.S. investment and manufacturing in the future, the United States can lose its lead in the areas where it is ahead and not be able to catch up in the areas where it lags.

For example, the United States has severe weaknesses today in its semiconductor, computer memories, fiber-optics communications, and consumer electronics (e.g., high-definition television [HDTV]) industries. These weaknesses are mostly a function of the lack of long-term financial incentives and cheaper capital, poor management, and weak downstream engineering, manufacturing, and marketing.[34] The huge, vertically integrated Japanese companies compete better in these areas. Bobby R. Inman and Daniel F. Burton have noted the weaknesses in the U.S. consumer electronics and semiconductor industries due to aggressive foreign competition, mostly from Japan, and the lack of U.S. commercialization efforts in, for example, superconductor technology and high-definition TV applications. They point out "the absence of U.S. government institutions capable of dealing with complex technological issues that have both commercial and military implications and that cut across several industries." They also state that the U.S. policy debate on global competition "revolves around four issues: strengthening the American manufacturing base, improving the U.S. policy making machinery for advancing the creation and use of technology, rebuilding the nation's technological infrastructure, and encouraging wider national R&D efforts."

They also point to "the relatively high cost of capital in the United States for investments in new manufacturing plants, the pressure on American management for short-term results, and the pressing need to incorporate economic issues related to industrial technology into the decision-making process that determines U.S. foreign policy." Their prescriptions are essential to formulating policies for continued U.S. international economic competitiveness.[35]

The need for increased capital investment is crucial. Ralph Gomory has postulated the *cyclic process of development*: once a strategic or enabling technology is created and a successful product is developed, then successive improved models are developed via simultaneous development and downstream engineering. Cycle time is the determinant factor in economic success of a product where the technology is still evolving. A group that can develop a new product in three years is better organized, capitalized, and managed than one that takes five years. Each model is a discrete business case that can be costed and marketed. The successful process generates continuous profits for successive R&D and plant investments. Without success, no capital is attracted to the process, resulting in a downward spiral for firms that fall behind.

Ralph Landau states that his Stanford colleagues "conclude that stable government policies (fiscal, monetary, trade, and tax) favoring higher rates of investment may be essential for higher rates of economic well-being in both the short and long runs. . . . In a study of the economic performance of five industrial countries, Michael Boskin and Lawrence Lau have found that technological progress is capital-augmenting and that the benefits of technological progress are higher when a larger capital stock is deployed per worker."[36]

Landau further states that "Japan is on a capital spending binge that will surely strengthen its growth and export capability."[37] The annual growth rate of gross capital per worker from 1964 to 1985 has been greater than 6 percent for Japan compared to less than 2 percent for the United States.[38] Thus, the case for increased savings and for more investment in physical plant, education, and technology is grounded in the economic and technological opportunities facing the United States.

The semiconductor or integrated-electronics industry is a prime example of how huge, vertically integrated Japanese corporations have come to dominate the market at the expense of the United States. Of the top twenty semiconductor suppliers in the world, only three derive greater than 50 percent of their sales directly from semiconductors; all three are U.S. companies. For example, Toshiba, the large, vertically integrated Japanese corporation, started in the semiconductor business in 1982 by initiating a $3 billion investment program in equipment and materials to manufacture semiconductors. By 1988, they attained number one rank in the world in semiconductor sales of $4 billion, beating out the Hitachi Group. Toshiba and Hitachi represent one part of the dual-structure economy in Japan, where large, internationally competitive industries pull forward the rest of the relatively unmodernized economy.

U.S. semiconductor manufacturers are now about 80 percent dependent on foreign suppliers, mostly in the Orient, in terms of dollars spent for equipment and materials. The massive capital investments that are required to develop such equipment and materials make it difficult for the United States to compete with the Japanese. U.S. firms have resorted to alternative means to appear vertically integrated, given that antitrust regulations generally inhibit vertical integration in the United States. Cross-licensing of new technology is the means used to substitute for vertical integration and the capital it provides to target massive investments.

Cross-licensing augmented by joint ventures and partial equity financing also helps to open global markets, especially in Japan and in Europe, where "frontier-free" trading within the European Community starting in 1992 looks like it may provide a decided disadvantage to outsiders.[39] This trend to cross-licensing and joint ventures will continue the growing interdependence of markets and competitors by spreading the risk and enormous costs of developing next-generation processes and fabrication facilities. For example, U.S. international joint ventures in the integrated electronics industry include VLSI Technology/Hitachi, ATT/NEC, AMD/Sony, Intel/NMB Semiconductor, IBM/Toshiba, IBM/Siemens, Motorola/Toshiba, Texas Instruments (TI)/Hitachi, TI/Philips/Signetics, TI/Taiwan, TI/Kobe Steel, and so on. These agreements involve hundreds of millions to billions of dollars to develop next-generation electronics technology and manufacturing capabilities. Such alliances also involve technical and operational cooperation, thereby alleviating intellectual property problems. These alliances also allow manufacturing capabilities to be retained in the United States, thereby increasing both national security and the fungibility of services that make up a large part of the U.S. economy.

Finally, there remain the questions of the role and function of the U.S. government in civil R&D and whether a more activist government role in sustaining the commercial industry's technology base is needed. The Congress recently created a Technology Administration in the Department of Commerce, and changed the National Bureau of Standards to the National Institute for Standards and Technology with a new mission to foster industrial technology. Senator John Glenn proposes to con-vert the Department of Commerce to the Department of Technology and Industry and install in it the Advanced Civilian Technology Agency, a counterpart to DARPA (Defense Advanced Research Projects Agency). Representative M. Levine proposes to establish a Technology Corporation of America to manage government funded civil research. Representative J. Saxton suggests that a National Environment Institute be established.

Some of the new initiatives and mechanisms to perform R&D in critical areas, such as superconductivity and manufacturing technology, propose consortia that bring government, universities, and industry together for the long term by mandating industry contributions to the effort, and by awarding government money on the basis of real competition in proposals. These consortia or technology centers are designed to be large enough to provide a critical mass of R&D effort, and they have real commercial applications to pursue through the industry element. The DARPA/MIT/industry efforts in high-definition television is an example of this kind of effort. The DARPA/industry funding of SEMATECH is another example in the field of semiconductor manufacturing processes. The MIT Lincoln Lab/Bell Labs/IBM effort in electronics superconductivity is a third example. However, the scale of these efforts may be many times below Japanese efforts in these areas.

The Bush Administration has a negative attitude about government funding of commercially oriented R&D. John Sununu has stated the administration case well, saying in interviews[40] that the United States ought to make changes that help the whole system respond to overcoming foreign competition, rather than funding special areas that plead for help and that compete with private R&D. The changes that the administration is pushing include reducing the cost of capital through deficit reduction, capital gains tax reduction, R&D tax credit, tort reform, product liability reform, permitting more cooperative private R&D, supporting more basic research in both small and big science, and maximizing defense R&D and dual-use technologies. Sununu also says the private sector has an obligation to manage well and to be smart and long term in its thinking.

We have seen only the beginning of the debate on the role of government in civil R&D. The Congress sees a need to spend some of the peace dividend from reduced defense spending on civil R&D, but government mechanisms and institutions that spend this money effectively to benefit the commercial economy are difficult to design and to make work, in part because of political interference in making program decisions and because of the difficulty in resolving intellectual property problems. The case for government involvement in more environmental research is strong, as are the cases for research in education and certain areas of health care.

The case for a direct government role in commercial exploitation of technology has yet to be made convincingly. Part of the difficulty in formulating an effective government role in this area is that commercially oriented projects will likely be opposed by the losers in the competitions and the funding decisions, resulting in continuous political review and disruption of projects as alliances in the losing states and companies petition their congressional representatives for changes and additions. The synthetic fuels program in the late 1970s represents an example of this phenomenon. Also, this situation is akin to the increasing opposition to "big science" projects by some in Congress and the scientific community where projects such as the human genome, the national aerospace plane, and the space station, face ongoing criticism by many groups nationwide; some of it is well justified; the rest is disruptive.

Joint government, industry, and university projects that are commercially oriented will not succeed unless the competition for the projects and their review remain depoliticized, streamlined, and renewable over the long term, rather than being short-term oriented as many are now. Projects should be managed by institutions and professionals who are accountable for the money they are awarded, who follow clear policy and priorities, and who provide accurate data on the projects to the sponsors and for public review. Institutions similar in form to the National Science Foundation, SEMATECH, COMSAT Corporation, and Federally Funded Research and Development Centers can possibly meet these objectives if the appropriate arrangements are made with private industry to assume responsibility for the projects and to exploit them at the appropriate time and with full intellectual property rights.

ARMS PROLIFERATION AND THE U.S. DEFENSE INDUSTRIAL AND TECHNOLOGY BASE

Two technical trends dominate military security issues today: the globalization of defense technology, production, and markets; and the proliferation of high-technology weapons worldwide.[41] The U.S. defense base depends increasingly on foreign or offshore resources, tooling, and components and on joint projects with allies. The U.S. defense community can no longer count on controlling its sources; they are too global in ownership, R&D, manufacturing, and materials. In addition, much cutting-edge R&D and many state-of-the-art products used in defense systems are now commercial; they are inseparable from the intangibles of software, maintenance, and training. Dual-use technologies (military/commercial), especially in Europe, have grown abroad.

This confluence of military and commercial technologies has been accelerated by mergers of defense firms with large multinationals that are headquartered in Europe, the United States (e.g.,

Hughes Aircraft with General Motors), and Asia; cross-licensing among the multinationals; and the pressure to pursue more foreign trade. Coincident with the reduction in defense budgets, major restructuring and shakeout are taking place in the defense industry with worldwide codevelopment and production increasing and some restrictions on technology transfer being lifted. Massive technology transfer and diffusion are taking place, leading to the development of indigenous capabilities to make high-technology defense weapons in such countries as Brazil, India, Israel, Korea, China, and others.

Arms proliferation is occurring worldwide in aircraft, ballistic and cruise missiles, chemical weapons, nuclear weapons, con-ventional ordnance, submarines, communications, sensors for surveillance and intelligence, air defense systems, and space launch vehicles.[42] Such forces currently are deployed in many countries outside the Western bloc and the Soviet Union in numbers useful for defense and local wars, but they now lack the capabilities for major power projection at long distances. In the future, proliferated cruise missiles based on land, ships, submarines, and aircraft will engender concern worldwide because of their capabilities to attack ships, ports, airbases, and other fixed targets. Thus, proliferation is occurring both within countries with respect to their broader base of capabilities and across countries.

In the United States, defense industries at the prime contractor level increasingly have become system integrators, buying many of their components from commercially oriented industries.[43] For example, consumer electronics firms, especially in Japan, are leaders in introducing new technologies, designing sophisticated components, and manufacturing them cheaply and with unprecedented reliability. Many U.S. defense firms now lack consumer electronics expertise and the market that goes with it, thereby weakening their revenue base and also forcing them to buy many components from foreign firms.

The Department of Defense (DoD) business environment and market are now highly unstable, and DoD discourages mixed defense and commercial activities by its contractors. With defense R&D and procurement budgets likely to decrease up to

25 percent in real terms in the next five years and with reductions in forces of up to 50 percent, U.S. defense contractors now have few incentives to invest for the long term in the defense market and to establish an integrated technology and manufacturing base. Coupled to the changes in threat, this raises the question of how to create and maintain a restructured defense industry and technology base. The only practical mechanism is to integrate the defense industrial base with the commercial industrial base and to mandate that the DoD use as much U.S. commercial technology as possible, while it continues to develop the technologies unique to defense[44] and maintains critical design teams.

Thus, the twin issues of arms proliferation and the defense industrial and technology base present a highly complex situation to the United States. In the case of planning for missions such as nuclear deterrence, protection of lines of communication and other vital facilities, maintenance-of-force worldwide, special operations, and short intervention capability, the DoD would have to assure a priori that its forces were of sufficient size and reliability, with a capability for maintenance and spares. In the case of planning for protracted interventions or wars and as a hedge against the Soviet residual threat or other new threats, the DoD would also have to maintain development and production capabilities and reserve forces that could be put into use when needed and that would maintain both U.S. technological leadership and modern forces.

To help achieve these objectives, Ashton B. Carter and William T. Perry have suggested that the basic research and exploratory development budget of the DoD be increased significantly and the advanced development budget and that the industrial independent R&D budgets be held at a constant level, while the rest and much larger part of the R&D and procurement budgets are being greatly decreased.[45] Defense technologies developed in this restructured development system would also be tested operationally and, if necessary, the appropriate systems could be designed and manufactured in efficient, low-rate production lines. The DoD would have to restructure its acquisition system to manage these developments so as to provide the appropriate hedges for alternative futures. The development of two-way dual-use technologies would be encouraged where feasible by reducing DoD acquisition and security barriers to integration with the commercial industrial base. To be effective, such a restructured acquisition system must remain dynamic to avoid obsolescence in the production processes and in design teams and staff skills and training. The current intercontinental ballistic missile (ICBM) modernization and strategic defense iniative (SDI) programs, although inadvertently, roughly fit this definition and provide a model of sorts for the future of how to develop new weapons technologies without having to deploy them in large numbers.

In the case of new electronics capabilities, however, a special opportunity exists. Most defense systems intensively use electronics, which, among other things, now require high maintenance costs. Two recent developments change this situation. First, electronic components now become obsolete in about six years and if, obtained from Japan, for example, in less than six years. Second, modern electronics, if properly designed and tested, can be ultrareliable. It is therefore feasible that a modernization program for existing defense platforms (command and control centers, communications nodes, aircraft, ships, and so on), which completely replaced the electronic subsystems of these platforms with modern electronics on a planned basis of about a six-year cycle or less, would provide new operational capabilities for these systems at a relatively low cost compared to producing completely new systems. It would also greatly reduce the maintenance costs compared to the status quo. The net cost would be highly affordable in an era of declining defense budgets. Recent MITRE studies lend some validity to this proposition to use modern electronics to replace existing subsystems on a planned basis in order to make all existing forces more deployable (lighter and smaller) and reliable, and thus maintainable with significantly fewer people and requiring reduced lift capabilities.[46] At the same time, planned modernization by subsystem—guidance, propulsion, software, etc., as well as electronics—will allow expensive new platform procurements (ships, aircraft, vehicles, submarines) to be stretched out to twenty-year cycles or more.

Finally, the trend in conventional defense forces for the United States will be to reduce greatly the size of the current forces and numbers of personnel and to opt for highly mobile, deployable forces capable of world-wide swiftness of action, high flexibility, and accuracy, and able to operate independent of nuclear forces. Electronic systems will therefore play a key role. Ogarkov, former Soviet defense chief, has termed these kinds of capabilities *reconnaissance strike complexes*. They are characterized by:

- all-weather, night and day, real-time reconnaissance, intelligence, warning, surveillance, and target acquisition of air and ground targets from space, air, and ground-based sensor systems (microwave, electro-optical, and infrared) to provide air order of battle, ground order of battle, and targeting data through fusion of multisource data;

- improved anti-armor forces—ground and helicopter-based antitank missiles, mobile multiple-launch rockets with terminally guided submunitions, high-velocity 120 mm cannons, and smart mines;

- high quality weapons vision subsystems—imagers, seekers—to recognize targets automatically;

- a variety of nonnuclear ordnance, both precision and wide-area, with terminally guided submunitions, shaped charges, sensor-fused munitions, self-forging fragments, penetrating warheads, etc., with essentially near zero error in guidance systems;

- theatre-wide real-time command and control networks for effective combined arms—air, tanks, antitank systems, artillery, air defense, and infantry;

- very-high-survivability strike missiles and aircraft, achieved through a combination of stealth and electronic warfare (EW) capabilities to overcome air defenses and deliver ordnance with high probability of kill;

- interceptors with long-range, fire and forget, air-to-air and air-to-ground missiles;

- similar surveillance, communications, and weapons capabilities at sea for Navy task forces and battle groups.

This array of potential new capabilities promises to increase the cost-effectiveness of conventional forces by factors of two to ten in firing rates, sorties, and ammunition required per target kill. Such capabilities can provide reliable intelligence and warning and targeting data; delay, disrupt, and destroy tank armies; and destroy fixed-based infrastructure, such as airfields and rail yards, and mobile targets, such as surface-to-air missile sites. In some cases, existing forces, such as artillery and aircraft, cannot perform these missions except at prohibitive costs in firing rates, sorties, and ordnance per target kill.

Aircraft are effective against point targets (e.g., bases and massed armored columns), or densely packed area targets. Identifying those targets is the function of reconnaissance and surveillance. By adding this ability to identify and track clustered area targets in real time, and by adding wide-area and homing munitions with high probability of kill to aircraft and artillery delivery systems, antitank and anti-artillery capabilities can be increased greatly, probably by factors of ten or more in kills per shot. Precision-guided munitions would be used against relatively isolated high-value fixed targets. In all cases, air defenses would also have to be attacked in order to keep aircraft attrition rates at acceptable levels. As a result of these factors, all-out, modern conventional war can destroy assets such as aircraft and tanks rapidly, and therefore requires robust reinforcement capabilities.

These new technical capabilities would also greatly reduce the need for logistics support of weapons systems because of the weapons' high accuracy and probability of kill and their day and night, all-weather, survivable, autonomous, multiple-kills-per-pass weapons capabilities. The sorties and bombs needed per weapons kill will be reduced by up to an order of magnitude, compared to current weapons systems, thereby reducing vulnerability of the weapons as well as overall costs.

In the long run these technologies, because of their very high reliability, levels of automation, and quality, can also reduce operations and maintenance costs by reducing the needs for surveillance, communications, and other operational personnel and also for maintenance personnel.

The transition to these capabilities in air, land, and sea forces will require major research, development, and testing activities and high capital investments before effective and affordable modernization can be achieved. Such capabilities will also require tactical intelligence and operational information to support existing forces, and they must be adequate to avoid surprises and to cover potential actions worldwide. Also, the increased vulnerability of ships, port facilities, air bases, and of airborne aircraft to missiles must be addressed with defensive mechanisms. Nevertheless, such capabilities represent the best option reduce reliance on nuclear weapons and to meet U.S. conventional defense needs in a changing world of arms proliferation, while having the performance characteristics to make them affordable because of the reduced numbers of weapons and people needed.

SUMMARY CONCLUSIONS

The developed world is in the midst of a new period of technological revolution and application. The technological imperative has taken hold worldwide. It has become:

- the prerequisite for increases in productivity leading to economic growth and competitiveness;

- the mechanism by which new knowledge is gained via research and development and the education of a skilled work force;

- the agent to achieve an environmentally sustainable economy through the ecological modernization of industry and agriculture (a paradigm that has been adopted by many leading environmentalists with respect to pollution prevention and energy conservation);

- the path by which cleaner energy generation systems will be achieved;

- the basis for highly effective, deployable conventional military forces;

- the source of the emerging biotechnology revolution in medical diagnostics and care, new wonder drugs, and agrogenetics that can bring about long, healthy, disease-free lives and change demographic and social trends greatly.

The social, economic, and political barriers to the widespread application of the new technologies are huge. Sweeping changes in industrial systems and massive technology transfer will be necessary to achieve the objectives discussed above. Investment in infrastructure—research, education, and manufacturing systems—will be critcal. Technology modulates demographic, economic, and environmental trends over time scales of several decades, and its potential impacts are important in formulating policies and investment choices for the economy and defense.

The globalization of technology and production is increasing and is likely to prove irreversible. Coupled to arms proliferation worldwide, these twin issues present a complex situation for U.S. policies and programs designed to maintain economic competitiveness and the U.S. defense industrial and technology base. There is a strong need for the U.S. government to recraft its role in technological competitiveness and to restructure its defense industrial and technology base.

The high priority needs for U.S. investments in the 1990s include:

- greatly increased environmental research in the common problems that affect everybody—air pollution (acid rain, ozone depletion, greenhouse warming); processes to prevent pollution at the source; techniques to clean up and treat toxic and hazardous wastes and to manage wastes; and measures to preserve water resources, forests, coastal areas, and agricultural and plant gene pools;

- legislation that will encourage and support investment for the insertion of new process technologies that will increase productivity and reduce pollution in energy systems, manufacturing, transportation systems, and agriculture;

- the application of information technologies to mass education in cognitive skills on an individualized learning basis;

- greatly increased research in new energy-generation systems, and the application of streamlined, acceptable licensing procedures for safe nuclear power plants and waste storage;

- legislation and policies that will increase economic competitiveness by increasing private savings and incentives for investments that can strengthen the U.S. research and manufacturing base and the U.S. position in world trade;

- the establishment of new DoD acquisition policies and procedures that will restructure the defense industrial and technology base by making maximum use of commercially developed technologies and the commercial industrial base;

- the continued modernization of U.S. conventional defense forces to make them more deployable, effective, and affordable to operate and maintain.

NOTES

1. *Business Week*, May 14, 1990, pp. 98–106.
2. Joseph S. Nye, Jr., *Bound to Lead:The Changing Nature of American Power* (New York, Basic Books, 1990), pp. 249–253.
3. Charles A. Zraket, "Understanding and Managing the New Benefits and Problems of the Information Society," Proceedings of the National Conference on the Advancement of Research, October 18–21, 1981, Hot Springs, Arkansas, and MITRE Corporation Paper, M82-44, July 1982.
4. Ibid.
5. Peter F. Drucker, *The New Realities: in Government and Politics, in Economics and Business, in Society and World View* (New York: Harper and Row, 1989).
6. Anthony Smith, *The Geopolitics of Information: How Western Culture Dominates the World* (London: Oxford University Press, 1980).

7. Zraket, "Understanding and Managing the New Benefits and Problems of the International Society."
8. Edward N. Luttwak, "The Shape of Things to Come," *Commentary* (July 1990), pp. 17–25.
9. Jesse H. Ausubel, "Hydrogen and the Green Wave," *The Bridge*, National Academy of Engineering, Vol. 20, No. 1, Summer 1990, pp. 17–22.
10. J. Gustave Speth, "The Global Environmental Agenda," *Environmental Science & Technology*, Vol. 23 (July 1989), p. 793.
11. Robert M. White, "The Great Climate Debate," *Scientific American*, Vol. 263, No. 1 (July 1990), pp. 36–43.
12. G. J. F. MacDonald, "Environmental Security Issues," Summer Seminar on Global Security and Arms Control, University of California, Los Angeles, July 1, 1990.
13. Thomas F. Homer-Dixon, *Environmental Change and Violent Conflict*, American Academy of Arts and Sciences, Occasional Paper No. 4, June 1990.
14. William Clark, "Global Interactions of Population, Technology, and Environment," Science, Technology, and Public Policy Program, Kennedy School of Government, Harvard University, 1990.
15. Ibid.
16. Charles A. Zraket, "Technology Trends and Alternatives for Economic Development," Watch Tower '74 Conference, January 18–20, 1974, Cocoyoc, Mexico, published as MITRE Paper MTP-390, February 1974.
17. Charles A. Zraket, "Environmental Situation in the United States," in A. T. Amr, D. E. Egan, K. R. Krickenberger, and S. V. McBrien, *Pollution Prevention: Opportunities and Constraints Workshop Presentations and Summary*, August 1–6, 1989, MTP-89W00006. Available from The MITRE Corporation, Civil Systems Division, McLean, VA 22102.
18. Ibid.
19. Ibid.
20. G. J. F. MacDonald, "Policies and Technologies for Waste Reduction and Energy Efficiency," in ibid.
21. Ibid.
22. Also see, for example, "Biotechnology Fosters New Era in Agricultural Investigation," *The Scientist*, February 5,1990, p. 22.
23. Department of State, Bureau of Intelligence and Research, *Potential for Expanding World Food Production by Region and Country*, October 15, 1985.
24. Zraket, "Understanding and Managing the New Benefits and Problems of the Information Society."
25. Jean-Claude Derian, *America's Struggle for Leadership in Technology* (Cambridge, Mass., MIT Press, 1990), pp. 273, 263–272.
26. Smith, *The Geopolitics of Information*.
27. *Wall Street Journal*, June 25, 1990, last page.
28. Ibid.
29. Charles A. Zraket, "Software as a Dual Use Technology," Chapter IIG of *Beyond Spinoff: Relating Military and Communication Technologies in a Changing World*, a project of the Science, Technology, and Public Policy Program, Kennedy School of Government, Harvard University, 1990, forthcoming.
30. Ausubel, "Hydrogen and the Green Wave."
31. Luttwak, "The Shape of Things to Come."

32. "Europower 1992," *IEEE Spectrum*, June 1990, pp. 22–23.
33. Technology Administration, U.S. Department of Commerce, *Emerging Technologies, a Survey of Technical and Economic Opportunities*, Spring 1990.
34. See for example, Michael L. Dertouzos, Richard K. Lester, and Robert M. Solow, *Made in America, Regaining the Productive Edge* (Cambridge, Mass.: MIT Press, 1990).
35. Bobby R. Inman, and Daniel F. Burton, Jr., "Technology and Competitiveness," *Foreign Affairs*, Spring 1990, pp. 116–134.
36. Ralph Landau, "Capital Investment: Key to Competitiveness and Growth," *The Brookings Review*, Summer 1990, pp. 52–56.
37. Ibid.
38. Ibid.
39. Lee H. Hamilton, "Europe 1992: The View from Congress," *Issues in Science and Technology*, Summer 1990.
40. See, for example, *Business Week*, February 5, 1990, p. 59.
41. See, for example, The Aspen Strategy Group Report, *New Threats: Responding to the Proliferation of Nuclear, Chemical, and Delivery Capabilities in the Third World* (Lanham, Md.: University Press of America, 1990). Janne E. Nolan and Albert D. Wheelon, "Third World Ballistic Missiles," *Scientific American*, August 1990, pp. 34–40. W. Perry, B. Inman, Joseph S. Nye, Jr., and Roger Smith, "Third World Threats," *Aspen Institute Quarterly*, Vol. 2, No. 3 (Summer 1990), pp. 10–32.
42. Ibid.
43. Charles A. Zraket, "Dual-Use Technologies and National Competitiveness," *The Bridge*, National Academy of Engineering, Vol. 19, No. 3 (Fall 1989), pp. 14–20.
44. Ibid.
45. Ashton B. Carter, and William T. Perry, *New Thinking and American Defense Technology*, a report of the Carnegie Commission on Science, Technology, and Government, New York, 1990.
46. Barry M. Horowitz, "Modernizing Electronics in DOD Systems," published as MITRE Paper M90-48, August 1990. Available from The MITRE Corporation, Bedford, MA 01730.

Appendix 4

AWAY FROM THE PAST:
EUROPEAN POLITICS AND SECURITY 1990

Stanley Hoffmann

I

The events of the last year in Europe have been analyzed almost to death, and yet a few important points still need to be made, if one wants to understand how we got to where we are today, and what the present condition of Europe is like. This will be the subject of the first part of this paper. The second part will examine the implication of the current scene for the security of Europe's nations.

"Nothing in history is inevitable, except in the formal sense that, for it to have happened otherwise, the antecedent cause would have had to be different."[1] This remark of E.H. Carr applies perfectly to the European events. Soon historians and political scientists will tell us why what happened had to occur. We should not too easily cross the line that separates an explanation of why the division of Europe and communist rule in much of Central and Eastern Europe came to a sudden end, from an assertion of necessity. *Things could have been different.* At every point, in every country, choices were made. During the hectic weeks of the late summer and fall of 1989, in each of the Communist nations of the Soviet *glacis*, a threatened leadership had to choose between repression and retreat, force and suicide. Only in Romania and in Bulgaria did the Communists succeed in staying in power. It is not enough to say that in Poland, Hungary, and Czechoslovakia, the satellite regimes were swept away by their fundamental illegitimacy, which was a permanent condition. What led to their demise was the decisions the demoralized leaders took, their disarray when the challenge of a revived opposition struck them, and their reluctance to use brute force on a large scale once they were on their own.

Similarly, the way in which Germany has marched, or rather run, to its unification was by no means inevitable. One can without too much trouble imagine a very different scenario, one in which the pace of events would have been slower, and all the other powers concerned by the "German problem" would have tried to guide the change, to subordinate unity to a host of "architectural" concerns and constructs. Indeed, in December of 1989, I suggested such a scheme.[2] It is not pointless to compare it with what actually happened; not only has German unity been accomplished in one year instead of ten, but the role of the other players has been very different from the one I was, in effect, advocating. Once again, choices were made—openly or implicitly—that could have been very different.

The reason why I emphasize this point is of special importance to students of international relations: academics with their baggage of theory, practitioners with their operational code. The dominant theory, the customary code stress the decisive importance of the structure of the international system, the way in which the distribution of capabilities (usually those that constitute, in Joseph Nye's terminology, "hard power": military might and economic resources) shapes the policies of states. It is high time to get rid of the sterilizing hold that this notion has had. As a "first cut" in analyzing international affairs, it has some validity, but no more. In 1989, the capabilities of the Soviet Union, in "hard power" terms, were not significantly lower than before, and the same can be said of the United States. What was weaker in both cases, (much more, of course, in the Soviet one) was what Raymond Aron had called the capacity for collective action—the ability of the state to extract those resources for foreign and military policy goals. The economic system is more important than, and vastly different from the sum of the material resources of a nation. Above all, the goals of the two countries—and again especially the Soviet ones—had significantly changed, and both the nature of relevant power and the interplay between such power and goals are far more complex than the "structural" approach to world politics suggests.

What the student of world affairs needs to examine above all, in order to understand what happened and to be ready for what might now occur, is a set of two factors that the structural approach has neglected. The most obvious is the role of leadership. As a student of Charles de Gaulle's statecraft—which the events of 1989 have made appear prophetic—I have made this point long ago: leaders matter. The European events have been shaped by the decisions of two men, and by the stance of several others. The two men are Mikhail Gorbachev, of course, and Helmut Kohl. It was Gorbachev who decided that the Soviet Union would no longer play, in Eastern Europe, the hegemonic role that his predecessors had forged and preserved—several times by force—even if this meant the demise of communist regimes. As debates in the Soviet Union have shown, this was not an uncontroversial decision; it is, indeed, one that most Western analysts had not considered likely. It is possible to imagine other Soviet leaders engaged, like Gorbachev, in attempts to reform the Soviet economy and to reduce military expenditures, but determined nevertheless to safeguard the satellite regimes and the preponderant position of the Soviet Union in Eastern Europe. Retreat from Empire was not dictated by the plight of the Soviet economy; a sharp reduction in the cost of Empire undoubtedly was, but that is not at all the same thing. It may be true that Gorbachev did not intend the communist regimes to fall, and might have preferred communist reformers to take over, but he was willing to let these regimes fall if such reformers could not be found or could not stem the tide, and determined not to use the massive Soviet forces in the area in order to hold on. He may himself have been a mere reformer when he came to power in 1985. By 1989, both in foreign and in domestic affairs, he was a revolutionary, intent on dismantling totalitarianism at home, and the whole foreign policy of Joseph Stalin and his successors. It was his decision not to prop up the satellite regimes thus depriving them of the one support they had been able to count on: their legitimacy in Moscow, which compensated for their lack of legitimacy at home. It was he who decided not to forfeit German goodwill by using Soviet forces in Germany as an instrument to blackmail Bonn and to prevent Germany either from uniting or from remaining in NATO after unity; he had weak cards, but it was his decision not to use them at all, or almost not. He may ultimately be able to show that his choice was beneficial to his country. But the returns of the gamble are not in, and not everybody deemed that gamble inevitable. Few people had taken Gorbachev's remarkable speech at the General Assembly of the United Nations in 1987 seriously; those who did turned out to be right. It was not mere rhetoric; it was policy.

As for Helmut Kohl, this man who had so often been accused of being without a vision, a mere tactician, a skillful politician rather than a statesman, a somewhat reluctant follower of his foreign minister Hans-Dietrich Genscher rather than an initiator, acted as if the spirit of Konrad Adenauer had suddenly seized him. We now tend to remember the old chancellor as a champion of Western European integration and of NATO, but he had also been a German patriot, keen on restoring as much of German sovereignty as the circumstances allowed, on making the Federal Republic an actor and not an object, and on improving its rank and status. What is striking about Kohl's leadership is his decision to make of German unity an issue for the Germans alone and to act accordingly. All the key initiatives have come from Bonn. The European Economic Community (EEC) was not consulted, even though the absorption of the DDR amounts to the entry of a thirteenth member; Brussels was not always even informed. Both political unification and economic aid have been shaped on Bonn's terms. To be sure, the Federal Republic had to accept the "four plus two" formula, but it was directly with Gorbachev that Kohl negotiated the acceptance by Moscow of German membership in NATO, the limitation on the size and nature of German armed forces, and the departure of Soviet forces from East Germany and of the occupying forces from Berlin. To be sure, like Adenauer, Kohl proclaims his intention to work for Western European monetary and political union, and to keep Germany in

NATO, but he has acted in such a way as to present these courses as a sovereign German choice, not a constraint imposed, or even a collective option adopted, by a coalition of nations. At every turn, including in NATO summit meetings, he has preempted or evaded control, while providing what might be called sovereign reassurance about his intentions and destination.

A third feat of leadership, more circumscribed in nature, has been that of Jacques Delors within the EEC since 1984.[3] While the progress of the EEC—and as a result its power as a magnet—have depended on a series of bargains among its main members, Delors has skillfully prodded them, and enlarged the opportunities for further integration. But the picture would not be what it is today if it had not been for the peculiar leadership of three other actors. George Bush, or his advisers, have seen to it that all summits, in 1989 and 1990, appear to have followed his script and endorsed his positions, but images and substance are very different. Essentially, he has accepted a much reduced role for the United States in Western Europe, allowed the EEC to be the main actor (after the Federal Republic!) in Eastern Europe, and adopted a kind of minimalist policy based on three notions: helping Gorbachev diplomatically (if not financially), supporting Germany's national aspirations, and saving NATO, the last instrument of America's preponderance in Western Europe. He has been skillful in taking into account Soviet security interests, German desire for sovereignty in unity, and the need to preserve a Western European and a North Atlantic "roof" over the new German house. He has been lucky insofar as the three goals have turned out to be compatible—thanks to Gorbachev and Kohl. But his performance has been that of a supporting player, not a key actor.

François Mitterrand appears to have been somewhat left behind by events. He has allowed Kohl to dominate the scene, after creating, last fall, an impression of disarray. A period of Franco-German pique was caused by the failure of the chancellor to inform his partner about his plan for German unity. Mitterrand's embrace of further Western European integration and of NATO does not entirely fit what remains a highly Gaullist defense policy, and the French, worried about France's role in world affairs, compare nostalgically de Gaulle's forceful and eloquent pedagogical leadership with Mitterrand's sparse statements and impressionistic nuances.[4]

As for Margaret Thatcher, nobody can deny that she is a forceful leader, but her own strong performance shows the difference between great leadership and wrong leadership. Great leaders exploit the opportunities provided by *la conjoncture* and use their nations' resources to affect the course of history. They may—as de Gaulle often did—have to resort to obstruction in order to prevent something they deems contrary to the national interest, but they must first assess correctly whether they can make their obstruction stick. Thatcher has consistently made it clear that she disapproves of the directions taken by events—deeper integration in the EEC, speedy German unity, even the pace of conventional arms control in Europe or changes in NATO's nuclear strategy—yet she has been unable to affect these events, and has preferred being dragged along reluctantly to being isolated. The muted performance or counter-performance of Bush, Mitterrand, and Thatcher has left the field to Gorbachev and Kohl, and thus contributed in its own way to the outcome.

A second factor neglected by the structural approach is, in a sense, an extension of the previous one. It is the importance of domestic factors for the understanding of foreign policy, and particularly the need to look at the configuration of political forces and at the relations between what is often called "civil society" and the state. In the 1980s, in all the Eastern European countries as well as in the Soviet Union, the ability of the regimes to provide their peoples with the economic benefits that the citizens expected had declined or collapsed, and faith in communism had been replaced by a combination of cynicism and routine. Moreover, thanks in part to détente, the isolation of these citizens had decreased, and many of them—particularly those among the more educated—had become able to compare their condition with that of the West Europeans and North Americans whom they visited or who visited them. Later, in the Soviet Union, *glasnost* and *perestroika* unleashed, revived, or created a host of tendencies, currents, and national or ethnic movements, protests, etc., whose claims, quarrels, and demands make it difficult to imagine any foreign policy other than one of retrenchment and retreat. The state of the Soviet economy, as well as the discontents it fosters, explains why Soviet diplomacy is so eager to reintegrate the Soviet Union both into the world economy and into what its spokespersons often call our common civilization. In Eastern Europe, while it was Gorbachev's decision that doomed Communist regimes, it was the deterioration of the economy and the partial revival of "civil society"—variable in scope and shape from country to country—that created the challenge in the first place.

Both in the Soviet Union and in Western Europe, many observers missed a generational change. In the Soviet Union, Gorbachev was only one member of a new generation of *cadres* who seemed to have come to the conclusion that the Stalinist system did not work—either at home or abroad—and who, thanks to *glasnost*, were finally able to put their private thoughts and their public stands in harmony. In Western Europe, there also exists a new generation of leaders: businessmen, civil servants, politicians, and media representatives, who have acquired the habit of cooperation across barriers, and who seem capable of reconciling their national perspectives and their "European" outlook (this is the case even in England). This distinguishes them often quite sharply from their elders; it explains in great part why, especially on the continent, Germany's partners did not appear excessively worried by Germany's new prominence, why the German leaders themselves were able to move toward their national goals without gloating or *hubris*, and why the German public, especially the young, often appeared rather ambivalent about unification. As for the United States, its relative timidity—after the years of Reaganesque posturing—would be difficult to understand if one did not take into account the size of the American debt, the two deficits, domestic social concerns, the new importance of economic worries about Western European and above all Japanese competition, and the taboo about raising taxes: a complex set of domestic, economic, political, and "mood" factors that explain in part the paradox of Bush's foreign policy, which often presents the United States as still number one but broke.

It is difficult to theorize about what aspects of domestic politics (in the broadest sense of that term) need to be examined.

"Structure," in the international system, has a deceptive simplicity; domestic factors are fluid and complex. In the first analysis, the opinions, passions; and interests of what is often referred to as the enlightened public, and the way in which it is organized politically and economically, should be the focus of attention. This is so, especially because of one fundamental transformation that has affected much (although not all) of world politics. The structural theory was geared to a world in which states, as discrete actors, sought power or sought to balance power, in a game that entailed the possible resort to war. The structural constraints that resulted from this condition limited the importance of the variations in behavior caused by the peculiarities of each actor's domestic regime or politics. Remove that possibility of war, or relax those constraints: the nature of the game changes—not because the actors will cease seeking power and influence, but because the way of acquiring gains, the nature of the desired gains, and the means of provoking international change will change. In traditional international politics, war provided the most visible and, often, quick instrument of change. Remove war: change in international affairs, or in the pecking order of states, will tend to result either from revolutions or from those modifications in the goals or in the power of states that domestic politics and internal efforts bring about. This is certainly not what has happened in the Middle East, those "Balkans" of the new international system, but it is exactly what has happened in East-West relations in Europe; here, the common desire to avoid a nuclear war and a conventional conflict capable of generating into a nuclear one froze the surface, under which major shifts took place, such as the development of the EEC and the decline of communist Eastern Europe. This is what happened in Eastern Europe, once the sword of Soviet military intervention was removed.

When we turn from the cause of recent events to the scene they have created, one is struck by a phenomenon that Pierre Hassner has often stressed:[5] institution building and political decisions by states and social movements interact, but they move at different speeds (and often paradoxically; after all, the rush to German unity, i.e., the decision of the Federal Republic to skip stages and to absorb, in effect, the DDR, was largely caused by the desire to keep the inhabitants of the DDR from moving into the Federal Republic, as would have happened if the two states had remained side by side). One is also struck by another paradox. The iron curtain is gone, and the artificial division of Europe and of Germany, the grip of the superpowers that maintained it, are things of the past. And yet there is no unity of Europe: its heterogeneity is blatantly apparent.

East Germany will soon cease to exist as a state—it never was a nation—but it will take years and probably more than the $70 billion allocated by the Federal Republic for its economy to be fully integrated into that of the West. Economically, Europe remains divided, between essentially free market, capitalist systems and nations that are either still in the throes of a command economy, or just beginning to move—without models—from a communist to a capitalist system. The dismantling of state property has barely begun. Politically, there are three distinct zones: the democracies of the EEC and the other European members of European Free Trade Association (EFTA), the remaining communist regimes, and the new parliamentary systems of Czechoslovakia, Hungary, and Poland; the distinction between communism and aspiring democracy runs across Yugoslavia. From the viewpoint of international affairs, the "western" parts of Europe have strong structures of cooperation: the EEC, EFTA, NATO, but the nations of the East remain separate, rather jealous or suspicious of one another; ethnic rivalries are fostering secessionist movements or interstate conflicts, and the former structures of the Warsaw Pact and the Council of Mutual Economic Assistance (COMECON) are deserted or crumbling shells.

There is no longer a liberal and capitalist Europe facing a communist one, but there is a settled Europe and an unsettled one. In settled Europe, nations are either governed by consensus or have well established political procedures and rituals, as well as a host of cooperative channels for their interactions. Unsettled Europe bears some resemblance to the postliberation scene in the western half forty-five years ago. This means that the priorities are widely different. In the West, the hidden agenda is the digestion of the new Germany; the open one is, in Germany, the digestion of the former DDR, and, everywhere, the further development of cooperation along well-laid tracks. In the East, the priority is national reconstruction and reform. One side looks toward the future, the other rediscovers its past.

II

The points made in the first part of this paper are meant to place a realistic net under the countless exercises in "architecture" for European security after the Cold War, in which so many commentators and scholars have indulged in the past few months. Statesmen, by necessity, have been more prudent: after all, the Vienna talks on conventional forces have not yet been concluded, and the leaders have had to concentrate on the very near future. The contest of designs has its picturesque aspects, but the institutional suggestions that have proliferated are less interesting than attempts to look seriously at the security needs facing the new Europe, and which the schemes in question would have to satisfy. Too often, writers have argued either as if the security scene was going to be the same as before, only at a lower level of danger and with a displacement of a few hundred miles toward the east—providing the West now, instead of the Soviet Union, with a *glacis*, or else as if the declining weight of the superpowers in Europe was going to bring back the troubled world of competing and hostile states that had led Europe to so many wars for so long, and to two catastrophes in twenty-five years of this century. But things are not so simple, or so grim.

What drives statecraft, more often than not, is ambition and fear. Ambitions, in present-day Europe, are largely fastened on domestic reconstruction or domestic progress, which requires a stable and cooperative external environment, and, in the eyes of many Europeans (East as well as West), the further development or expansion of the European Community. Current fears seem to be focused on two key actors: the Soviet Union and Germany. Many Europeans see in the Soviet Union—or in Russia, should the Soviet Union itself disintegrate—a potential threat, because of the disproportion between its might and the military power of the European states, which will remain contiguous to the Russian bear. To be sure, any resurgence of Soviet aggressiveness seems remote at present, but internal turmoil could—as has happened in so many revolutions—spill over into external diversions, especially if anti-Western, nationalistic, and militaristic forces should prevail in a domestic power struggle. Also, turbulence and conflict in Eastern Europe could under certain circumstances provoke new Soviet interventions caused by a fear of spreading insecurity. This lingering suspicion of Soviet or Russian moves, combined with continuing awe at Soviet capabilities and with a fear of the unpredictable effects, especially of the control of nuclear weapons, of an eventual breakdown of law and order, or of a triumph of centrifugal forces in a collapsing Soviet Union, explains the attachment of the European members of NATO to the organization (as well as French and British reluctance at downgrading the threat of nuclear weapons in NATO's strategy). It also explains in part why the leaders of the key nations of Eastern and Central Europe have made it clear that they want NATO to survive and why, so far, all these countries want U.S. forces to remain in Europe, and the U.S. nuclear guarantee to its allies to persist.

As for Germany, the anxieties that have been expressed are much more varied, and quite contradictory.[6] Some fear a return to the past—pre-1914 or even pre-1939, with a dominant Germany driven to nuclear rearmament by security worries or eager to exploit the "power vacuum" in Eastern Europe, or even to recover lost territories in the East.[7] Others fear various acts of collusion between the new, strong Germany and the new weakened Soviet Union, with Germany giving a more "Eastern" orientation to its foreign policy, and gradually emptying NATO of its military content, reducing it to "a symbolic compact"[8] and relying instead on the Soviet-sponsored Conference on Security and Cooperation in Europe (CSCE) for collective security. In this conception, the dynamic but naive Germany would in fact let the Soviet fox into the European barnyard, and, in Hassner's words, the price for not having the neutralized Germany that the Soviets first said they wanted would be a neutralized Europe. The two nightmares are incompatible, but both lead, once again, to a desire to preserve a strong NATO, as a barrier to both kinds of "German peril."

In turn, the logic of the fears that many Europeans have both of the Soviet Union (or Russia) *and* of Germany leads to some sort of a collective Western guarantee to the nations of Eastern and Central Europe in order to protect them altogether from German revanchism, from a Soviet aggressive resurgence, and from a new variant of the Nazi-Soviet Pact. Practically nobody suggests extending the membership of NATO or the scope of the territory covered by the North Atlantic treaty toward the east—such an extension is deemed unacceptable to the Soviets, and would be opposed by France, always on its guard against any change in NATO's sphere of action. Moreover, two other fears are rampant in Western Europe and would interfere with any such expansion of the Atlantic Alliance.

One is the fear of a return, in the eastern half of Europe, to the kind of conflictual anarchy that people associate with the interwar period and with the concept of balkanization. This could result either from interstate clashes provoked by antagonistic nationalisms (cf. Romania vs. Hungary), or from secessionist movements, as in Yugoslavia or Czechoslovakia, or from internal turmoil in countries that face simultaneously the talk of establishing democratic political systems and of administering enormous shocks to their economies in order to become part of the capitalist world. Nobody has analyzed the difficulty of succeeding in both tasks at once better than Timothy Garton Ash;[9] he has warned that the transition from the moralistic unity of anti-Communist resistance to pluralistic politics—a transition that reminds one of the difficult births of postwar politics in France and Italy after 1945—is likely to be made more difficult by the absence of "many elements of civil society," long suppressed by the Communists regimes. There is a real danger of authoritarian, antidemocratic regimes taking over, as happened before in Poland and Hungary, if democratic politics cannot "absorb the larger part of the inevitable popular discontents" that drastic economic reform will generate. What is obvious today is the desire of the rest of Europe *not* to be dragged into the domestic or external conflicts of Eastern and Central European nations, *not* to let itself be pushed back into a past that the West Europeans pride themselves on having overcome at last and for good.

There is another fear—particularly but not exclusively in France; one has seen a version of it in the Federal Republic in the summer and fall of 1989. It is the fantastical fear of an invasion by outsiders—Moslem fundamentalists and terrorists, starving Africans, refugees from the Third World's conflicts, or East Europeans in quest of jobs and prosperity. In history, economic and political success usually brings smugness, and yet it also breeds anxieties, dark suspicions of subversion by evil forces of greed and envy. To many West Europeans in their wealthy nations, capitalist Europe appears like a besieged and coveted island surrounded by hungry pirates who would like to land and to plunder, or like the Roman Empire facing the barbarians. The demographic state of Western Europe feeds these phobias, which are—as is usually the case—based on genuine cultural clashes and worries about national identity. The fear of having to grant free entry and circulation to 100 million Turks dooms Turkey's application for membership to the EEC. An unspoken but nevertheless real fear of an exodus from Eastern Europe caused by rising unemployment and higher prices is one of the many obstacles to an early entry of Western-oriented countries like Hungary, Poland, and Czechoslovakia into the EEC's club.

One reason why many Europeans—especially the French—continue to emphasize the importance of the North-South dimension of world politics, and the need for greater efforts to reduce the debt of and provide assistance to the developing countries, is the conviction that misery will breed political and economic disasters, and produce uncontrollable masses of refugees and emigrants who will knock at or break the door of the rich. This same fear of a world in which the East-West confrontation will have been replaced by a contest between the rich nations and the poor masses of often ramshackle states explains in part the prudence shown by the West European leaders (except Thatcher) in supporting the American military buildup against Iraq. (This fear is reinforced by the belief that the failure to resolve the Palestinian issue and America's support for an intransigent Israel, are partly responsible for Saddam Hussein's popularity, as well as for America's unpopularity in many Arab countries.) The debate on European security has, in recent months, turned around the respective virtues and defects of the CSCE versus NATO, and around the ability of these two very different institutions to cope with some of the fears I have listed. As happens so often, each camp is better at pointing out the flaws of the other position than at proving the strength of its own. Critics of the CSCE have an easy task reminding us of the failures of collective security: "nations are loath to sacrifice their *sacro egoismo* on the altar of abstract justice."[10] They point to the inconveniences entailed by a vast membership and by Soviet participation in the CSCE: a weak and troubled Soviet Union could wreck the institution; a strong one could dominate it. They tell us that both a multipolar balance of power system and world peace through world law are less reliable than "permanent or preventive integration or entanglement through physical presence."[11]

Much of this is true. Collective security, in the sense of a commitment to forcible resistance to aggression independently of the character of the aggressor and of the victim, remains not very compatible with the essence of foreign policy behavior. On the one hand, the integrated system of NATO is endangered by the fading away of the common enemy, by the collapse of the Warsaw Pact (which dooms the whole doctrine of forward defense and much of NATO's strategy), and by developments in the two key countries. The United States plans drastic force reductions in Europe (while pretending to believe that this will not affect American predominance in the integrated command and in strategy); and Germany has made its objections to the presence of short-range nuclear systems on its soil very clear indeed.[12] NATO may thus effectively "contain" neither Moscow nor Bonn (or Berlin). Also, as we have seen, NATO provides no answer to the security problems of the new free neighbors of the Soviet Union, its former allies of the Warsaw Pact, whether one thinks of their protection from future Soviet threats or of the problems of nationalisms, minorities, and borders that could threaten their relations with one another or their existence. On the other hand, the CSCE has the merit of keeping the superpowers involved constructively in the security issues of a continent whose turbulence could adversely affect both of them, of providing for one important channel of cooperation between the nations of Eastern and Central Europe and the West, and of offering a framework for the negotiation and enforcement of arms reductions and possible procedures for the resolution of disputes; tasks that are not within NATO's domain and will be of considerable importance.

There are two major tasks that the combination of an aging NATO and a strengthened CSCE will not be able to accomplish. The first is to preserve the Western orientation of a united Germany, to see to it that Germany's quite legitimate concern with defusing any potential Soviet threat by helping Moscow to become a member of the "common European house" does not lead to the emasculation of Western Europe's defenses. It is not simply French paranoia that fears a convergence of America's deep reluctance toward the idea of fighting a nuclear war over Europe and of Germany's "nuclear allergy." NATO, dominated by the German-American "special relationship," could easily become, in a few years, little more than a clearing house. U.S. nonstrategic nuclear forces would only be air-based systems in England and sea-launched cruise missiles, and if the sense of threat from the East declines further, American forces may be asked to leave the sovereign soil of Germany. Much here depends on the future evolution of German politics: there lies the key to NATO's future substance, if not to its formal existence. Moreover, how enthusiastic will the U.S. Congress be for keeping U.S. troops in Germany, if no nuclear weapons are stored nearby? If NATO becomes a largely empty shell, the Soviets would have reached their goal of a largely neutralized and denuclearized continent, but in exchange Germany might acquire a dominant diplomatic and economic influence in Eastern Europe, and a kind of partnership with an economically dependent Russia.

The second task is to further the integration of Central and Eastern Europe—especially Czechoslovakia, Hungary, and Poland—into the rest of Europe, so as to help these nations overcome the enormous obstacles they face on the road to democracy and market economics, and to reduce the risk of nationalistic explosions or exploitation of domestic discontent. The task, here, is both psychological and economic, but it has a military dimension as well, insofar as these nations need reassurance both against their Soviet neighbor, and against any revival of a German peril—although German economic predominance is far more plausible than the military threat of a Germany that accepts limited forces and armaments.

The key to a satisfactory performance of both tasks lies within the European Community. *On paper*, it is easy to imagine that its move toward monetary and political union will be accompanied by an attempt at setting up, directly or through the West European Union, a defense system for its members. In this system, the separation between France's independent strategy and forces, and the integrated strategy and forces of her NATO partners, would at last come to an end. This separation was not too harmful as long as the old American-dominated NATO functioned well. It would have far worse effects in the new NATO one can now foresee. In a Western European security organization, the British and French deterrents would be coordinated with the conventional forces of the participants, and joint military procurement would be systematically undertaken. As American leadership fades in NATO, a British-French-German triumvirate would play the leading role in defense coordination, in order to prevent an atrophy of the military dimension of Western cooperation, and also in order to put an end to the partial isolation of France from the defense arrangements in Western Europe. This defense system could, if they desire it, provide the three states of Eastern and Central Europe with a military guarantee. One can also imagine the EEC, through its new Bank for European Reconstruction and Development, and through the Commission, which plays a major role in the EEC's foreign economic policy, providing substantial economic aid to these states, on condition—as in the Marshall Plan—that they cooperate with one another. Their grouping could thus gradually become capable of negotiating with the EEC agreements similar to those negotiated with EFTA. Mitterrand's idea of a confederation—one that would go from the Atlantic to the Bug—would thus be carried out on the economic front, and a reformed or reenforced Council of Europe could serve as a political coordinating body.

These are ways in which functions relinquished by or not appropriate to a fading NATO could be performed. The Alliance would become, under the vague and flexible 1949 treaty, an agreement between the United States and Canada on the one hand, a European Defense Organization on the other; the nuclear forces of Britain and France and those of the United States (air-based systems in England, as well as sea-launched nuclear weapons) would carry out the deterrent and reassurance roles that will remain necessary. At the same time, links between the different parts of Europe could be established, without any hasty "broadening" of the EEC that would jeopardize its attempt at "deepening" the integration of its twelve current members. Ultimately, if the political systems and the economies of Eastern and Central Europe meet the tests that the EEC has, more or less informally, set up for new members and if these nations become willing to pool and to transfer parts of their recently recovered sovereignty, they could join the EEC, but in the interim they would not be abandoned.

We should, however, not underestimate the factors that could prevent such schemes from moving from paper to reality. I will list them, for purposes of discussion; they all bring us back to the problems of leadership, domestic affairs, and European heterogeneity.

- European security in the aftermath of the Cold War requires the definition of a new relationship between the nations of Europe and the "superpowers." With the United States, the general direction is clear: American influence on the various European processes will continue to decline, without, however, vanishing, given America's economic and residual military presence, Western European needs for reassurance, and Western European dependence on American force for the security of its oil supplies from the Middle East. The links between Washington and Western Europe will largely remain attached to NATO, even if the makeup of NATO and its strategy change, and links between the United States and the rest of Europe are likely to be assured through the EEC and the CSCE. An important variable will be America's prosperity. A recession in the United States would affect Western Europe, probably accelerate the decline of traditional, i.e., American-dominated NATO, and undoubtedly limit the willingness and ability of the EEC's members to devote to Eastern Europe the amounts of aid, and the attention, that are required.

- With the Soviet Union, the new relationship will depend primarily on the outcome of the new Russian revolution. Protracted turmoil, violent conflicts among nationalities, political paralysis at the top would both impede cooperation between the European nations and its troubled neighbor, and perpetuate the fears of an external overflow or transfer of violence. The successful establishment of a radically decentralized Soviet Confederation—accompanied by Baltic independence—would have exactly the opposite effects. It is not clear that the United States and its Western European allies can affect the evolution deeply, even if they provide considerable economic help.

- The linchpin of the various organizations mentioned here will be Germany. Today's apparent paradox is the recovery of full German sovereignty, just as the Western European economies move toward a single market and, soon, a central banking system with some form of a common currency. One must remember that the single market and a monetary union dominated by the Bundesbank are net assets for Germany, and that the united German Republic may well be able to attain a result comparable to the one France had achieved in the 1960s: just enough integration to serve the interests of German farmers, businesses, and services, just enough diplomatic coordination to provide Germany with a seal of European legitimacy, but also enough freedom of diplomatic maneuver to prevent unwelcome constraints in foreign policy and defense. Until today, German governments have remained extremely reluctant to move toward a Western European Defense system. They have preferred the certainties of NATO (even when there were tensions over nuclear issues between Washington and Bonn) as long as the Cold War and the Soviet threat defined the Federal Republic's security condition. They may still prefer NATO, with a central role for German armed forces (whatever their limits) and a convergence between Washington and Bonn on the role of nuclear weapons, to a Western European scheme in which they would have to deal with the quite different nuclear doctrines of their two main partners. Nor has Bonn shown more than verbal enthusiasm for a coordinated diplomacy of the EEC in Eastern Europe. Talk about German "domination" of the EEC is excessive: interdependence in a single market means mutual vulnerability, and influence in the EEC has never been proportional to economic power. A united Germany could, if its leaders so desired, set the limits beyond which they would not accept further constraints and burdens. Moreover, the cost of integrating East Germany is likely to affect the amount of public assistance and private investment available for the rest of Eastern and Central Europe, as well as for assistance to the poorer nations of the EEC and to the countries overseas.

- Neither France nor Britain are fully committed to the course suggested here. Under Thatcher, British policy shows both a strong suspicion of Germany, *and* obstinate unwillingness to "deepen" the EEC in order to limit German freedom of maneuver. What a Labour government would do, given Labour's own divagations on defense, is hard to predict. French policy is not that much more consistent. France's Defense Minister presents France as the only nation capable of and willing to fill the security void created by U.S. "fashions" and German antinuclear illusions, despite the persistent Soviet threat;[13] France's insistence on nuclear independence still impedes any explicit French guarantee to its neighbors or any statement that the deterrence of an attack on them is a vital French interest. The French president—like Chancellor Kohl—remains unwilling to move foreign policy coordination from pure intergovernmentalism into a status comparable to that of the EEC's foreign economic policy (in which there are qualified majority decisions by the Council and a major role for the supranational Commission).

- The willingness and ability of the three nations of Eastern and Central Europe to cooperate and to deal jointly with the EEC remain in doubt. Much will depend on their success or failure in creating the "strong, freely elected coalitions" that Garton Ash deems essential for economic reform—or rather for gaining popular support for such reform, despite the extensive hardships it is likely to produce at first—and, I would add, in establishing institutions strong enough to prevent such coalitions from exploding over every crisis. It is too soon to tell whether they will succeed, although the fragmentation of the initial anticommunist fronts should not be seen as a proof of fiasco.

- We are no closer than before to a common Western European policy and strategy for what is called in NATO jargon "out of area" issues. The French continue, and will continue, to deem such issues beyond the jurisdiction of NATO. The attempt to have the West European Union deal with the crisis provoked by Iraq is a small step forward, but there is no common direction yet, given France's (and Italy's) desire not to alienate countries in which the government or the public sympathizes with Iraq, Britain's determination to reinvigorate a "special relationship" with the United States that had shown signs of fading in favor of a German-American one, and Germany's reluctance to use force abroad. The tendency that prevailed during the oil crisis of 1973—when each of the Western European governments had its own strategy, and several preferred making separate deals with Arab suppliers—has not disappeared. A common policy toward the Arab world, including the Palestinian issue, would require overcoming the pull of historical traditions and the push of competing private interests. Not only has there been only minimal European cohesion, but the crisis also threatens to raise tensions between the United States and its allies. In the short term, America's willingness to deploy vast forces against Saddam Hussein has allowed the Western European countries once more to rely on American actions for the protection of their supplies of oil, but the United States, given its economic difficulties, has raised the old issue of burden sharing with a new sense of urgency (as well as an old sense of self-righteousness). While the allies have responded to the pressure by providing aid to Turkey and other countries hurt by the embargo on Iraq, this has been deemed insufficient by many Americans (and their ire, focused largely on Germany, enlarges the cracks among West Europeans). Moreover, the common front of the allies with Washington against Iraq conceals serious divergences, both within each of the Western European nations and among them, about the possible use of force, and that front could collapse should the United States resort to force without a clear provocation in order to expel Saddam Hussein from Kuwait or in order to destroy his arsenal and evict him from power.

Thus the problems remain immense. And yet the optimists who bet on historical discontinuity and discount the gloomy precedents of European folly may well turn out to be right. Europe has been a zone of security and stability because of the physical presence of superpowers armed with nuclear weapons; and while the decreasing involvement of those powers, and the retreat of nuclear weapons from the front row of European politics may provoke the return of long-repressed rivalries and animosities, Europe is likely nevertheless to be, in a troubled world, an oasis of relative security and stability. Europe as a whole might become a "security community," in the sense defined years ago by Karl Deutsch and his associates, for a variety of reasons. One is a palpable "battle fatigue" about war and violence, especially among the younger generations—it is a factor that accounts in part even for the relative restraint shown by most of the major contenders in the debate over the future of the Soviet Union. Another is the attraction of prosperity, or, if you will, the priority of wealth over might, or the choice of economic influence over territorial control, that has inspired the policies of Germany and the development of the EEC, and now attracts the countries to its East. Finally, while there is nothing inevitable about the further "deepening" of the EEC—it will continue to depend on political bargains among its member states—economic integration and habitual cooperation among elites profoundly affect the conditions and scope of national independence. Indeed, the greatest peril in coming years may well be neither the German nor the Soviet "threats" discussed above, but—especially if economic growth should stop—an egoistic Western Europe keen only on protecting its assets, indifferent to the plight of the nations of Eastern and Central Europe, unwilling or incapable of making the effort to help the developing countries to its South and the struggling nations to its east, and thus turning its fears of external "invasions" and chaos in the east into a self-fulfilling prophecy. But—with the help of good leadership—this peril too could be kept at bay.[14]

NOTES

1. E. H. Carr, *What is History?* (London: Penguin, 1964, p. 96), quoted by Paul Kennedy, "Fin-de-siècle America," *New York Review of Books*, June 28, 1990, p. 40.
2. "A Plan for the New Europe," *New York Review of Books*, January 18, 1990, p. 18ff.
3. For an analysis of his role, see Robert Keohane and Stanley Hoffmann, "European Community Politics and Institutional Change," Harvard Center for European Studies, *Working Paper Series #25*.
4. On French foreign policy, see my essay in *Politique Etrangère*, March 1990. On nostalgia for de Gaulle, see "Histoire et Mémoire," *French Politics and Society*, Vol. 8, No. 3 (Summer 1990), pp. 65–71.
5. I am referring especially to a forthcoming paper by Pierre Hassner, "Beyond Division and Unity: The Dialectics of European (de) recomposition."
6. See Stanley Hoffman, "Reflections on the German Question," *Survival*, Vol. 32, No. 4 (July–August 1990). This essay is a prolongation of, or complement to, the piece in *Survival*.
7. For one example, see John J. Mearsheimer, "Back to the Future: Instability in Europe After the Cold War," *International Security*, Vol. 15, No. 1 (Summer 1990), pp. 5–56. This essay is, in part, an elaboration of my objections listed in this correspondence, and a reply to Mearsheimer's own response.
8. See Josef Joffe, "One and a Half Cheers for German Unification," *Commentary*, Vol. 89, No. 6 (June 1990), p. 32; also, recent articles by Pierre Lellouche in *Le Point*.
9. See, in particular, Timothy Garton Ash, "Eastern Europe: Après le Déluge, Nous," *New York Review of Books*, August 16, 1990, pp. 51–57.

10. Joffe, "One and a Half Cheers," p. 33
11. Hassner, "Beyond Division and Unity."
12. A sketch of a new role for nuclear weapons in Europe is provided by Karl Kaiser in "From Nuclear Deterrence to Graduated Conflict Control," *Survival*, Vol. 32, No. 6 (November–December 1990, forthcoming). The notion of relying increasingly on multinational corps for NATO, endorsed by the North Atlantic Council in London in July 1990, strikes me more as a gimmick for collective self-reassurance about NATO's permanence than as a likely prospect. Multinational forces did not develop when the threat was real—either in the Atlantic Alliance or among the six of the European Coal and Steel Community of Western Europe at the time of the European Defense Community (EDC). It is unlikely that they will appear now.
13. See Jean-Pierre Chevènement's interview in *Le Monde*, July 13, 1990.
14. See the reference in *The New York Times* of July 27, 1990, p. A7, to a plan by Spain, France, Italy, and Portugal for a "Conference on Security and Cooperation" in the Mediterranean, aimed at dealing with the threat of insecurity coming from North Africa, and modeled after the CSCE.

Appendix 5

THE ASIAN PERIMETER, MOVING FRONT AND CENTER

Daniel I. Okimoto

OUTLOOK FOR ASIA

As the world heads into the next century, the outlook for peace and prosperity in Asia appears brighter today than at any time since 1850. For the past 140 years, a period of revolutionary transformation in Asia, the region experienced almost continual upheaval and violence. Even with the creation of a more enduring regional order in 1945, Asia continued to be plagued by a combination of economic backwardness, social unrest, political instability, big-power maneuvering, and lethal warfare. Indeed, extrapolating from certain indicators (like human casualties), historians might be tempted to designate Asia, from 1945–1989, as arguably the world's most turbulent region. During that time, Asia experienced more bloodshed—leading to a far heavier loss of lives—than any other region in the world, including the volatile Middle East. Recall the number and scope of the conflicts in Asia: long, drawn-out civil wars in China and Cambodia; intractable insurgency movements and frequent coup d'état attempts in the Philippines; massive internal uprisings in Indonesia and China (most notably the Cultural Revolution); and savage and protracted conventional warfare in Korea and Vietnam. Add them together and the casualty toll is staggering—far in excess of any other region of the world.

143

Asia today is still far removed from the threshold of structural stability that North America and Western Europe have already crossed. It is still groping to find a point of equilibrium that will provide the gyroscopic stability necessary to handle conflicts, turmoil, and crisis without witnessing severe dislocations. Most of the old sources of instability persist, and new ones are appearing all the time. Given its blood-stained past and unpredictable present, why are there grounds for optimism about Asia's near-term and long-run future? What, if anything, has happened to change the outlook?

To the extent that optimism is warranted, such optimism emerges out of an assessment of how far Asia has advanced *relative* to where it used to stand. Problems and setbacks are bound to occur; but overall conditions in Asia have improved measurably. There are definite signs of progress and they point toward a future which is less turbulent, offering a basis for hope not readily apparent even as recently as a decade ago.

Although the grounds for guarded optimism are too involved to discuss fully, a few obvious factors can be cited: the world's fastest, sustained rate of growth; the possession of healthy, competitive fundamentals—such as high rates of savings and investments, abundant human resources, a strong work ethic—to continue the steep economic ascent; the dynamism of what might be called the Asian perimeter, Japan, the Asian newly industrialized economies (ANIEs)—Taiwan, South Korea, Hong Kong—the Association of Southeast Asian Nations (ASEAN) states (Singapore, Malaysia, Thailand, Indonesia, and the Philippines), and Oceania (Australia and New Zealand); movement across (or toward) a critical threshold for the kind of political stability that comes from the establishment of an advanced socio-economic infrastructure (including mass education, and extensive information networks; mobility based on merit; the expansion of secondary organizations; and more pluralistic political representation, and so forth); the synergy and stability associated with proliferating ties of economic interdependence not only within Asia but between Asia and outside regions (especially North America); the relaxation of military tensions between the major military powers (the United States, Soviet Union, and

China); the easing of tensions in historic trouble spots, especially the Korean peninsula; a preoccupation with domestic priorities on the part of the continental communist states (China, Vietnam, North Korea), which are absorbed in the all-consuming goal of economic reform; and somewhat more favorable conditions for successful economic reform by the Asian communist economies (compared to the Soviet bloc), especially given the proximity of, and opportunities for synergistic interaction with, the dynamic Asian perimeter. These and other factors give rise to a tentative and fragile feeling of optimism concerning Asia's short- and long-term future.

COMPOUND GROWTH RATES

Dynamic economic development is the first and foremost reason for optimism. The economies of Northeast Asia have completed lift-off already and can be located somewhere over or near the threshold of advanced industrial development. There is every reason to expect the ASEAN countries to join them in the second wave of non-Western countries managing to escape the mire of perpetual "developing" status. The process will take time, and the road to economic maturity may not be straight-lined or smooth. But the logic of compound growth rates is compelling. Assume compound rates continue: simple arithmetic means that much of the Asian perimeter will be fully industrialized by the beginning of the next century. While the relationship between rapid economic change and regional security is complex (including both stabilizing and destabilizing elements), the prospects for peace and prosperity appear substantially more encouraging in Asia than at any point since its opening to the West—and more hopeful today than those of Africa, Central or Latin America, the Middle East, the Indian subcontinent, and the Soviet empire.

Not only is the economic outlook more bullish than ever, Asia's relative weight in the world appears to be on the rise. Even excluding the Indian subcontinent, Soviet Siberia, and the Pacific Islands, Asia is one of the globe's vastest regions, stretching from the northern tip of Hokkaido all the way down to the bottom of

New Zealand. Over 1.6 billion people, representing about one-third of the world's population, live and work in this demarcation of Asia.[1] They are producing an expanding share of the world's goods and services. In 1990, economic output in Asia accounted for 22 percent of world gross national product (GNP). In another ten years, econometric estimates place the figure for Asia at 28 percent of world GNP.[2] By the middle of the next century, it is expected to climb all the way to 50 percent of the world economy.[3] The growth rates in Asia far exceed those anywhere else—and are measurably faster than the world average (see Figure 1).[4]

Placed in historical perspective, Asia's pacesetting growth rates can be understood as the long-delayed but full unleashing of what has constituted for centuries, going all the way back to Tokugawa Japan (1603–1867), the region's immense economic potential. Indeed, the post–World War II realization of that potential might even be viewed, in longer time horizon, as a return to an era of historical normalcy.[5] For nearly a millennium, dating back to the heyday of Sung China (960–1276), Asia stood at the forefront of the world in terms of cultural sophistication, population size, economic output, state of technology, and scope and advancement of market infrastructure. Asia's recent surge, moving into the next, so-called Pacific Century, can be seen as the reassertion of its centuries-long prominence, a strong comeback by one of the world's seedbed civilizations.

What is impressive about Asia's emergence is the fact that the success goes beyond mere aggregate output; it is also characterized by significant advances in production quality and technological complexity. Not only is Asia producing more, it is making better goods at higher values.[6] Consider, for example, three key manufacturing sectors—consumer electronics, automobiles, and steel. All three can be considered "strategic" or "core" industries, and all three rank high on the ladder of value added and technological sophistication. Asia accounts for the lion's share of world output in three representative products: 80 percent of television sets and 50 percent of semiconductors in consumer electronics; 50 percent of automobiles; and 45 percent of crude steel.

Such dominance suggests that old stereotypes of Asia as a low-wage, import-substituting sweatshop turning out semi-

Figure 1 GDP Growth Rates by Region

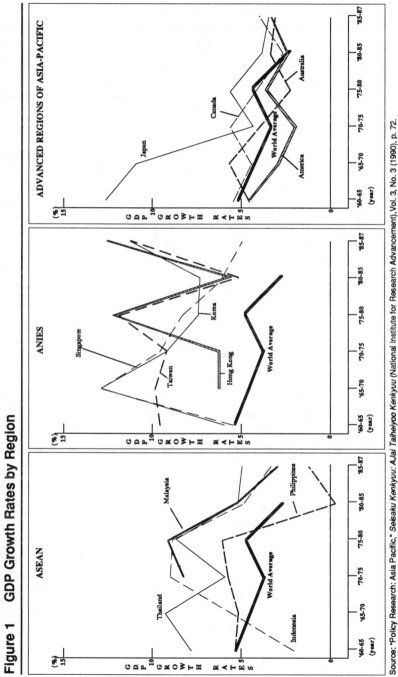

Source: "Policy Research: Asia Pacific," *Seisaku Kenkyuu: A.Jai Taiheiyoo Kenkyuu* (National Institute for Research Advancement), Vol. 3, No. 3 (1990). p. 72.

processed, light industrial goods (like pens and pencils, foot-wear, and cotton textiles) are obsolete. Asia has become one of the world's leading centers of manufacturing excellence, and its ascent into upmarket segments of production is almost certain to continue.[7] Asia's peaceful integration into the world economy and its swift adjustments to ongoing shifts in international comparative advantage are two of the remarkable trends in twentieth century history.

The United States' percentage of trade with Asia today is nearly 60 percent of its world total—and climbing. Quantitative measures of trade interdependence indicate that the United States and Japan have stronger linkages with Asia than they do with Europe (see Figure 2).[8] The likelihood is that such ties will continue to proliferate. Hence, by virtue of its record-breaking pace of growth, Asia is making its presence felt throughout the world. It is putting distance between itself and the Third World and is closing up fast on the First World.

THE ASIAN PERIMETER

Perhaps the most intriguing feature of Asia today, one replete with important implications, is that the region's pacesetting rate of growth is concentrated on the geographic perimeter rather than on the mainland of the continent. The impetus for growth got underway in Japan, spreading southwest to the ANIEs and subsequently sweeping all the way down to the ASEAN belt. In an economic sense, one can say that the perimeter has moved front and center and is serving as the fountainhead of Asia's remarkable spurt forward. The continental heartland has been left behind.

This inversion of the geographic concept of core-periphery is, at first glance, puzzling. Looking at the distribution of factor endowments, one would expect the resource-rich continental powers to dominate, just as they have throughout long centuries of Asian history,[9] but the data make clear that the wellspring of Asia's enormous economic vitality is gushing out of the resource-poor perimeter. With less than one-third the population, living

Figure 2   Measures of Trade Interdependence

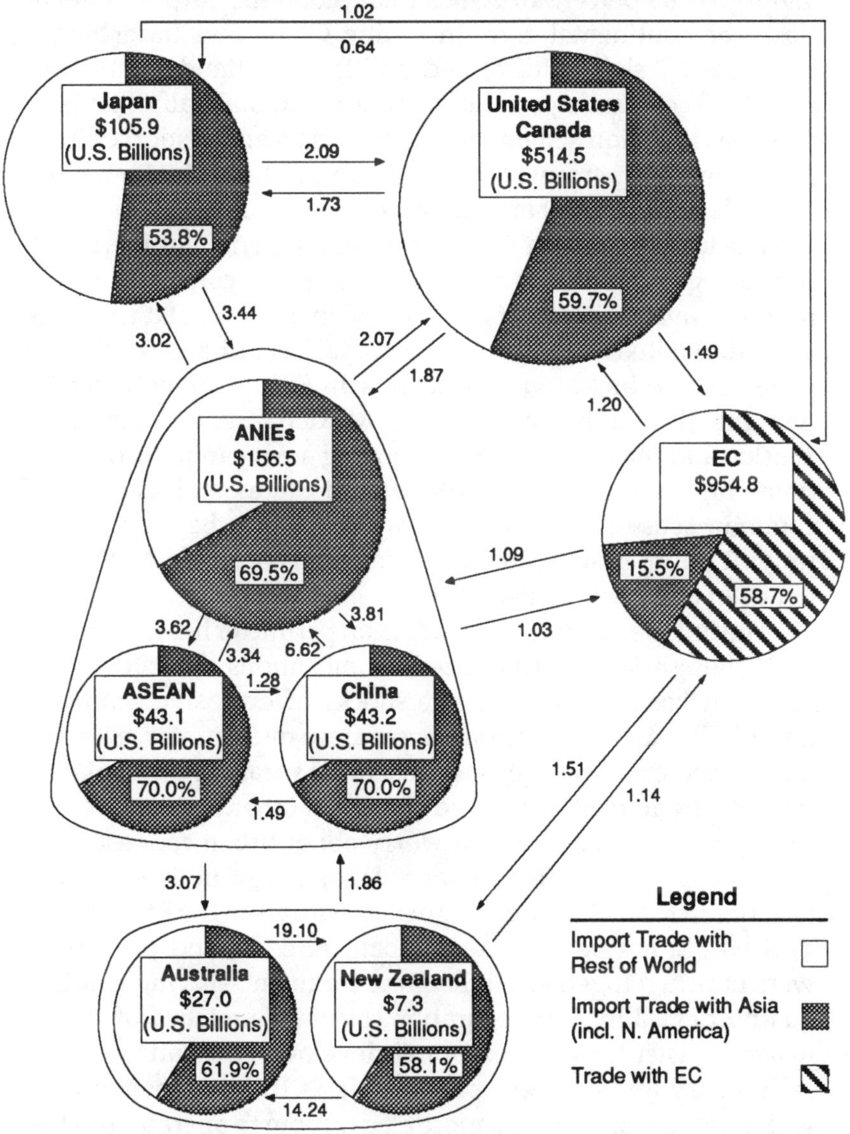

Note: The numbers associated with each arrow represent a measure of trade dependence for the involved regions or countries, and are calculated as:

$$\frac{\text{Country A's Exports to Country B / Country A's Total Exports}}{\text{Country B's Total Imports / Total World Imports}}$$

on 15 percent of the region's land area, Asia's periphery produces a lopsided 85 percent of Asia's total economic output. By contrast, the continental core, including China and Indochina—historically Asia's cultural and political heartland—with over two-thirds of Asia's population, more than one-half of its land mass, and the lion's share of raw materials and resources, produces a mere 15 percent of the region's output and lags far behind in the development of an industrial infrastructure.

The incredible dominance of the Asian perimeter is without parallel, geographically and historically. To come up with a rough equivalent, think of Europe, and imagine what it would be like if the United Kingdom, Scandinavia, Iceland, and the Iberian peninsula produced twice as much as the European continent. Or imagine the Caribbean islands, Mexico, Central America, Alaska, and the Pacific islands enjoying a per capita income ten times higher than that of the United States and Canada. If common sense notions of geography have to be stretched to provide counterfactual models, the annals of world history do not even offer rough analogues.

The unique geography of the Asian perimeter has had significant, though largely unnoticed, ramifications. To cite an example, it has softened the aftershocks of explosive economic growth. Because long distances separate one country from another, each country enjoys a substantial measure of insulation from the tremors of very rapid change in other perimeter countries. Japan does not have to worry about urban congestion in Bangkok, air pollution in Jakarta, labor unrest in Seoul, ethnic tensions in Kuala Lumpur, or guerilla warfare in the Philippines. This would not be the case if Japan, ASEAN, and the ANIEs were bunched together on the same continent, sharing contiguous borders. Physical separation, by vast stretches of ocean, makes it easier to isolate economic development from the political, military, and strategic spillover effects. It allows each country wider degrees of freedom, more elbow room to operate, and less danger of conflict, confrontation, and national war. Although the threat of domestic violence still exists within individual countries, the likelihood of border wars erupting is reduced. Thus, the unique geography of the Asian perimeter has made it possible for the region to undergo what amounts to an economic revolution without having to endure the destablilizing political and military aftereffects.

At the same time, however, geographic dispersion has also worked to Asia's disadvantage in several respects. It has limited the diffusion of knowledge and ideas, diminished somewhat the natural intensity of competition, constricted the migration of labor (while capital has flowed fairly freely), and truncated the emergence of a sense of common regional identity. Geographic dispersion has thus reduced the chances for genuine regional integration. It has led to greater fragmentation, bigger differences across nation-states, and troublesome divergences in national interests. Dispersion means that a single, unified, common market, *à la* European Community (EC), is unlikely to be organized. Ties of economic interdependence will expand over time, but true regional integration—with common laws, binding political institutions, and monetary union—will probably never be realized. So the geography of the Asian perimeter brings both benefits and limitations.

THE LOCOMOTIVE AND FIRST ZONE: JAPAN

To understand the nature and significance of the phenomenon I call the "Asian perimeter," it is necessary to divide Asia into its five subregional components, the five geo-economic zones that define the boundaries of this perimeter. I shall analyze the patterns of economic interdependence linking each zone with the United States and with each other. The five geo-economic zones are 1) Japan; 2) the Asian newly industrialized economies, Taiwan, South Korea, and Hong Kong; 3) the Association for Southeast Asian Nations, consisting of Singapore, Malaysia, Thailand, Indonesia, and the Philippines; 4) Oceania (Australia and New Zealand); and 5) the continental mainland: China, Vietnam, North Korea, Laos, Cambodia, and Burma. The first four zones make up what is called here the "Asian perimeter," the economic epicenter for the entire region.

Of the five zones in Asia, Japan is by far the biggest. Its economy is several times larger than the rest of Asia put together. According to Nikkei Shimbun figures, Japan's economy boasts a GNP of $2.5 trillion (using an exchange rate of 140 yen to the dollar), which places it about 70 percent the size of the U.S. economy (see Table 1). To convey a sense of the phenomenal speed of Japan's postwar growth, mention should be made of the fact that, in 1952, the year that the Allied Occupation ended, Japan was only 5 percent the size of the United States. The Nikkei Shimbun projection of growth rates by the year 2000 forecasts that Japan will have a GNP of $3.7 trillion, with the United States at $4.6 trillion, making Japan roughly 80 percent America's size (Table 1). In only a decade, therefore, Japan will narrow the size gap by 10 percent. In both 1990 and 2000, Japan's output is four times greater than that of Southeast Asia. Thus, the rise of Asia is, in large measure, the rise of Japan, not only in terms of its disproportionate size but also with respect to Japan's role as a high horsepower locomotive pulling Asia along behind it.

As Japan's economy has moved past industrialization into the stage of postindustrialism, some writers have predicted a significant slowdown in growth rates.[10] The most often cited obstacles threatening to slow the Japan juggernaut include plummeting rates of savings and investments, a pent-up consumption binge, a rapidly aging population (soon to be the oldest in the

Table 1   The World and Japan in the Year 2000

	1990	2000	1980–1990	1990–2000
\<JAPAN\>				
Demand Items (¥ tril.)				
Nominal GNP	412.8	715.3	5.6	5.7
Real GNP	361.5	524.4	4.2	3.8
Real private final consumption	197.2	286.4	3.4	3.8
Real private housing investment	21.1	28.3	3.2	3.0
Real private capital investment	88.5	145.8	8.9	5.1
Real government final consumption	30.3	39.3	2.6	2.6
Real public fixed capital formation	25.7	35.6	1.2	3.3
Real exports, etc.	72.7	117.1	7.4	4.9
Real imports, etc.	75.3	129.6	7.1	5.6
Price Indexes				
GNP deflator (1980=100)	114.2	136.4	1.3	1.8
Wholesale price index (1980=100)	89.2	104.6	−1.1	1.6
Consumer price index (1985=100)	105.5	136.3	1.9	2.6

Table 1   The World and Japan in the Year 2000 (continued)

	1990	2000	1980– 1990	1990– 2000
Population, Labor Force, and Income				
Population (mil. persons)	124.4	129.8	0.6	0.4
% of labor force made up of women*	49.2	51.2	48.5	50.3
% of population over 65 yrs.*	11.9	15.4	10.5	14.0
Real income of working family (¥ 1,000)	6,335	10,246	4.2	4.9
Government Finance				
Bond issues accounted for budget (%)	8.9	4.0	19.9	5.8
Bond issues outstanding as a percentage of GNP	42.0	31.1	41.3	36.6
External Transactions				
Current account ($ bil.)*	64.6	52.3	49.7	58.5
Net assets overseas ($ bil.)*	464.8	1,078.1	188.4	812.3
Yen rate (yen/dollar)	133.8	100.0	–5.1	–2.9
<U.S.>				
Real GNP ($ bil.)	3,598.9	4,559.6	2.8	2.4
Wholesale price index (1980=100)	128.3	198.9	2.5	4.5
Current account ($ bil.)*	–114.8	–77.2	–90.6	–96.3
Net assets overseas ($ bil.)*	–716.8	–1,268.8	–266.0	–1,063.4
Effective rate of dollar (1980=100)	98.2	78.3	–0.2	–2.2
<EC>				
Real GDP ($ bil.)	3,677.3	4,636.6	1.9	2.3
Wholesale price index (1980=100)	166.6	233.1	5.2	3.4
Current account ($ bil.)*	–15.7	12.3	2.2	9.3
Exchange rate index (1980=100)	134.4	129.0	3.0	–0.4
<SOUTHEAST ASIA>				
Real GDP ($ bil.)	522.7	787.8	5.5	4.2
Wholesale price index (1980=100)	175.7	276.2	5.8	4.6
Current account ($ bil.)*	23.1	–23.6	2.6	4.8
Exchange rate index (1980=100)	142.0	132.7	3.6	–0.7
<LATIN AMERICA>				
Real GDP ($ bil.)	893.6	1,205.6	1.9	3.0
Wholesale price index (1980=1)	2,438.0	74,748.0	118.0	41.0
Current account ($ bil.)*	–16.9	1.6	–11.6	–7.0
<MIDDLE EAST/OPEC>				
Real GDP ($ bil.)	446.7	566.1	0.8	2.4
Wholesale price index (1980=100)	198.5	357.8	7.1	6.1
Current account ($ bil.)*	–21.5	13.2	–15.0	–4.4
<WORLD> AGGREGATE OF 8 REGIONS				
Real GDP ($ bil.)	12,775.0	16,791.1	2.8	2.8
Real global exports ($ bil.)	2,649.2	3,760.2	3.5	3.6
Population (bil. persons)	5.16	6.04	0.117	0.16

Note: Figures for 1980–1990 and 1990–2000 are average % change; those with * are mean values of 1981–1990 and 1991–2000.

Source: Japan Economic Journal, *Japan Economic Almanac, 1990*, p. 17.

world), an erosion of the work ethic, skyrocketing land prices, an overinflated and gyrating stock market, the hemorrhaging effects of massive capital outflows, a loss of comparative advantage in manufacturing, a shortage of labor, the revolt of women, and the closure of foreign markets. One cannot ignore the existence of these and other bottlenecks. Such problems are real and cast a pall of uncertainty over Japan's economic future.

However, what is not clear—what is very much open to debate—is the severity of these problems and their likely impact on growth rates and economic performance. How far and how fast will savings and investments fall, for example? And how big and bulimic will be Japan's consumption binge? Such questions are subjects of considerable controversy. On the question of Japan's future, it should be pointed out that at critical junctures throughout its postwar history (such as the late 1940s, 1960, 1974, and the mid-to-late 1980s), we have heard the weeping Cassandras of doom predicting the apocalypse: the sinking of the Japanese archipelago, the demise of the ruling conservative party, the end of parliamentary democracy, the collapse of Japan's industrial structure, the bursting of Japan's financial bubble, the disintegration of the United States–Japan alliance, and yes, even the eruption of the United States–Japan Third World War. All such prophecies of doom have proven to be wrong. Perhaps the 1990s may turn out to be the exception to the pattern, but the evidence is still unclear.

The prophets of pessimism do not take account of the positive developments that might compensate for, or help Japan overcome, the stumbling blocks they see ahead—to cite only a few: the continuation of heavy capital investments, the substitution of automated equipment for labor, rising rates of investments in research and development, steep increases in patent applications and approvals, advances in productivity growth, progress in custom-made and batch production, competitiveness in high technology, the globalization of business, massive holdings of foreign assets, greater recruitment of women into the work force, and so on. Such developments cast a very different light on Japan's economic prospects. They suggest that the age of post-industrialism will bring both problems and progress.

As Japan encounters increasingly stiff competition from Asian producers, who possess comparative advantage at the low-end and mid-range of manufacturing, Japan has strong incentives to move progressively higher up the ladder of value-added goods. The structure of a horizontal division of labor seems to be taking shape in Asia, albeit in crude form, and if the trend continues, the gains to trade will continue to rise. Although Japan has served as an engine for Asia's takeoff, and still plays that role, Asia's considerable momentum today is serving, in turn, to push Japan forward. A dynamic synergy involving Japan and Asia has developed. Most economists, who follow the Japanese econ-omy, expect Japan to continue its powerful thrust forward, driven in part by the dynamism of Asia that Japan itself helped to kick-start and sustain.

For the United States, Japan's faster rate of growth will probably continue to generate serious frictions. Japan is, without a doubt, America's highest priority interest in Asia. Maintaining and strengthening the United States–Japan relationship is of overriding importance. But the framework of the alliance, which is already showing signs of wear, will be further strained in the years ahead. As long as American and Japanese rates of savings and investments stay stuck at opposite ends of the spectrum—with the U.S. saving too little and spending too much and Japan presumably saving too much and spending too little—the imbalance in merchandise trade will not disappear. Nor will the rancor and threats.

As the world desperately needs surplus savings to fuel growth in Eastern Europe, Latin America, Africa, and other capital-starved regions, the surplus of savings over spending in Japan must be regarded as a scarce and immensely valuable world commodity, one that must be husbanded and invested wisely. From a global point of view, American pressures on Japan to reduce savings as a corrective to the United States–Japan trade deficit makes little sense. The more desirable corrective, by far, is for the United States to raise its savings and cut consumption. In that way, the zero-sum competition can be converted into a variable-sum gain.

If the United States does nothing to reign in its profligate spending habits, the problems that will be created or exacerbated (both at home and abroad) are almost too depressing to consider—severe trade tensions, lopsided current account imbalances, high interest rates, the continuation of America's costly and dangerous dependence on capital inflows from abroad, worldwide capital scarcity, and so forth. A great deal is riding on the health of America's macroeconomic condition. What is at stake is nothing less than America's long-term capacity to lead, its commercial capacity to compete, GATT's (the General Agreement on Tariffs and Trade) future survival, and the quality of U.S. interactions with countries in Asia. If the United States fails to restore balance to its savings and spending ratio, it may run headlong into a storm of conflicts, including trade disputes with Japan and the ANIEs. Should trade disputes turn nasty, leading to the imposition of punitive sanctions (in the form, say, of Super 301), then the whole structure of free trade may be placed in jeopardy. Clearly, the United States, Japan, and ANIEs have a huge stake in working out their differences, without destroying the structure of free trade. This is an item of utmost urgency on America's foreign policy agenda for the 1990s.

In scanning the horizon for other Japan-related issues, mention should be made of the Soviet Union's strong desire to normalize ties with Japan. The Soviet Union needs access to Japanese capital, production technology, and marketing know-how in order to develop Siberian resources and to expedite the processes of economic reform. As the precondition for signing a peace treaty, Japan is demanding the return of the four northern territories. However, even if the territories are returned, and a peace treaty is signed, there appear to be clear limits to the scope of Soviet-Japanese economic ties, owing to the small size of potential Soviet demand and the paucity of products that the Japanese would want to buy.

Japan's perception of its own security might be deeply affected by developments towards a reunification of the Korean peninsula. The astounding speed of German reunification raises hopes, in some circles, that the Koreans might proceed with equal dispatch, but the circumstances in Germany and Korea are sufficiently different that steps toward reunification will be far slower and more difficult in Korea. Nevertheless, the possibility of some form of integration is greater today than a year ago, and if reunification does take place, the whole situation in Asia may be transformed. A dangerous tinderbox in Asia will be defused, creating opportunities to harness the considerable economic potential of the Korean peninsula. This would add yet another dynamic locus to the already dynamic Asian perimeter. On the other hand, it is possible that Japan will feel threatened by a unified Korea, just as France, Poland, and the Soviet Union have feared German reunification. Japan's reactions to the emergence of a formidable economic rival only a stone's throw across the Sea of Japan—heavily armed, nationalistic, and perhaps not kindly disposed towards its former colonizer—might conceivably be one of alarm (depending on the form reunification takes). For centuries, dating back to the Tokugawa period, Japan's sense of security has been closely intertwined with that of the Korean peninsula.

Thus, Japan faces the possibility of conflict and change in all of its most important foreign relationships: with the United States, the Soviet Union, and Korea, not to mention Europe, China, and the rest of Asia. Of these, the prospects for change appear the least worrisome in Asia, where ties of interdependence are binding Japan and its regional neighbors ever more tightly together.

THE SECOND ZONE: ANIEs

Located in the Northeast Asia arc nearest Japan is the second geo-economic zone, the ANIEs: Taiwan, South Korea, and Hong Kong. This zone completed economic lift-off later than Japan but earlier than ASEAN. Its industrial structure is slightly more advanced than ASEAN, but it produces about as much aggregate output as ASEAN and Oceania, about $250 billion per year. The three ANIEs share several characteristics in common, including a paucity of raw materials, an educated and industrious work force, inclusion in the Confucian orbit, and political partitionment. Two of the ANIEs, Taiwan and South Korea, also share bitter memories of Japanese colonialism, a strong aversion to communism, large military forces, a strong and interventionist government, and popular pressures for greater participation and political liberalization. All three ANIEs have enjoyed robust rates of growth, led by a vigorous export sector making inroads in the huge U.S. market.

The ANIEs' export-led growth has given rise to an interesting multilateral pattern of trade linking the three ANIEs with the two Pacific giants, Japan and the United States. To explain the dimensions of trade, standard statistics will be cited, showing dollar amounts as well as percentage shares of exports flowing from one country to another. These data are straightforward and are listed in parentheses within the small rectangular boxes giving measures of trade interdependence in Figures 1–8. However, in order to provide an added dimension, standard statistics need to be supplemented by other measures of bilateral trade interdependence. The measure selected for use in this paper is based on the ratio of export shares of seller countries to the purchaser country's share of imports relative to world imports. Crunching data into this formula yields a handy numerical measure of bilateral trade interdependence and is listed in the small rectangular boxes just above the parentheses on Figures 1–8. The computed value of 1 represents an average level of interdependence; this is the level that would be expected, given the export-import ratios described above. Anything above 1 represents a higher than expected degree of interdependence.

It is wellknown that all three ANIEs rely heavily on exports to drive economic growth. Trade as a percentage of GNP is 55 percent for Taiwan, 70 percent for South Korea, and 187 percent for Hong Kong. This pattern of heavy reliance on foreign demand remains the same, even when we use a slightly different indicator, measuring the multiplier effects of foreign demand on domestic growth rates. Foreign-led demand is 50 percent for Hong Kong; 60 percent for Taiwan; and 40 percent for Korea (see Table 2). Compare these percentages with those calculated for Japan (10 percent) and the United States (8 percent). We see immediately that the ANIEs lean very heavily on overseas demand. In this sense, they bear a resemblance to the small European states, which must export in order to achieve competitive economies of scale.[11]

Table 2   Demand Multiplier Effects Matrix – United States, Japan, ANIEs, ASEAN

Demand Creating Country / Multiplier-Effect Country	Japan	America	Korea	Taiwan	Hong Kong	Singapore	Thailand	Indonesia	Philippines	Malaysia
Japan	249.12	22.47	43.60	45.21	45.99	53.35	41.40	31.40	28.76	40.45
America	18.89	430.85	48.99	40.60	69.70	66.20	38.10	19.20	53.86	58.90
Korea	1.76	2.79	141.85	5.72	2.28	4.32	2.62	1.78	3.42	3.07
Taiwan	1.29	3.28	1.53	9.21	129.48	5.67	3.11	2.40	5.33	3.45
Hong Kong	0.22	0.73	0.50	74.06	1.74	1.91	0.81	1.10	1.82	0.95
Singapore	0.17	0.41	0.40	1.63	0.59	49.69	2.27	0.78	1.18	4.43
ANIEs	3.44	7.21	2.43	16.56	4.61	11.90	8.81	6.06	11.75	11.90
Thailand	0.59	0.71	0.71	2.09	1.05	5.68	195.37	0.65	1.09	4.30
Indonesia	2.16	1.04	2.76	2.09	2.20	6.82	1.90	228.84	1.79	3.74
Philippines	0.49	0.64	0.51	1.21	0.87	1.43	1.54	0.65	223.64	1.59
Malaysia	0.65	0.63	1.82	1.69	1.67	13.94	3.43	0.97	2.38	121.88
ASEAN	3.89	3.02	5.80	7.08	5.79	27.87	6.87	2.27	5.26	9.63
Domestic-Led Growth	90.48	92.95	58.45	40.36	50.66	23.77	67.24	79.52	69.18	50.21

Note: Individual countries' Demand Multiplier Effect can be calculated as follows:

$$Y_i = A_i + c_i + \sum_{j-1}^{10} a_{ij}Y_j \text{-} B_iY_i$$

Y_i : GDP of i
A_i : Independent Demand of i
c_i : Average consumption tendency of i
a_{ij} : Average import tendency of j from i
B_i : Average imports of i

Source: Tsusansho Hakusho, MITI White Paper, 1989, p. 302.

Figure 3   Measures of U.S./Japan–ANIEs Trade Dependence

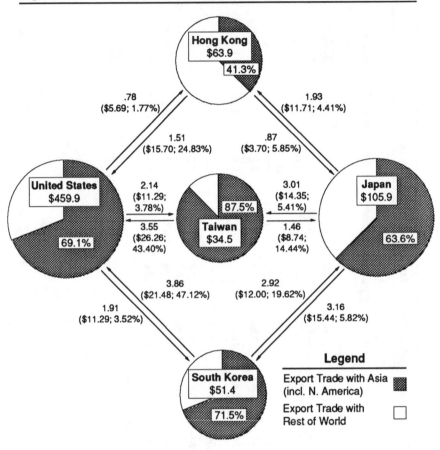

Note: The set of numbers associated with each arrow indicates the following:

1.00 ———— Trade dependence of the involved countries, calculated as: A's Exports to B / A's Total Exports / B's Total Imports / Total World Imports
($1.00; 1.00%)— Percentage of A's Total Exports
Value (in $U.S. Billions) of A's exports to B

Figure 3 also shows that the lion's share of trade for Taiwan and South Korea takes place in Asia (which should be thought of as the Pacific, since the data used for these calculations include the United States and Canada); Asia (so defined) accounts for nearly 90 percent of Taiwan's exports and over 70 percent of South Korea's. Owing perhaps to its membership in the Commonwealth, Hong Kong is the exception, with only about 40 percent of its exports going to Asia.

In looking at measures of export and import dependence, one might ask: Which is the more important? The answer depends on variables too complex to discuss here, but if importance is assessed in terms of the *costs of substitution*, then exports clearly count for more than imports. For the ANIEs, the costs of finding alternative buyers for their exports would be far higher than that of finding alternative sellers of foreign-made imports. In other words, it is easier to strike deals with different sellers than it is to find alternate buyers. Foreign buyers have the power to pick and choose, or to decide against purchasing, but when it comes to imports, the ANIEs possess the right of choice. Thus, the export imperative is overriding, particularly because the ANIEs lack raw materials and must sell what they manufacture in order to survive.

By disaggregating the data, Figure 3 shows that the ANIEs' dependence on the U.S. market is exceedingly high. Nearly half of South Korea's exports and almost 45 percent of Taiwan's exports find their way to the U.S. In contrast, South Korea exports only about 20 percent of its goods and services to Japan, and Taiwan even less, a surprising 15 percent. This means that the United States buys more than twice as much from South Korea and Taiwan as Japan. This fact may run counter to expectations, given Taiwan's and South Korea's proximity to Japan and the recent history of Japan's colonial presence. Some analysts might cite the disparity as *prima facie* evidence of the openness of the U.S. market and the closed nature of the Japanese market. However, the disparity can be explained, by taking into account the similarity of Japanese, Taiwanese, and Korean factor endowments and the greater degree of complementarity with the resource-rich United States. Since all three ANIEs lack natural resources, their economies do not have the natural complementarity with Japan that they have with the United States.

Lumping the United States and Japanese import markets together, we see that they account for over 60 percent of ANIEs' total exports. What happens in the world's two largest markets, therefore, cannot help but have big ripple effects in South Korea and Taiwan. To invoke an old metaphor: When the United States and Japan sneeze, the ANIEs catch cold. In terms of demand multiplier effects (Table 2), America is the ANIEs' most important customer. The index for America's impact on South Korea is 2.79 while Japan's is 1.76, and America's effect on demand in Taiwan is 3.28 while Japan's is 1.29. If one looks at the figures for the ANIEs as a subregional entity, the figures are even more striking. The United States, at 7.21, has twice as much impact as Japan, at 3.44. Both have relatively minor impact on Hong Kong (the United States has 0.73, and Japan has 0.22).

One can say, then, that the stereotype of Japan sitting astride Northeast Asia like a colossus is misleading. The United States is at least as large. In fact, focusing only on exports—the more telling indicator—the United States wields more clout in Northeast Asia than does Japan. The ANIEs are more vulnerable to fluctuations in U.S. demand, in other words, than they are to Japanese demand. High levels of export dependence often carry correspondingly high degrees of vulnerability, measured in terms of substitution costs. Should a serious and sustained recession hit the United States, the high-flying economies of South Korea and Taiwan would encounter tremendous turbulence and might even be forced to be grounded, temporarily. When dependence on the United States in other areas, such as political and military security, is added, America's level of influence can be said to far exceed Japan's. But the influence of the United States and Japan together is simply overwhelming.

The import picture is different. Both South Korea and Taiwan buy more from Japan than they do from the United States. Imports from Japan account for 30 percent of South Korea's total while those from the United States make up 22 percent; Taiwan purchases 41 percent of its imports from Japan and 33 percent from the United States. This means that both South Korea and Taiwan ring up big trade surpluses with the United States, as does Hong Kong. Indeed, if Japan is included, the countries of Northeast Asia run a collective trade surplus of $85 billion with the United States, which is well over half of America's $140 billion deficit worldwide. Given the political volatility of the trade issue in the United States, Northeast Asia's lopsided surplus could give rise to political conflicts that put America's relationship with Japan and the ANIEs under significant strain. How the trade imbalance affects U.S.-Japan-ANIE relations in the post–Cold War environment will bear close watching. Even in an environment of reduced military threat, the United States still has a major stake in maintaining non-conflictual, mutually beneficial ties with an economically flourishing ANIE belt on the Asian perimeter.

The ANIEs look at the trade problem with Japan from the opposite end of the lens used to view their relationship with the United States. That is, the problem is reversed. The three ANIEs run substantial trade deficits with Japan, amounting to over $17 billion, or over 20 percent of Japan's overall trade surplus. Just as America feels frustrated about its chronic deficits with Japan, so too the ANIEs feel thwarted in their efforts to penetrate the Japanese market. The difference is that the ANIEs have little leverage over Japan, lacking large domestic markets that they might threaten to close off. The ANIEs also have to be concerned about getting caught in the cross-fire of any deadly United States–Japan trade shoot-out. Like Japan, they have an enormous stake in seeing the United States improve its economic fundamentals.

Intrazone trade is on the rise, even though it is dwarfed by the ANIEs trade with the United States and Japan. As Figure 4 shows, Hong Kong is closely linked to both Taiwan and South Korea; the level of interdependence is particularly noteworthy between Hong Kong and Taiwan, especially with respect to Taiwanese exports to Hong Kong. The trade relationship between South Korea and Taiwan is much less extensive; the value of Taiwanese exports to South Korea is low. Overall, the magnitude of intra-regional trade is limited and clearly of secondary importance compared to the nexus of ANIEs' ties with the United States and Japan. The United States and Japan serve as the central axis around which the ANIEs revolve. By itself, the second geo-economic zone has no core or autonomous identity.

On the other hand, ties of economic interdependence are expanding rapidly between the ANIEs and ASEAN. The measures of trade interdependence shown on Figure 5 are high (3.62 and 3.34), much higher than comparable measures with the

Figure 4   Measures of Intra–ANIEs Trade Dependence

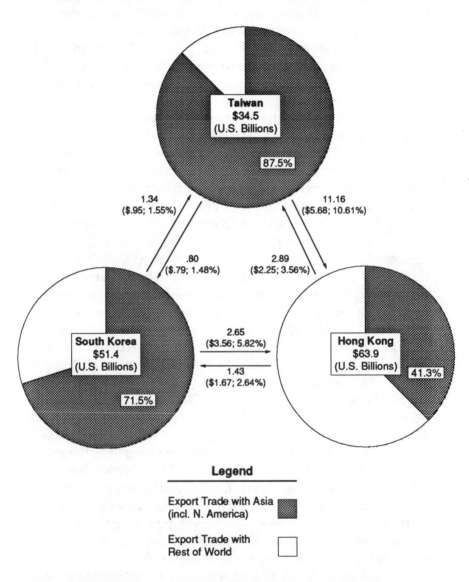

Figure 5   Measures of Asian Trade Dependence

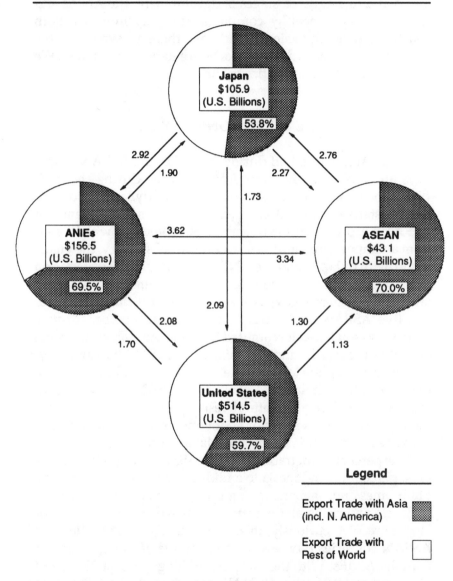

Note: The set of numbers associated with each arrow represents a measure of trade dependence for the involved regions or countries, and are calculated as:

$$\frac{\text{A's Exports to B / A's Total Exports}}{\text{B's Total Imports / Total World Imports}}$$

United States and Japan. Thanks to differences in factor endowments and to staggered stages of development, the ANIEs and ASEAN enjoy a healthy complementarity of interests. Both benefit from the expansion of trade, and there is a synergy in the simultaneous growth dynamics of both geo-economic zones. We can thus expect economic ties to continue flourishing.

THE THIRD ZONE: ASEAN

If the ANIEs lifted off during the 1970s, the ASEAN economies accomplished the same feat sometime during the mid-1980s, forming a third zone of economic dynamism on the Southeastern arc of the Asian perimeter. It was no accident that ASEAN's growth spurt in the mid-1980s coincided with its shift from an import substitution to an export-led strategy, the vigorous growth of Japan and the ANIEs, and the sharp appreciation of the yen against the dollar (and local currencies). These and other developments gave ASEAN a powerful thrust forward. The five ASEAN economies (minus a sixth member, Brunei, which is so small that it is omitted here) generate about the same output as the ANIEs and Oceania, about $250 billion annually, representing slightly less than a tenth of Asia's total GNP. Unlike the ANIEs, but similar to Oceania, the ASEAN third zone contains an abundance of natural resources, and owing to pronounced differences in factor endowments, the ASEAN economies are natural trade partners for Japan and the ANIEs.

The percentage of trade to GNP in ASEAN ranges from a low of 30 percent for Indonesia to a mid-range of 44 percent for the Philippines and Thailand, going up to a high of 103 percent for Malaysia and rising all the way to an incredible 266 percent for Singapore. Yet, curiously, in spite of the high trade ratios, the ASEAN countries rely less on the stimulus of foreign demand than the ANIEs. With the exception of Singapore, at 23.77, and Malaysia at 50.21, the ASEAN economies depend far more heavily on domestic demand to stimulate economic growth; the proportion of domestic-led demand for Thailand is 67.24; for the Philippines, 69.18; and for Indonesia, 79.52 (refer to Table 2). This is not contradictory or abnormal. It is in keeping with ASEAN's industrial structure and distinctive distribution of factor endowments. Thailand, the Philippines, and Indonesia possess far richer resources than Singapore. The better endowed, more diversified ASEAN zone thus poses a sharp contrast to the ANIEs, which are more dependent on, and vulnerable to, the vagaries of world demand.

Like the ANIEs, the bulk of ASEAN's trade, upwards of 70 percent, takes place within the Pacific (again including the United States and Canada). What is striking about ASEAN, compared to the ANIEs, is that the degree of trade interdependence is measurably higher with Japan, 2.76 and 2.27, than it is with the United States, 1.30 and 1.13 (refer to Figure 5). Japan is a much bigger actor in Southeast Asia than the United States. Except for the Philippines and Singapore, where quantitative measures of trade interdependence are comparable, the rest of the countries of Southeast Asia have developed far closer ties with Japan than with the United States (see Figure 6). According to the quantitative measure used in Figure 6, Japan's index of trade interdependence with Malaysia is twice as strong as America's, more than twice that with Thailand, and three times as strong with Indonesia.

As one would expect, Japan sells far more to ASEAN than the United States. For every ASEAN country, except the Philippines, Japan outsells the United States by a factor of nearly two. Moreover, in key product markets, like capital goods, Japan sells substantially more to Malaysia and Indonesia than the United States. In terms of quantity and quality, therefore, Japan is deriving far greater benefits from its economic involvement in Southeast Asia than the United States. Japanese exports to ASEAN amount to about 22 percent of ASEAN's total, a figure that falls below what the ANIEs import from Japan, 28 percent. The United States sells much less, only 13 percent, which also falls below U.S. exports to the ANIEs, 19 percent. Taken together, Japan and the United States account for only 35 percent of ASEAN's total imports, compared to 47 percent of ANIEs' imports. This disparity can be explained by the greater distances between Southeast Asia and the United States and Japan and by the lower U.S. level of involvement.

Figure 6   Measures of U.S./Japan–ASEAN Trade Dependence

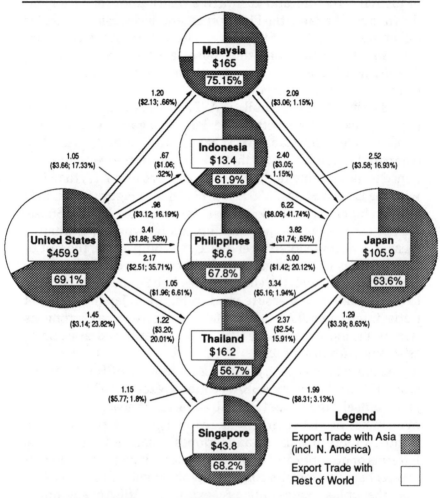

Note: The set of numbers associated with each arrow indicates the following:

1.00 ————— Trade dependence of the involved countries, calculated as: $\frac{A's\ Exports\ to\ B\ /\ A's\ Total\ Exports}{B's\ Total\ Imports\ /\ Total\ World\ Imports}$
($1.00; 1.00%) — Percentage of A's Total Exports
                  — Value (in $U.S. Billions) of A's exports to B

Somewhat surprisingly, Japan's share of ASEAN exports is much higher, at 28 percent, than its share from the ANIEs, at 17 percent, but America's share, 23 percent, is only about half that from the ANIEs, 44 percent. Thus, Japan absorbs proportionally more of ASEAN exports and is the largest single importer from, and exporter to, ASEAN. On a country-by-country basis, Japan buys about as much as the United States from Malaysia and Singapore, only slightly less from Thailand, significantly less from the Philippines, but twice as much from Indonesia. The extraordinary scope of Japanese ties with Indonesia and Malaysia is not hard to understand, since Indonesia and Malaysia possess many of the raw materials that Japan needs: namely, oil, liquefied natural gas (LNG), timber, rubber, and coffee. What is surprising, though, is the comparatively large volume of products that Japan purchases from Singapore and Thailand, two countries on which Japan is not reliant for natural resources.

Looking at the pattern of American/Japanese interdependence with ASEAN, using the second zone as a point of comparison, we note that the two Pacific giants sell about as much to ASEAN, 45 percent, as they do to the ANIEs, 47 percent; but that the two import a far smaller share from ASEAN, 41 percent, than they do from the ANIEs, 61 percent. The total figure for U.S. and Japanese imports from ASEAN disguises the fact that Japan imports proportionally more from ASEAN, 28 percent, than it does from the ANIEs, 17 percent, while the U.S. imports far less, 23 percent, compared to 44 percent. Thus, unlike the ANIEs, the ASEAN countries are less dependent on the United States and proportionally more dependent on Japan. Here again, we should remind ourselves that ASEAN as a whole is less reliant than the ANIEs on exports to drive economic growth (Singapore being the notable exception). If the United States and Japan sneeze, ASEAN need not necessarily die of pneumonia. Nevertheless, the American and Japanese demand does have measurable effects on the ASEAN economies; Japanese demand for ASEAN goods yields a slightly bigger multiplier effect on ASEAN growth than American demand does (refer to Table 2). Thus, while Japan maintains an equally pervasive presence in both Northeast and Southeast Asia, the U.S. presence is far-reaching in the second zone, Northeast Asia, but limited in the third zone, Southeast Asia. This asymmetry is the source of some anxiety. Feeling vulnerable with respect to Japan, virtually all ASEAN countries would welcome higher levels of American involvement, if only as a counterweight to their lopsided dependence on Japan.

In contrast to the ANIEs, the ASEAN nations run a substantial balance of trade deficit ($13 billion) with the United States; not surprisingly, ASEAN runs an even bigger trade deficit with Japan, amounting to $22 billion, or nearly twice that of the United States. Its combined deficit (with both the United States and Japan) exceeds $25 billion. On the matter of merchandise trade imbalances, therefore, the ASEAN economies are not nearly as likely as the ANIEs to incur Washington's wrath. Even if a country like Singapore begins to run bilateral surpluses with the United States, the trade flows for individual ASEAN states are sufficiently small that they probably would not give rise to the same degree of tension that trade imbalances with South Korea or Taiwan would generate. ASEAN need only worry if America's global deficit becomes so big that all surplus countries are vulnerable to an indiscriminate political backlash or if ASEAN trade practices stand out as egregiously in violation of the accepted norms of fair trade. This implies that if Japan wants to invest overseas in order to export whatever is produced to the U.S. market, the incentives to invest in the third zone (ASEAN) are far greater those in the second zone (the ANIEs).

Asia's very rapid rates of growth and rising purchasing power make it an especially attractive market for countries like Japan, which are constantly searching for alternative outlets to the U.S. market. Indeed, faced with severe strains in its trade relationship with the United States, Japan is looking to Asia to expand sales and thus relieve some of the mounting pressures on U.S.–Japanese relations. The desire to diversify is, in part, a conscious objective and national plan, based on detailed analysis by Ministry of International Trade and Industry (MITI) of promising sectors for expansion into Asia. But it is also the by-product of market-driven decisions made by a myriad of private Japanese corporations seeking to find the best business opportunities overseas; diversification as an explicit government goal is thus an acknowledgement of what is already taking place in the private sector. Here is an instance, like so many others, where private and public interests converge, and the government gives its imprimatur on decisions already being made by private enterprise.

Although the United States has always been Japan's biggest single market, absorbing about 35 percent of Japanese exports, Asia now accounts for over 30 percent, and the percentage is sharply on the rise. Monthly trade data in 1990 suggest, in fact, that Asia may be in the process of overtaking America as Japan's biggest customer. Given the steep trajectories of growth in domestic demand, especially in the second and third zones of Asia's perimeter, Japan quietly hopes that it can scale down its level of dependence on the U.S. market and diversify into Asia's fast-growing markets. For this and other reasons, Japan places very high priority on strengthening its nexus of ties with the second and third zones on the Asian perimeter.

Beyond merchandise trade, the depth of Japan's involvement in Southeast Asia is also evident in Japan's position as the region's largest donor of foreign aid and its biggest direct investor. Most of Japan's $9 billion in official development assistance goes to Asia, with Indonesia the largest recipient, followed by China, the Philippines, Thailand, Burma (Myanmar), and Malaysia. Its cumulative foreign direct investments in Asia reached $32.2 billion by 1989, less than half the size of total investments in North America ($75.1 billion) and only slightly larger than South America ($31.6 b.) and Europe ($30.2 b.), but much larger than that in Oceania ($9.3 b.), and the Middle East ($3.3 b.) (Tables 3 and 4). As ASEAN is short of savings, member countries have welcomed capital inflows from outside investors like Japan and Taiwan, two of the few countries in the world that find themselves awash in surplus savings. Japan channels more than one-quarter of its investments in Asia into sectors of relatively high value-added and technological sophistication, like metals, chemicals, electrical machinery, general machinery, and transportation equipment. Japanese companies often sell or transplant capital equipment to Southeast Asia (like Malaysia) and then buy back intermediate goods, like integrated circuits, for assembly in end products made in Japan.

What we are witnessing, then, is the development of what might be described as a crude but evolving regional division of labor—*between* the United States / Japan and the ANIEs, between Japan and ASEAN, between the ANIEs and ASEAN, as well as

**Table 3   Japan's Foreign Direct Investment by Country
FY 1984 – FY 1988 (in millions of dollars)**

	FY 1984	FY 1985	FY 1986	FY 1987	FY 1988	Cumulative March 31, 1989
United States	$3,360	$5,395	$10,165	$14,704	$21,701	$71,860
Canada	184	100	276	653	626	3,231
North America	3,544	5,495	10,441	15,357	22,328	75,091
Indonesia	374	408	250	545	586	9,804
Hong Kong	412	131	502	1,072	1,662	6,167
Singapore	225	339	302	494	747	3,812
Korea	107	134	436	647	483	3,248
China	114	100	226	1,226	296	2,036
Thailand	119	48	124	250	359	1,992
Malaysia	142	79	158	163	387	1,834
Taiwan	65	114	291	367	372	1,791
Philippines	46	61	21	72	134	1,120
Asia	1,628	1,435	2,327	4,868	5,569	32,227
Panama	1,671	1,533	2,401	2,305	1,712	12,858
Brazil	318	314	270	229	510	5,596
Caymans	1	132	930	1,197	2,609	5,085
Bahamas	97	298	792	734	737	2,718
Mexico	56	101	226	28	87	1,671
Bermuda	29	148	16	36	337	991
Neth. Antilles	66	62	66	199	172	747
Peru	6	101	—	1	—	696
Latin America	2,290	2,616	4,737	4,816	6,428	31,617
United Kingdom	318	375	984	2,473	3,956	10,554
Netherlands	452	613	651	829	2,359	5,525
Luxembourg	315	300	1,092	1,764	657	4,729
West Germany	245	172	210	403	409	2,364
France	117	67	152	330	463	1,764
Switzerland	229	60	91	224	454	1,432
Spain	140	91	86	283	161	1,045
Belgium	71	84	50	70	164	1,027
Europe	1,937	1,930	3,469	6,576	9,116	30,164
Australia	105	468	881	1,222	2,413	8,137
Oceania	157	525	992	1,413	2,669	9,315
Liberia	281	159	289	267	648	3,658
Africa	326	172	309	272	653	4,604
Kuwait	55	34	41	54	20	1,383
Iran	0	0	—	—	1	1,005
Middle East	273	45	44	62	259	3,338
Total	**10,155**	**12,217**	**22,320**	**33,364**	**47,022**	**186,356**

Source: Ministry of Finance, Japan

Table 4 Japan's Foreign Overseas Investment By Region and Industry (as of March 31, 1988)

	North America		Asia	
	Amount		*Amount*	
	No. of Cases	*U.S.$ million*	*No. Of Cases*	*U.S.$ million*
Iron & Nonferrous Metals	235	1,650	709	2,064
Chemicals	304	1,499	903	1,585
Electrical Machinery	641	4,451	1,319	1,562
Transportation Equipment	199	2,221	357	1,028
Textiles	157	397	768	1,231
General Machinery	545	1,716	781	778
Lumber and Pulp	112	952	326	212
Manufacturing, total	*3,316*	*14,753*	*7,174*	*10,111*
Mining	277	1,440	217	6,677
Commerce	6,061	9,727	2,452	1,482
Finance and Insurance	312	9,149	312	1,447
Transportation	190	188	171	393
Total	*16,408*	*52,763*	*13,691*	*26,658*

Source: Ministry of Finance, Japan; *Japan 1989: An International Comparison*, Keizai Koho Center, Japan Institute for Social and Economic Affairs, p. 57.

within the second (ANIEs) and third (ASEAN) geo-economic zones. All countries derive multiple benefits from participating in this unfolding horizontal division of labor. By supplying capital, technology, and business know-how to countries on the Asian perimeter, Japan can offset its own dwindling supply of unskilled labor while establishing, at the same time, a profitable presence inside the flourishing Asian markets. Countries in the second and third zones benefit from the influx of investment capital, greater employment opportunities, the transfer of technology, and a head start in certain manufacturing sectors.

Intrazone trade is extensive in ASEAN. As shown in Figure 7, measures of intra-ASEAN trade are far higher than those within the ANIEs. In every bilateral exchange, except that between Indonesia and the Philippines, ASEAN countries surpass the average or expected levels; in some cases, the index reaches astounding numerical values—9, 12, and 22—numbers that cannot be found anywhere else in Asia. Of the ASEAN five, Singapore is, by far, the most extensively tied in with fellow ASEAN countries, followed by Malaysia, with Indonesia having the weakest links of interdependence. Singapore's ties with its

Figure 7   Measures of Intra–ASEAN Trade Dependence

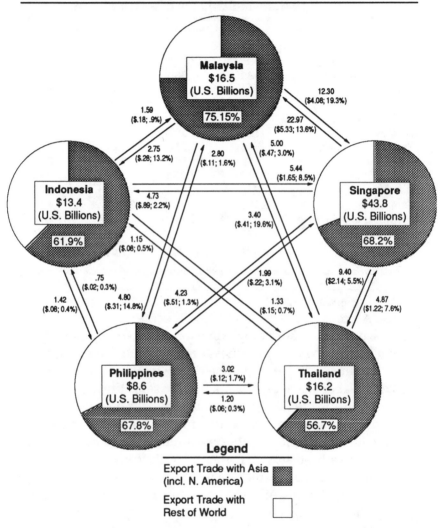

Note: The set of numbers associated with each arrow indicates the following:

1.00 ——— Trade dependence of the involved countries, calculated as: $\frac{\text{A's Exports to B / A's Total Exports}}{\text{B's Total Imports / Total World Imports}}$
($1.00; 1.00%) — Percentage of A's Total Exports
— Value (in $U.S. Billions) of A's exports to B

neighbor, Malaysia (with which it was once joined), are especially strong, and this dynamic duo serves as the hub of trade activity in Southeast Asia. Thailand is also securely tied into the third zone. Here again, we see clear evidence that there is an emerging structure of regional interdependence cutting *across and within* the various geo-economic zones.

REGIONAL INTEGRATION?

As ties of trade, investment, and technology interdependence proliferate, we are witnessing, for the first time in Asia's modern history, the emergence of a vibrant, increasingly open and interconnected periphery. Asia has finally managed to produce the rudiments of a regional system that had been an essential but missing element for several centuries—namely, the structure of intensely competitive, interlinked, pluralistic centers of commercial activity. Except for Japan's colonial empire (created by military aggression and of short-lived duration), Asia had never developed anything comparable to the scope and density of economic interactions in Europe from the fifteenth century forward.[12] Now, within the Asian perimeter, we see heavy commercial transactions, dense communications networks, stiff competition, and rapid transmission effects—all essential components of an economically dynamic region.

The embryo of economic integration is starting to take shape, even though the kind of integration in Asia differs significantly from that of the European Community (EC). In contrast to Europe, integration in Asia is still in gestation, spontaneous, informal, ad hoc, uneven, and totally lacking in central coordination. Because it is not as well planned or as sweeping, the process will not unfold as fast or as smoothly and will not proceed as far as integration in Europe. It will certainly fall short of maturing into Asia's version of the EC, the Asian Pacific Economic Community (APEC). Nevertheless, the emergence of increasingly integrated geo-economic zones in Asia is an exciting and potentially momentous development, given the region's immense long-run potential.

As the biggest economy in the region, Japan is bound to play a central role in any trend toward regional integration. The smaller countries in Asia, still haunted by memories of the

Second World War, do not want to fall under Japanese domination. Nevertheless, owing to its overwhelming size, Japan cannot
help but have a disproportionate impact on the region, regardless of the anxieties and fears gripping the smaller countries on
the perimeter. Do the Japanese want to exercise dominant
power? Do they aspire to assume the role of regional leader? The
answer is not clear. The Japanese themselves seem to have no
idea what kind of role they want to play or feel they should play.

The ultimate answer to the question may lie not so much in
an explicit Japanese plan of action but may emerge, instead, out
of a myriad of incremental decisions having to do with such
mundane matters as the daily buying and selling of Japanese
and Asian goods, yen or dollar denominated transactions, exchange rates, international capital flows, and reserve currency
holdings. The cumulative effect of thousands of daily decisions
may have a greater bearing on the question of Japan's regional
role than any grand strategy. The key, indeed, may reside in the
future role of the yen as the preferred currency for trade, investments, and reserve holdings. If the various countries in Asia
find it in their interests to peg their own currencies to the yen,
they will be compelled, somewhere down the road, to harmonize
their own policies with Japanese monetary and economic policies; for the smaller economies in Asia such harmonization
would be the only means of containing inflation and maintaining
stable currencies. It would take Asia down a path toward the
establishment of a yen bloc, and this would transform Japan's
power in the region.[13]

Note, however, that the prospects of a yen bloc appear remote. The yen's share of world foreign exchange holdings is only
about 7 or 8 percent compared to over 60 percent for the U.S.
dollar. True, the 7 or 8 percent represents a doubling since 1980,
when yen holdings amounted to a minuscule 4 percent (see
Table 5); but the figure is far below the 16 percent level for the
Deutsche mark, which is bound to rise in the wake of European
monetary union. For a variety of reasons (perhaps the most
central of which has been the desire to retain national control
over money supply), the Japanese have preferred to limit the
yen's role as a reserve currency. On the other hand, the yen's

Table 5 Share of National Currencies in Total Identified Official Holdings of Foreign Exchange, End of Year 1980–1988 (in percent)

	1980	1981	1982	1983	1984	1985	1986	1987	1988	Memorandum ECUs Treated Separately 1988
All Countries										
U.S. Dollar	68.6	71.5	70.5	71.2	69.4	64.2	66.0	66.8	63.3	54.5
Pound Sterling	2.9	2.1	2.4	2.6	3.0	3.1	2.8	2.7	3.1	2.9
Deutsche Mark	14.9	12.8	12.3	11.6	12.3	14.9	14.9	14.7	16.2	15.1
French Franc	1.7	1.3	1.2	1.0	1.0	1.3	1.2	1.2	1.7	1.5
Swiss Franc	3.2	2.7	2.8	2.4	2.1	2.3	1.9	1.6	1.5	1.4
Netherlands Guilder	1.3	1.1	1.1	0.8	0.8	1.0	1.1	1.2	1.1	1.0
Japanese Yen	4.3	4.0	4.7	4.9	5.6	7.8	7.6	7.1	7.2	6.7
Unspecified Currencies	3.1	4.4	5.0	5.5	5.8	5.4	4.4	4.7	6.0	17.0
Industrial Countries										
U.S. Dollar	77.6	78.7	77.1	77.4	73.6	65.4	68.4	70.7	67.4	54.9
Pound Sterling	0.7	0.7	0.8	0.8	1.6	2.1	1.5	1.4	1.9	1.7
Deutsche Mark	14.3	12.8	12.2	12.8	14.8	19.4	17.5	16.5	18.3	16.5
French Franc	0.5	0.4	0.3	0.3	0.4	0.5	0.6	0.8	1.6	1.4
Swiss Franc	1.7	1.7	1.7	1.4	1.4	1.8	1.4	1.0	1.0	0.9
Netherlands Guilder	0.7	0.8	0.7	0.5	0.6	1.0	1.1	1.1	1.1	1.0
Japanese Yen	3.3	3.7	4.4	5.1	6.3	8.8	8.2	6.6	6.4	5.8
Unspecified Currencies	1.2	1.2	2.8	1.7	1.2	1.1	1.1	1.8	2.3	17.7
Developing Countries										
U.S. Dollar	59.8	64.1	63.8	64.8	64.9	62.8	62.1	58.2	53.9	53.0
Pound Sterling	5.0	3.5	4.1	4.4	4.4	4.4	4.6	5.3	5.7	5.6
Deutsche Mark	15.5	12.8	12.4	10.3	9.7	9.8	10.8	11.1	11.9	11.7
French Franc	2.9	2.2	2.1	1.8	1.7	2.1	2.2	2.0	1.9	1.9
Swiss Franc	4.7	3.8	3.8	3.4	2.8	2.9	2.8	2.9	2.6	2.5
Netherlands Guilder	1.9	1.4	1.6	1.2	0.9	1.0	1.2	1.2	1.0	1.0
Japanese Yen	5.3	4.4	4.9	4.7	5.0	6.7	6.8	8.3	9.0	8.8
Unspecified Currencies	4.9	7.7	7.3	9.5	10.6	10.3	9.5	11.0	14.1	15.5

Table 6   Share of Yen-denominated Exports and Imports of Japan

Year	1970	1975	1980	1981	1982	1983	1984	1985	1986	1987	1988	1989
Exports (%)	0.9	17.5	29.4	31.2	32.2	34.5	33.7	35.9	35.3*	33.4	34.4	34.7
Imports (%)	0.3	39	2.4	—	—	—	—	7.3*	9.7*	10.6	13.3	14.1

* Figures are from a fiscal year that is 12 months from April of the year to March of the following year.

position in international trade has expanded significantly. Table 6 reveals a sharp increase over the past twenty years. Yen-denominated exports have jumped from 0.9 percent (1970) to 34.7 percent (1989) while yen-denominated imports have risen from 0.3 percent to 14.1 percent in 1989. As the dollar weakens, and exchange rates fluctuate, the incentives to hold yen and to transact in yen may continue to grow. Thus, the future role of the yen bears close watching both as a barometer and as an instrument of Japanese influence in Asia.

Given the dominance of the dollar, the size of the U.S. market, and America's politico-military commitments, the United States is already a central player in Asia. The only question is whether the United States can keep up with Japan, particularly in Southeast Asia and on the mainland (zones three and five). And what about major actors outside the Pacific? Will Europe, the third major actor in the tripolar structure of advanced industrial areas, ante up the resources necessary to participate in Asia? The question is crucial because it will affect Asia's links to the large and distant European continent. Western Europe may decide against straying too far into Asia's five zones, not only because Asia is far away, but also because Western Europe is preoccupied with integration on its own continent and because it has more immediate responsibilities and opportunities in Central and Eastern Europe.

Returning to Figure 2, observe that Europe's trade interdependence with Japan and the rest of Asia is only average. Compared to the United States and relative to Europe's size, the index of interdependence can only be described as very "weak." Whether Europe takes steps to strength its trade ties with the Asian perimeter remains to be seen; it is already active in financial transactions, with several banks and financial service corporations operating in Asia, and with a backlog of capital investments. How far Europe decides to pursue commercial opportunities in Asia is bound to have far-reaching effects on the shape of the international system. If Europe chooses to stay close to home, it will deprive itself of the opportunity to share in the manifold returns from Asia's economic growth. Although the trends towards globalization in the private sector may make this scenario seem unlikely,[14] Europe's level of engagement must be regarded as a question mark, given the strong tug of involvement exerted by its neighbors in the Soviet bloc.

THE FOURTH ZONE: OCEANIA

Tucked away at the bottom of Asia's perimeter is Oceania (Australia and New Zealand), the fourth geo-economic zone in Asia. Oceania is an anomaly in the region: a Western outpost, far away from the Asian continent and Northeast corridor. Because it is blessed with an abundance of natural resources, including natural gas, coal, and non-ferrous metals, Oceania is an important economic zone in the region. With a combined GNP of $300 billion, Australia and New Zealand are somewhat larger than the ANIEs and ASEAN.

Figure 8 sets forth Oceania's pattern of trade. Using the same measures of interdependence as the three other geo-economic zones, we see that Oceania is tied far more closely with Asia than it is with either Europe or the United States. Being members of the Commonwealth, the countries of Oceania might be expected to have far closer linkages with Europe (similar to Hong Kong's), but the value of its index of interdependence is extremely low (.62 and .38), reflecting rather tenuous ties of trade with Europe. Its linkages are stronger with the United States in terms of imports (1.70) but below average for exports (.69). The same is true of its relationship with China, except that the export and import indices are reversed.

Oceania enjoys its closest links with the first, second, and third zones in Asia. Its trade with Japan, both ways, is Oceania's most extensive (2.10 and 3.74). Its links with the ANIEs also stand out (1.46 and 1.96). That Oceania's heaviest involvement

Figure 8   Measures of Oceania Trade Dependence

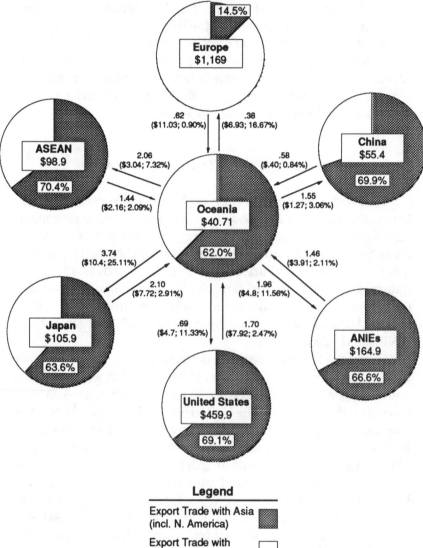

Legend

Export Trade with Asia
(incl. N. America)

Export Trade with
Rest of World

Note: The set of numbers associated with each arrow indicates the following:

1.00 —— Trade dependence of the involved countries, calculated as: A's Exports to B / A's Total Exports / B's Total Imports / Total World Imports
($1.00; 1.00%) —— Percentage of A's Total Exports
—— Value (in $U.S. Billions) of A's exports to B

should be with Northeast Asia is not at all surprising, given the complementarity of their respective economies. The resource-deprived economies of Northeast Asia, with vast installed manufacturing bases, look to resource-rich Oceania for energy and raw materials to convert into heavy industrial products. The gains to trade for all sides are substantial. Trade with Southeast Asia is also brisk, though not quite as active as that with Northeast Asia.

Hence, there is no question that Oceania, despite its European heritage, belongs to the regional economy of Asia. Already an important player, Oceania's ties of interdependence with the Asian perimeter will expand as the first, second, and third zones continue their compound growth rates. For the economies of Northeast and Southeast Asia, having access to Oceania's rich resources must be reassuring, especially in view of the perception that Oceania is a stable region, which poses no threat of any kind.

THE FIFTH ZONE: CONTINENTAL HEARTLAND

The fifth and final zone in Asia, which lies outside the Asian perimeter, are the countries located on Asia's continental landmass: China, Vietnam, North Korea, Cambodia, Laos, Burma, and Mongolia; Soviet Siberia might also be included in this zone, but because it is part of the Soviet Union, it has been excluded from this discussion. As pointed out earlier, the fifth zone constitutes, metaphorically, the economic and political back lands of Asia. The continent is home to the four communist regimes in the region, and all happen to be governed by rigid, highly authoritarian rulers. The continent also is home to the most unstable polities in Asia, including Cambodia.

Compared to the perimeter, the continent is still mired in the economic backwaters. Owing to China's sheer size, this zone is comparatively big—somewhat bigger in GNP terms than the second, third, or fourth zones; but aggregate output conveys a misleading sense of importance that belies reality. To restore some perspective, we should understand that on a per capita basis, the fifth zone is ten times poorer than the rest of the Asia. Not a single country deserves to be placed in the category of a newly industrialized economy. None has achieved lift-off. Indeed, though they have been at it for more than 150 years, the continental states are still a long ways from industrialization and find themselves lagging far behind Asia's other four zones.

Apparently incapable of moving forward on a smooth, linear path, continental Asia can only hope to be hauled out of its backwardness by the pull of the perimeter's powerful engine of economic growth. Although the potential for long-term growth is there for Vietnam, China, and North Korea, the road to industrial development is long and will be beset by roadblocks, detours, U-turns, and dead ends. For the foreseeable future, the continent will constitute what might be called a Third World subregion within Asia—a geo-economic zone starved for capital, lacking essential technology, in need of transplanting the market mechanism and building more effective public institutions and private sector organizations. To meet these needs, the core will turn to the perimeter.

Thus, Asia will have in its own backyard, local versions of problems that plague the international system: namely, the existence of distinct economic zones, a yawning gap between these zones, and the challenge of linking the more advanced and backward areas together in a synergistic loop. Japan is clearly in the front ranks of industrialized nations; the ANIEs can be placed in a second category of newly industrialized countries; ASEAN belongs to a third category, one which is well beyond economic takeoff but still a ways from industrial maturity; Oceania is a resource-rich, economically prosperous, Western enclave; and the Asian continent is an economically backward, politically unstable Third World subregion, still caught in the throes of attempting takeoff.

Although the continent suffers by comparison with Asia's perimeter, it holds its own when compared to other regions. Compared to Africa, the Indian subcontinent, and Latin America, for example, the Asian continent looks like it might have a much better chance of mobilizing to meet the challenge of economic takeoff. It is blessed with an abundance of human energy and talent[15] and has the advantage of being surrounded by the dynamic Asian perimeter. To free itself from the mire of perpetual development, the continental core will try to attract as much capital and technology from the perimeter as it can. If the continent can gain much of what it needs, the perimeter's engine of growth might impart enough momentum for the continental countries to accomplish lift-off.

The continental country with the biggest economy and potential for growth, China, is already tied fairly closely into the Asian perimeter. As shown in Figure 9, China's trade interdependence with Hong Kong is extraordinary (16.78 and 13.61); it is almost as if Hong Kong serves as China's main port of entry for world trade. Its ties with Japan are also substantial (2.52 and 1.81), and the same can be said of its linkages with ASEAN, especially Singapore. Moreover, China's trade with South Korea and Taiwan is on the rise, and Chinese imports from Oceania are significant (1.55). By contrast, and somewhat surprisingly, the measures of trade interdependence with the United States are quite low (.79 and .43), suggesting perhaps that China's destiny is more closely tied to the future of the Asian perimeter than to the United States or Europe. The major source of uncertainty in China is the instability of its political system, especially the periodic convulsions of popular unrest, such as the Cultural Revolution and Tiananmen Square riots, which delay the timetable for industrialization any number of years. In this regard, China is not unique. Political instability is a serious stumbling block for all countries on the Asian continent.

For the next twenty to twenty-five years, the heartland of continental Asia is apt to suffer from serious and recurring problems of governability. All four communist states, for example, face vexing problems of political transition, stemming from an impending generational turnover in leadership. How well the communist states handle the task of political succession, as the small cohort of aging revolutionary leaders disappears, will have a crucial bearing on their chances for advancing down the industrial learning curve. In pursuing simultaneously the twin goals of nation-building and industrial development, the communist states will have to deal with mounting pressures for

Figure 9 Measures of China Trade Dependence

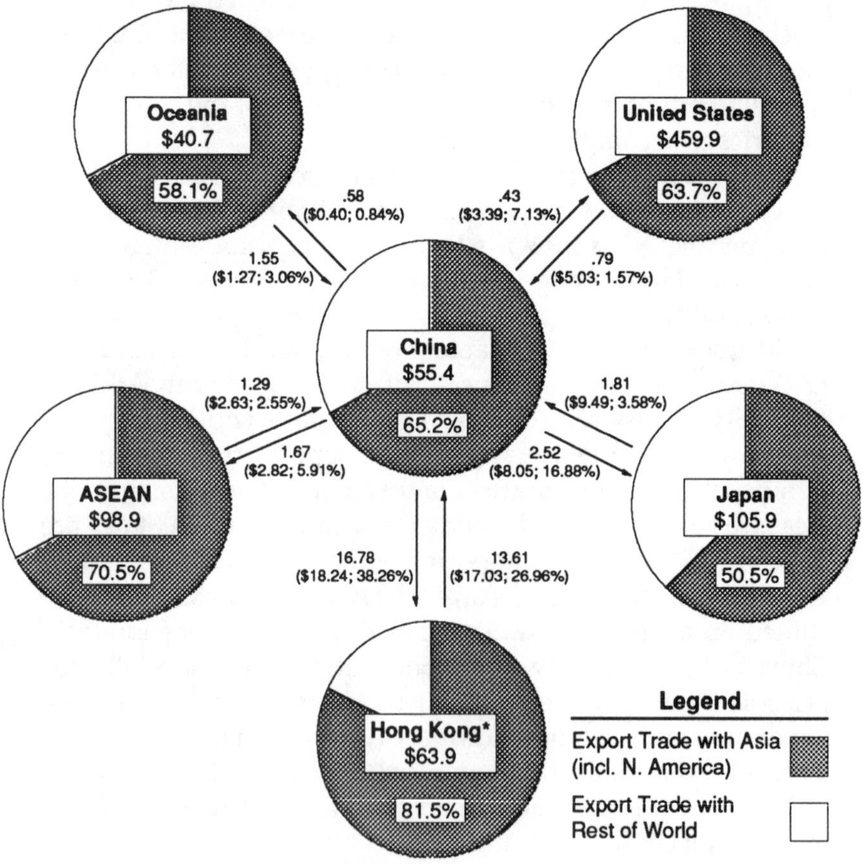

Note: The set of numbers associated with each arrow indicates the following:

1.00 ——— Trade dependence of the involved countries, calculated as: A's Exports to B / A's Total Exports / B's Total Imports / Total World Imports
($1.00; 1.00%) —— Percentage of A's Total Exports
—— Value (in $U.S. Billions) of A's exports to B

* Figures for Korea and Taiwan trade with China are unavailable, so trade dependence figures for the ANIEs in this chart are calculated by Hong Kong figures only.

both liberalization and national consolidation; and having witnessed the upheavals that took place inside the disintegrating Soviet empire, Asia's old communist leaders and their successors may try to cling to the levers of power and resist radical reform as long as possible.

CONTINENT AND PERIMETER: THE YAWNING GAP

Why is there, in Asia, so big a gap between the continental countries, which seem to posses relatively favorable factor endowments, and the resource-poor countries on the Asian perimeter, which have managed to turn an apparent weakness into a formidable strength? It may seem puzzling, a curious inversion of history.

Historically, China has always taken immense pride in its status as the "Middle Kingdom," the cultural and economic hub around which all tributary states on the Asian perimeter revolved.[16] Until the mid-nineteenth century, China's proud claims went unchallenged. No rival state, or alliance of states, rose up to displace the Middle Kingdom. But the mainland lost its position of preeminence when Japan embarked on a crash program of industrial development around the mid-nineteenth century. Even before then, Tokugawa Japan had slowly laid the foundations for economic takeoff, preparing the way for Japan's industrialization and eventually, for the postwar emergence of the Asian perimeter. Thus, the old relationship of core-periphery (with the continent at the core and everyone else on the periphery) started to shift around the seventeenth century. By the late twentieth century, the process had been completed. The Asian perimeter moved front and center as the economic core, with the mainland gravitating to the periphery. Why did this reversal take place, when the continent seems to possess all the advantages of favorable factor endowments?

One plausible explanation emerges out of traditional notions of international comparative advantage. According to orthodox trade theory, the export composition of resource-rich, late developing countries tends to be weighted heavily towards raw materials and semi-processed goods; resource-poor countries, on the other hand, have little to offer but the export of manufactured goods of high value-added. As resource-rich countries can be more self-sufficient, the ratio of trade to GNP tends to be lower, and the temptation to follow a strategy of import substitution can be harder to resist. As a result, resource-rich countries may not be as export-oriented as the resource-poor economies; this means that they may not be exposed as fully to the discipline of foreign competition. Hence, an abundant resource base can turn out to be an early handicap rather than a headstart. If this is the case, it may be no accident that the resource-rich ASEAN economies got off to a much slower start than the resource-poor ANIEs. It was not until ASEAN countries dropped the strategy of import substitution and reoriented their economies to export-led growth that they took off.[17]

The concept of comparative advantage, however, does not provide a complete explanation, since it would be odd to argue that favorable factor endowments prevent or impede economic development. A more compelling explanation must take political factors into account: specifically, the incompatibility of communist systems and economic efficiency (in the case of China, North Korea, and Vietnam), and the ineffectuality of political regimes in non-communist but authoritarian states (like Cambodia and Burma). The empirical evidence pointing to the deadening hand of communism on economic efficiency is overwhelming. It would be hard to cite a single case in which the rigid communist organizations did not undermine economic efficiency and retard dynamic growth.

Tangible evidence of the negative correlation between communist organization and market efficiency can be found in Asia's own backyard. Look at the dramatic divergence of growth trajectories in politically divided countries like North and South Korea, or China, Taiwan, and Hong Kong. In Europe, the contrast is just as dramatic if one looks at the divergent performances of the two German states, or those of Western and Eastern Europe.

What this pattern implies for Asia is that the communization of China, North Korea, and Vietnam was, and is, the main reason for their slow, zigzag pattern of economic and political development. Political institutions do make a decisive difference on the capacity of latecomer countries to break out of the rut of semipermanent stagnation,[18] and it is precisely for this reason that the outlook for the Asian continent is so much bleaker than it is for the perimeter.

Of the communist countries on the continent, those that are the most agrarian—those, that is, with the lowest levels of industrial infrastructure, may be in the best position to administer the painful medicine of far-reaching market reforms. The reason is simple: agriculture lends itself more readily to reform, and the cleaner the industrial slate—the less embedded the dysfunctional institutions and practices of manufacturing—the greater the degrees of freedom and better the chances at structural reform. By this logic, Laos and Vietnam, the two most backward communist economies, may be in a stronger position to undertake economic reform than China or North Korea, which are farther down the road of industrialization. By the same token, China and North Korea may stand a better chance than the Soviet Union or Czechoslovakia, where heavily subsidized and inefficient industries cannot be easily exposed to open competition.

The short-term outlook for the communist economies on the Asian continent is thus bleak, but not as bleak as that for the Soviet Union or most of Central and Eastern Europe. Laos and Vietnam may stand a chance of achieving a turnaround. At the present time, Vietnam is reeling from the effects of a Soviet cutoff in credits; the abrupt cutoff is intensifying the need to attract outside capital and technology, to gain access to foreign markets, and to win acceptance in countries within the Asian perimeter. Vietnam possesses impressive human resources, including entrepreneurial talent embodied in scores of overseas Chinese. If the government can disengage from direct intervention in the Cambodian conflict, and set its financial and institutional house in order, Vietnam may succeed yet in attracting much of what it needs over the next decade.

The future of both China and North Korea is harder to forecast but the prospects look brighter the farther out the time horizon is stretched. At some point in the twenty-first century, one can predict, with some sense of certainty, that China will join the circle of industrial states. Should the Korean peninsula be unified, or economically integrated, the Korean peninsula might become a formidable force in the region and world. What continental Asia possesses in greater abundance than, say, the Soviet Union is a disciplined, educated, and resilient work force, one which is less than a generation removed from first-hand experience in market activities (compared to the space of two-generations in the Soviet Union). Other things being equal, the freshness of the past experience with capitalistic endeavors may mean a faster turn around in Asia.

Is there a brighter side to the observable gap between the Asian perimeter and the continental heartland? Perhaps so. If one looks at it from an American, Japanese, or perimeter perspective, the relative backwardness and slow, jerky pace of growth in Asia's fifth zone may redound to the interests of the capitalist states. Sure, there are risks and costs accompanying the continent's struggles; and few analysts would quarrel with the notion that Japan and the United States ought to lend a helping hand so that the continental heartland can be peacefully integrated into the regional and world economy. On balance, the benefits of economic takeoff on the continent will outweigh the costs. But to date at least, the slower rates of growth on the communist continent have served to maintain a regional balance of power very favorable to American and perimeter interests. So long as the continental economies are mired in the bog of dysfunctional organization, their capacity to exercise power is limited. They cannot convert their rich resource base into the kind of military muscle or political-diplomatic clout that might give rise to high levels of tension. Forced to look inward, they have been stymied in their capacity to manipulate and intimidate their neighbors on the perimeter.

THE IMPACT OF THE COLD WAR

If domestic political factors have stunted the development of the communist economies on the continent, the international politics of the Cold War, in contrast, have contributed to the successes of the capitalist economies on the Asian perimeter. In particular, America's commitment to maintain a favorable balance of power established a climate of stability that Asia had not known for centuries. This stable environment permitted countries on the Asian perimeter to concentrate on nation-building and economic development.

In the minds of U.S. leaders during the late 1940s, the key to communist containment lay in effectively combining military deterrence with political stability and economic growth. They understood that economic stagnancy would serve as fertile breeding grounds for the spread of communism. The best way of containing that danger was to generate brisk rates of economic growth. Acting on this conviction, the United States did everything in its power to foster robust market economies on the Asian perimeter—providing most-favored-nation access to U.S. markets, making technology available for transfer, procuring military equipment and support services, injecting foreign aid, rendering valuable economic advice (like the seminal Dodge program in Japan), and serving as a sponsor for admission to various international economic organizations. The program was very similar to the one implemented in Western Europe—without massive Marshall Plan assistance but with similarly successful results.

It was no accident, then, that the economic momentum of the Asian perimeter got started in the first and second zones, for Northeast Asia formed the crucial arc of encirclement of the communist-dominated mainland. America's preoccupation with military security led it to bear a portion of the economic costs and consequences of reviving Asia's devastated economies. In the name of regional peace and security, the United States accepted asymmetric relationships with Japan and the ANIEs, involving differential market access, different standards of behavior, and asymmetric assumption of the costs of providing for the collective good. In seeking to foster industrial development, political stability, and regional prosperity as instruments for the containment of communism, America's Cold War strategy in Asia succeeded far beyond anyone's expectations. So successful was the strategy, in fact, that the United States is now having to deal with the ramifications of having overshot the mark. The U.S. economy now faces formidable commercial competition from Japan, the ANIEs, and increasingly ASEAN, and the rise of industrial Asia has altered the world distribution of economic power, reducing America's share of world production from dominant levels to more normal levels historically.[19]

Now that the Cold War is largely over, how will Asia be affected? Will America be less magnanimous in its dealings with Japan, the ANIEs, and ASEAN? Will the United States try to level the playing field? Will the United States want to redistribute the burdens of paying for the collective good? The answer is probably yes. We shall probably see a reorientation of America's role in Asia, from a preoccupation with military security to the assignment of high priority for the pursuit of economic interests. Indeed, national security will come to be redefined to incorporate a broader range of economic concerns, including trade balances, access to foreign markets, competitiveness in key industries, dual-purpose technology, technology diffusion, capital flows, exchange rates, direct foreign investments, savings and investments, monetary policy, Third World debt, economic development, utilization and preservation of natural resources, the global environment, and trade regimes— all factors considered relevant in the past but which have moved up in importance today.

The passing of the Cold War will also change the nature of bilateral alliances. It will erode the foundations for cooperation laid down and reinforced by common military threats. This erosion may accentuate, in turn, the sources of conflict emerging from the multiple arenas of economic competition. Such conflicts may become especially acute in America's relationship with Japan and the ANIEs. To hold together the network of alliances, the United States and its Asian allies may have to redefine the conceptual basis of their relationships, taking into account the post–Cold War environment in Asia. Articulating a new conceptual framework for the United States–Japan alliance—supplanting the old Yoshida Doctrine—will be crucial. It will have to incorporate a new vision for Japan's world role, one that encourages Japan to shed the free rider image. Without a new integrative vision, the United States–Japan alliance is vulnerable to the rough and tumble of economic friction and political backbiting.

It may be that the alliances with South Korea and the Philippines will also have to be reviewed. The old structure of bilateral alliances in Asia, based on U.S. forward deployments, has weakened, and with it, America's political influence in the region; but at the same time, as pointed out earlier, ties of economic interdependence have proliferated, driven by market opportunities and countless private-sector decisions. How the political-military structure will fit with the burgeoning ties of economic interdependence is not yet clear. Will the two coincide and reinforce each other? If so, perhaps we need not worry about the loosening of alliance networks. If, on the other hand, economic linkages are moving counter to political-military relationships, then there may be serious road blocks ahead. Based on the data presented in this paper, one can be cautiously optimistic. It looks as if the direction of economic linkage is serving to *stabilize* the region. It is providing the kind of reinforcement that purely political and military relationships cannot supply.

STRATEGIC SALIENCE

If Asia's explosive growth has transformed the international economy, events in Europe have brought about the dismantling of the Cold War's military structure. In terms of political-strategic considerations, there is no doubt that Europe has been, and remains, the fulcrum of struggle among the big powers, which maneuver constantly to maintain the balance of power.

The historical scene of incessant warfare among expansionist empires, rival religions, and aggressive nation-states,[20] Europe is still the vortex of the highest stakes competition between the military superpowers. Asia, by contrast, is a region where, for several thousand years, only one empire existed, China, and no local challengers arose to overthrow it.[21] In contrast to the Roman, Byzantine, or Moslem empires, China was content to exercise cultural suzerainty and not political or military hegemony.[22] What is historically intriguing, and of momentous long-term significance, is that China never sought to conquer the Asian perimeter through the use of superior maritime power, even though it possessed the ships, resources, and know-how to become a world seafaring power long before the Portuguese, Spaniards, or British. China never launched ships to conquer its offshore neighbors, much less expand its empire to North and South America, the Middle East, and Europe.[23] In military-strategic terms over the past five hundred years, therefore, Asia has occupied a place of secondary importance, subordinate to Europe, but characterized by over a millennium of comparatively peaceful coexistence.

There are marked differences in the worlds of power politics, on the one hand, and economics, on the other. In the delicate and ever-shifting world of power politics, the number and salience of geographic regions are large—much larger than in the world of economic activity. The Philippines, for instance, is of greater importance to the global balance of power than it is to the world of economic production. This implies that Asia, though secondary, can still occupy a pivotal place in the strategic scheme of things. With the end of the Cold War, the relative weight of economic factors in the mix of forces affecting international security is becoming heavier. Asia, by virtue of its pacesetting growth, is becoming steadily more central.

Nor is this assessment confined to the future. For the past half-century, Asia has been pivotal to the world balance of power. Recall an early development in Cold War history: When China severed its ties with the Soviet Union in the early 1960s, the impact on the global balance of power was both far-reaching and lasting, transforming the strictly bipolar structure that had existed until then into one of multipolarity. More recently, several of the momentous changes leading to the disintegration of the Soviet Union—particularly the acknowledgement of glaring deficiencies inherent in all Leninist economies and the need to undertake thoroughgoing reform—began in Asia before spreading to the Soviet Union. China shed Leninist doctrines and took steps to reform its economy during the mid-1970s, a decade before Gorbachev launched his programs of *perestroika* and *glasnost*. It did not take China long to acknowledge the superior features of market incentives, being surrounded by evidence of economic dynamism on its own periphery—Japan, South Korea, Taiwan, and Hong Kong. China's proximity to the vigorous zones of the Asian perimeter has yielded tangible benefits. Should the economic climate on the perimeter continue to be favorable, the impetus imparted to the backward communist countries on the continent—Laos, Vietnam, China, and North Korea—could turn out to be decisive, with significant spillover benefits, in turn, for the world system.

JAPAN: A NEW WORLD ROLE?

But this is a long-term scenario. Closer at hand, Asia is the home of an already established economic giant, Japan, which —depending on the directions it chooses to follow—is in a position to exert a profound impact on the world system. To date, and for the foreseeable future, Japan has chosen to eschew the acquisition and exercise of political-military power. Its historically unprecedented concentration solely on commercial interests, combined with a reluctance to convert economic strength into political and military leverage, has worked to everyone's advantage—not only Japan's but also the region's as a whole. Indeed, Asia's bright outlook today is due, in no small measure, to Japan's role in functioning as catalyst and loco-motive for growth while at the same time posing no political-military threat to the regional status quo. It is hard to imagine where Asia would be today if Japan had decided to travel down a different road—if, for example, Japan had pursued more aggressive political and military policies. In this sense—of not drawing on all its potential cards—Japan has already had a seminal impact on the stability and shape of the regional and world system.

Should Japan decide to break out of its one-dimensional mold—if it chooses to abandon its low political-military posture—the impact on the global political-strategic balance would be immense, to say nothing of the secondary-order effects on economic relationships. The potential to play an active role is there; the gap between Japan's latent and actual power is very large—larger than that of any country since isolationist America between World Wars I and II. Whether Japan opts to narrow the gap, or continues its policy of low posture, is an important question (though, to date at least, the answer is a resounding no).

In an increasingly intertwined and complex world, the opportunities, incentives, and pressures for Japan to assume a larger noneconomic role may be growing. Accordingly, Japan seems to be groping to define a new role for itself over the next century, a nonthreatening, nonmilitary role. Whether it formulates a new, long-term vision or merely acts in ad hoc response to changing external circumstances, Japan is in a position to play a leading role in such important issues as restructuring international economic institutions (like GATT), expanding foreign aid, relieving Third World debt, recycling current account surpluses to capital-starved countries, importing more manufactured products from Asia and the Third World, generating and diffusing more technology abroad, taking the initiatives in preserving the global environment, and serving as a mediator in regional conflicts. Whatever the issues, Japan will probably try to define and test its new international role in Asia first. Asia is a logical theater within which to explore, identify, sharpen, and ultimately implement a new world role.

Here again, Asia may be at the forefront of regional developments that have large ripple effects around the world. In the same way that a unified Germany will set the basic parameters for Europe—and thereby affect the global balance, Japan's search for a new world role is certain to have far-reaching implications for Asia—and the world system. Unlike Europe, there is in Asia a queue of emerging powers capable of altering the global balance well into the twenty-first century—Japan, China, and down the road perhaps, an economically integrated Korea.

Of the world's regions, therefore, Asia and Europe seem poised to make the biggest economic strides and to be the scene of the most consequential political realignments and developments. While few changes of comparable significance loom on the North American horizon, the U.S. economy will have a huge bearing on the health of the world economy. Here, too, Asia enters the picture, for the future of the U.S. economy will be closely tied to the future of its trade, investments, and competitive/cooperative involvements with the burgeoning Asian perimeter.

OLD AND NEW SOURCES
OF CONFLICT AND INSTABILITY

To this point in the paper, the outlook for Asia may seem one-sidedly positive. The forecast calls for continued growth on the perimeter, expanding ties of interdependence, nonlinear and fragile but steady progress toward political stability, reduced threats of Soviet and Chinese aggression, and Asia's emergence as one of the world's three powerful cylinders of economic growth.

We all know, however, that no forecast for a region as vast, complex, and rapidly changing, or as turbulent over the past half-century, can be free of turmoil and uncertainties. Asia is moving too fast for there not to be dislocations, crises, and points of punctuated equilibrium, particularly in the near term. Indeed, the nearer the time horizon—the closer up the scrutiny, the clearer the view of problems—the more pessimistic the prognosis. No matter how good Asia may look in long-run perspective, regardless of how much worse the situation may look in Africa, South and Central America, the Indian sub-continent, the Middle East, or the Soviet bloc, there is no denying that the region is nowhere as stable as North America or Western Europe. It faces problems and uncertainties aplenty.

Few of the postwar sources of conflict and instability in Asia have been remedied. If an inventory of the most troublesome were to be taken, the list would include: the difficulties of nation-building on the continent, in areas like Burma and Cambodia; the problem of political partitionment (the Korean peninsula, Taiwan, Hong Kong); unresolved territorial disputes (such as the Spratley Islands); domestic instability stemming from highly skewed income distribution (the Philippines), religious separatist movements (the Philippines), ethnic unrest (Indonesia), and authoritarian rule (Burma); popular demands for more participation and greater liberalization in the political system (South Korea, China, and the Philippines); historic and geostrategic rivalries (Sino-Soviet, Soviet-Japanese, Korean-Japanese, and Sino-Japanese); continuing tensions from relatively heavy force deployments (especially along the Sino-Soviet and Korean borders) and the slow pace of arms reductions in Asia (compared to Europe); anxieties concerning the staying power of American commitments in the region (that is, the fear of U.S. neo-isolationism); and Asia's heavy reliance on imported oil from the volatile Middle East and its vulnerability to supply and price disruptions.

Iraq's invasion and occupation of Kuwait in 1990 has revived the enormous latent dangers that deep-seated economic tremors could occur and rock the foundations of Asia's perimeter. Worst-case scenarios involving oil supply and price disruptions could see plummeting growth and investment rates, spiraling unemployment and inflation rates, plunging stock markets, escalating trade tensions, and spreading political instability in Asia. Best-case scenarios are based on assumptions of gradual, rather than sudden, change, and the availability of adequate time within which to make necessary adjustments. If price hikes are gradual, if they can be kept within the range, say, of $25 per barrel, the Asian economies will probably be able to adjust relatively easily to the higher prices, though they would have to deal with inflationary pressures over the short term. If, on the other hand, prices suddenly jump above $30–35 per barrel and stay there, the short-term effects in Asia could be crippling and the long-run adjustments necessary would be exceedingly costly, painful, and conflict producing. Sure, a few oil producing countries, like China and Indonesia, might reap immediate windfall benefits from the price hikes, but even they would be hurt by the primary and secondary-order effects of far-reaching economic dislocation. Within the dynamic Asian perimeter, the momentum of growth could come to a screeching halt; problem economies like that of the Philippines might suffer traumatic ripple effects; and the fragile structure of participatory democracy slowly being put in place in countries like South Korea could be put on hold or even crushed under the weight of widespread political unrest.

The Iraq-Kuwait crisis is thus a sobering reminder of the uncertainties and vulnerabilities surrounding Asia. Even if the world passes through the immediate crisis without incident, Asia's dependence on oil from the Persian Gulf to power its engines of growth will neither disappear nor diminish overnight. Indeed, unless new or alternative energy sources can be developed, the likelihood is that Asia's oil imports from the Middle East will increase over the next decade. Already it has climbed from 67 percent in 1985 to roughly 73 percent in 1990; assuming linear increases in demand, the level of dependence could exceed 80 percent by 1995 and reach 90 percent by the end of the century.[24]

Accordingly, optimistic forecasts for any region so dependent on the unstable Persian Gulf, even one as adaptable and resilient as Asia, must be tempered by the recognition that ongoing growth can only take place when the alignment of certain external circumstances continues to be favorable. This is true not just for oil. Asia's future hinges on a host of other external circumstances that optimistic forecasts often take for granted, including a healthy and open U.S. economy, a viable system of free trade, and the well-being of the Third World. In a world of deepening interdependence—in which Asia is an integral and leading-edge participant—regional forecasts cannot be made without taking into account what is happening outside of Asia.

On top of such recurrent concerns, new problems are looming on the horizon: long-run concerns about America's will and capacity to set its economic house in order (taming the twin dragons of budget and trade deficits); short-term concerns about continuing access to U.S., Japanese, and European markets and the possibility of damaging trade protectionism; the dangers of closed regional blocs; exchange rate per-turbations; progressive damage to the region (and world's) natural environment; apprehensions about Japan's intentions and goals, including fears of domination; generational turnover and succession crises, particularly in authoritarian states like North Korea and China; the need to make sometimes painful domestic adjustments in response to sudden shifts in international comparative advantage; the future of the United States–Japan alliance; the after tremors of a major recession in the United States or Japan, or both; and a crash on the New York, London, or Tokyo stock markets.

The inventory is not exhaustive. It merely illustrates the range and seriousness of the possible near-term problems. Essentially, the types of problems listed above can be grouped into several generic categories: internal instability stemming either from inept government or economic backwardness; the costs of making domestic adjustments to external changes; and uncertainties about the role of the United States and Japan in the region; unresolved territorial disputes; and instability in the Persian Gulf. Except for the last, none seems likely to ignite explosions that will embroil nations in a hot war. Perhaps the Asian perimeter, like North America and Western Europe, has crossed over the threshold of relative peace—that is, arrived at a stage of development in which the probabilities of external invasion have fallen so low that they can be considered relatively remote. In the years ahead, accordingly, domestic instability and economic conflicts of various sorts appear to be the most common, and perhaps troublesome, form of problems that will have to be dealt with.

FORECAST OF TRENDS: A BRIEF SUMMARY

This paper has sought to analyze the powerful historic forces at work in Asia and to assess what they might mean. Before turning to a discussion of the policy implications of the foregoing assessment, it might be useful here to review briefly the identification of central trends. For brevity, the summary will be presented in outline form.

The World System

- The collapse of the Cold War system; the unraveling of the Soviet empire; Leninist economies in disarray; a long and uncertain period of attempted economic reform.

- Serious problems of governability and political stability everywhere except North America, Western Europe, and most countries on the Asian perimeter.

- Widening gaps in the distribution of wealth between the advanced industrial states and late developing and communist-bloc countries.

- The simultaneous increase, without contradiction, of global interdependence, regionalism, nationalism, ethnic unrest, and localism.

- A redefinition of security—from military to economic concerns; from global to regional and local arenas; from ideological to political struggles; from nuclear war to the physical environment.

- The loosening of Cold War alliances; greater conflict among allies; and a restructuring of alliance groupings.

- The emergence of a tripolar world economy consisting of the United States, Western Europe; and Japan.

- Lingering doubts about America's capacity to reinvigorate its economy and reassert both its economic competitiveness and political influence.

Asia

- The rise in the relative importance of Asia in the world system in terms economic and political-military factors.

- The emergence of the Asian perimeter as the engine of dynamic growth; the expansion outward from Japan to the ANIEs in Northeast Asia, and through ASEAN.

- Proliferating links of interdependence tying together Japan, the United States, and ANIEs; between Japan and ASEAN; between the ANIEs and ASEAN.

- Growing commercial competition between the United States, Japan, and the ANIEs in such sectors as consumer electronics, steel, and automobiles.

- The growing presence and influence of Japan, which appears capable of sustaining vigorous growth rates well into the next century.

- Questions concerning the extent of Europe's involvement in the ongoing growth of the Asian perimeter; some danger of semi-closed regional blocs; the increasing linking of the Asian perimeter and North America.

- Slower and more uncertain growth patterns in the heart of the Asian continent; greater unrest; more volatility than on the perimeter; but gradual, sometimes halting, long-term movement toward economic and political maturity.

- Some major changes down the road: possible Korean unification, Vietnam's integration into the perimeter; and China's incorporation of Hong Kong.

Having summarized the underlying trends, we turn, finally, to a discussion of the policy implications and questions raised by these trends.

POLICY IMPLICATIONS AND QUESTIONS

What policy implications can be drawn from this analysis? As this paper has analyzed the broad economic trends at work, not focusing on the specific hot spots and near-term problems, the policy discussion will focus on the big issues and questions. For brevity again, the outline format will be used.

Policy Implications

- In dealing with Asia, the United States must come up with a clear definition of its economic interests, security objectives, and overall priorities; otherwise it will not be able to mobilize public support at home or allied support abroad.

- At the top of America's list of interests and priorities is the effective management of its relationship with Japan. No bilateral relationship is of greater importance, but the alliance is under severe strain on both sides of the Pacific, due to the escalation of head-to-head competition in key sectors and to the lopsidedness of the bilateral trade imbalance. Seeing the relationship through the next ten years should be among the highest priorities for both countries.

- To survive the conflicts that lie ahead, both governments must upgrade and streamline the policy-making apparatus for United States–Japanese issues so that the apparatus reflects the great and growing importance of the relationship to both sides and is fully capable of responding to the heavier and heavier demands made on it.

- For the relationship to endure, the United States also must fashion, with Japan, a bold new vision of what the United States and Japan can accomplish together in managing an ever more interdependent, complex, and multipolar world.

- Japan ought to be encouraged to define a bold new role in the region and world. Natural issue areas in which Japan can play a very constructive role include the following: wise channeling of its excess savings to priority areas; greater purchases of manufacturing imports, especially from developing countries; Third World debt relief; foreign aid (including nonmonetary assistance in the diffusion of organizational know-how); the transfer of manufacturing technology overseas; strengthening of international economic institutions, like GATT; preservation of the global environment; and greater support for basic research and development.

- Very quietly and unobtrusively Japan seems to have decided that lowering its level of dependence on the U.S. market lies in its national interests (given the intensity of trade-related conflicts) and that the Asian perimeter is the most promising area into which to diversify.

- The key to America's continuing capacity to lead, which is also the precondition of any hope to play a constructive role in Asia, is the necessity of setting its own economy in order; specifically, this requires cutting spending and raising savings and investments. If the United States fails to restore macroeconomic health, it is bound to continue suffering lopsided trade deficits, losing in the commercial competition to Asian producers, and becoming more dependent on capital inflows from Japan and Taiwan.

- The United States should consult with its European and Japanese allies to come up with a common and consistent policy stance with respect to questions of how to deal with the needs of the communist-bloc countries across a wide range of concrete issues: foreign aid, direct investments, extension of loans and credits, convertible currencies, membership in GATT and other international economic organizations, most-favored-nation treatment, economic advice, technology transfers, and so forth.

- Japan, together perhaps with the ANIEs, should be encouraged to play a more active economic role in Mexico and Latin America, which need the kind of capital investments, process know-how, business organization, and access to Asian markets that Japan can offer.

- Japan can negotiate from a position of strength on the northern territories issue and should be encouraged to stand firm on the return of all four islands. Japanese rapprochement with the Soviet Union is not something for the United States to fear, given intrinsic limitations on the scope of Soviet-Japanese economic cooperation; but it may lead to a weakening of domestic support for United States–Japanese relations, especially when concessions are required to pass safely through periods of severe economic conflict.

- As it would be undesirable to have Europe standing on the sidelines, cut off from the growth dynamic in Asia, the United States and Japan should find ways of increasing the incentives for Europe to participate increasingly in Asia, and conversely, for the Asian perimeter to expand ties in Europe; market incentives are working in this direction.

- Unless unexpected changes take place, the Asian perimeter appears sufficiently stable that the United States can continue cutting back force deployments.

- Facing a very difficult situation, Vietnam is eager to establish ties of economic interdependence with the West; if satisfactory progress in made on the Cambodian question, the United States and Japan should respond positively to Vietnam's overtures.

- To insure, healthy, sustained, and balanced growth in the second and third zones (ANIEs and ASEAN), there must be a proper mix of capital goods and consumer goods imports; the United States and Japan should monitor the mix over time to see that the import of consumer goods does not overwhelm those of capital goods.

Policy Questions

- Do the United States and Asia want Japan to play a bigger role in Asia and the world? If so, what kind of role? If not, who will assume the role?

- Should Japan be asked to expand the yen's role as an international reserve currency? What are the advantages and disadvantages? What would be the regional consequences?

- Is the level of debt in the U.S. economy about where it should be? Or should debt levels be cut back? To what levels? What are the worst-case consequences of America's capital dependence on Japanese inflows?

- How much pressure ought to be applied to countries in Asia with closed financial markets to open up and internationalize?

- How important is it to pressure Japan into more rapid deregulation of its financial markets?

- What policy position should the United States and Japan take toward Korean unification? Should it facilitate the process or stand back? How might Japan react to a unified Korean peninsula? What impact would it have on the region as a whole?

NOTES

1. Paul Knox and John Agnew, *The Geography of the World Economy* (New York: Edward Arnold, 1989).
2. Nihon Keizai Shimbun, *Japan Economic Almanac: 1990* (Tokyo: Nihon Keizai Shimbun, 1990).

3. Japan Center for Economic Research, *JCER Report*, Vol 2, No. 6 (July 1990).
4. National Institute for Research Advancement, *Policy Research: Asia Pacific* (Seisaku Kenkyuu: Ajia Taiheiyou Kenkyuu, Vol. 3, No. 3 (1990), p. 73.
5. E. L. Jones, *Growth Recurring: Economic Change in World History* (Oxford: Clarendon Press, 1988).
6. Organization for Economic Cooperation and Development (OECD), *The Newly Industrializing Countries: Challenge and Opportunity for OECD Industries* (Paris: OECD, 1988).
7. Ibid.
8. Ministry of International Trade and Industry (MITI), *Tsusho Hakushko (MITI White Paper) 1990* (Tokyo: Okurasho Insatsukyoku, 1990).
9. Mark Elvin, *The Pattern of the Chinese Past* (Stanford: Stanford University Press, 1973); and E. L. Jones, *Growth Recurring*.
10. Bill Emmot, *The Sun Also Sets: The Limits to Japan's Economic Power* (New York: Random House, 1989).
11. Peter Katzenstein, *Small States in World Markets: Industrial Policy for Europe* (Ithaca: Cornell University Press, 1985).
12. Fernand Braudel, *Afterthoughts on Material Civilization and Capitalism* (Baltimore: The Johns Hopkins University Press, 1977).
13. Emmott, *The Sun Also Sets*.
14. Kenichi Ohmae, *The Borderless Economy: Strategy in an Interlinked Economy* (New York: Harper Business, 1990).
15. Dwight H. Perkins, *China: Asia's Next Economic Giant?* (Seattle: University of Washington Press, 1989).
16. Jones, *Growth Recurring*.
17. OECD, *Industrializing Countries*.
18. Samuel Huntington, *Political Order in Changing Societies* (New Haven: Yale University Press, 1968); and Jones, *Growth Recurring*.
19. Joseph S. Nye, Jr., *Bound to Lead: The Changing Nature of American Power* (New York: Basic Books, 1990).
20. Fernand Braudel, *Civilization and Capitalism, 15th–18th Century: The Perspective of the World*, Vol. 3 (New York: Harper and Row, 1979).
21. Gerald Segal, *Rethinking the Pacific* (Oxford: Clarendon Press, 1990).
22. Jones, *Growth Recurring*.
23. Segal, *Rethinking the Pacific*; K.N. Chaudhuri, *Trade and Civilization in the Indian Ocean: An Economic History From the Rise of Island to 1750* (Cambridge: Cambridge University Press, 1985); and Janet L. Abu-Lughod, *Before European Hegemony: The World System A.D. 1240–1350* (New York: Oxford University Press, 1989).
24. Michael Westlake, "Over a barrel: Asia's economic prospects hinge on Gulf oil," *Far Eastern Economic Review*, Vol. 149, No. 35 (August 23, 1990).

Appendix 6

THIRD WORLD POLITICS AND SECURITY
IN THE 1990s:
"THE WORLD FORGETTING,
BY THE WORLD FORGOT?"

John Chipman

Far from the epicenter of the political earthquake that shook Europe in 1989, the developing states of the Middle East, Africa, Asia, and Latin America have nevertheless been affected by the ensuing shock waves. As if in reinforcement of their perceived position on the periphery of world politics, leaders throughout the developing world have pointed to the Eastern European revolutions of 1989 and the general Western response to a reforming (and imploding) Soviet Union and seen in the new nature of East-West politics challenges to their own standing in international society. The reemergence of traditional disputes in East Central Europe and the increased salience of local problems parallel the problems in the developing world that continue to derive from incomplete processes of state-building and the management of internal strife. The sources of insecurity in East Central Europe having become analogous to those of the political South, the nature of East-West relations, much to the dismay of many in the Third World, have come to imitate the previous concerns of North-South politics and therefore diminished the specificity (and possibly amount) of development aid to the Third World.

This still unproven thesis of marginalization from the flow of development assistance has been expressed at a time when, given the broad trend of superpower withdrawals from military engagements in the developing world, the management of most regional conflict in the Third World certainly appears less pressing. Superpower participation in often arcane Third World disputes and the sometimes fanciful strategic calculations that accompanied justifications for intervention lent international prestige to otherwise parochial quarrels. States in the developing world often lamented the participation of the superpowers in regional conflict. They also appreciated that they could draw advantages from this competition. The capacity to play East against West is gone, and the poorer states in the developing world are thus struggling with how to deal with great power acceptance of their geopolitical insignificance. Some of the richer Third World states are seeking to acquire with greater enthusiasm a wider array of the military instruments of power. In general, faced with the reality of continued, even intensified, local instability to which regional powers may not be so indifferent, states in the developing world cannot readily borrow power from the outside to buttress their own capacities. With competition for superpower patronage now less relevant, most developing states must rely on the uncertain assurance offered by existing national military power to bolster national identity and prestige, even if these are not always appropriate tools with which to address the problems they face.

An exception to this emerging rule of the post–Cold War era, by which actors in the Third World might be able to count on the indifference of the outside community to their actions, was provided by the Middle East crisis beginning in the summer of 1990. The special place still retained by the Persian Gulf in U.S. strategic calculations and the clear breach of international law committed by Iraq's annexation and thus attempted murder of the state of Kuwait in August 1990 produced an unprecedented international condemnation and military deployments by the United States and over twenty other states to the region. It demonstrated that the United Nations Security Council could act in unison on the basis of unanimous resolutions and that the superpowers could act in virtual loose alliance together and with a host of other countries to put pressure on a state which had made itself a pariah in a world system many thought would become more benign. The outcome of the 1990 Persian Gulf crisis will reshape attitudes toward the management of conflict in the Middle East, and to the utility of economic sanctions and military force in reversing the results of aggressive action in the developing world. In his speech to Congress on September 11, 1990, President George Bush argued that it was necessary to build a new world order where "the rule of law supplants the rule of the jungle" and deemed the crisis the start of "a new partnership of nations" and "the first test of our mettle." It is doubtful that the Persian Gulf crisis, almost no matter what its outcome, will prove the archetype for international responses to regional conflict in the 1990s. The particular political importance of the balance of power in the Middle East, the question of oil, and the nature of Saddam Hussein's actions were a truly special combination of features that allowed for quick and unambiguous action by the United States and most of the rest of the world.

The sources, implications, relevance, and balances between "good" and "evil" in most other cases (actual or prospective) of regional conflict are much less clear. In fact, much regional conflict simply does not matter. The United States continues to see itself engaged in the problems of Latin America, now primarily because of the drug problem, and the Soviet Union will be affected by developments in Central Asia, especially insofar as these are related to the management of an Islamic revival. By and large, superpower concern for regional conflict—even in the Middle East—is expressed through irregular diplomatic efforts to bring parties to a negotiating table. While in 1990 the superpowers are still supporting opposite sides in civil wars—in Angola and Afghanistan—their participation is not at a level that either inspires international concern or gives them substantial influence over the course of these wars. Great power attachment to the international diplomacy of conflict resolution should not, however, be confused with the same urgency of purpose that previously accompanied competitive military intervention.

In this international environment, where the role of the superpowers in regional conflict is in general decline, and where the developed countries of Europe and North America will concentrate on encouraging and creating new conditions of security in Europe, the direction of Third World politics and security will more than ever before be locally determined. The likelihood of domestic forces multiplying and of local actors diversifying their regional ambitions is high. This pluralism of domestic and regional activity will, in turn, make it difficult for great powers to engage themselves easily again in regions from which they have withdrawn. The increasing autonomy of local actors (whether states or insurgent groups) and their appreciation of their own local influence will create facts and contexts that will complicate the assessments of outsiders and make the effects of political, economic, or military intervention often incalculable.

In the 1990s, therefore, understanding regional security in the Third World will mean appreciating, more than ever before, the international relations of parochialism. Regional security in the Middle East, Africa, Asia, and Latin America is regularly affected by the external effects of policies implemented to attenuate domestic problems and by the domestic consequences of the external reactions to locally inspired change. Policies pursued by governments to deal with ethnic disputes, secessionist movements, national revival groups, economic depression, or drug issues become security problems for others and inspire reactions that are not always pacific or neutral. The domestic policies of one's neighbor quickly become part of one's own.

The differences between national and regional perceptions of security, as well as the challenge of managing domestic demands for change are among the overarching dilemmas of Third World politics and security. In the bipolar world of the past—for which many in the Third World appear sadly nostalgic—the complexity of state security was hidden by the simple geometry and simplistic politics of East-West and North-South relations. The issues that now define Third World security are far more subtle, and the definition of regional relationships no longer simply corresponds to the rules of geography.

Five elemental sets of pressures impose themselves on many developing societies: the persistence of feudal or traditional structures and the desire for modern systems of state management; the pressure for democracy and the perceived need of political leaders to maintain more autocratic forms of order; the challenge of maintaining national cohesion and the attractiveness of regional systems of political organization; the aspirations to political and economic independence and the reality of reliance on external aid; and the preeminent desire for military self-reliance, which sometimes obscures the urgency of nonmilitary threats to security.

The coexistence of many of these in numerous Third World states perhaps justifies the tendency of the great powers to disengage themselves from the intricacy of most Third World insecurity. Nagging doubts about whether influence abandoned is peace gained will mean that outside powers will not be able to ignore entirely the outcome of these pressures in some regions. The dramatic events of the Persian Gulf in the summer and autumn of 1990 will result in changes in the balance of political influence, domestic stability, and the military balance of power in the Middle East that will change interstate relations and domestic relationships significantly. After months of musical chairs, diplomacy, and alliance shifts (likely to occur at an *allegro vivace* pace), the Middle East will still be unstable and although a vital principle of international law will have been defended, some will ask whether it was all worth it. Equally, outside powers and the United States, in particular, are denied the luxury of simply redefining the nature of threats in and from the Third World to construct new defense policies as coherent and comprehensive as those that could be elaborated in the period of the Cold War. It will be almost impossible to construct overarching themes to guide policy in an age where regional conflict is *sui generis*, interests are variable, and the distribution of power and influence so diffuse.

FEUDALISM vs. MODERNITY

Problems of political stability—and therefore security—in many states of the developing world are often conditioned by the competition between central state power and more traditional forms of influence within state boundaries. The tension between aspirations for modern forms of state management at the center and the reality of long established—sometimes ancient—practices of local control acutely affects domestic order and perceptions of national identity. The current instruments of political organization (bureaucracies and parties) can rarely displace entirely the more archaic systems of social order that persist in developing countries. Their inevitable coexistence means that leaders in capitals may have to compromise their desire for a unitary system of government with the practical needs of managing complex social orders. Almost by definition, this also means that the capacities of outsiders to influence local events using the traditional mechanisms of international diplomacy are limited.

In the Afghanistan of the 1990s, for example, recognition of the local influence of tribal groups has persuaded the communist regime to make arrangements that effectively devolve power to provincial leaders. In 1985, Babrak Karmal, then general secretary of the People's Democratic Party of Afghanistan (PDPA), complained that party life was "rife with factionalism, tribalism, corruption, and regionalism."[1] These did not represent ideological currents or opposition opinion within the Communist party so much as the tribalism inherent in Afghan society. By 1989 the Najibullah regime had decided to recognize this reality by offering local autonomy, weapons, money, and even titles to local leaders in the country (such as Ismailis in Baghlan province) who could help by keeping open communication to the cities.[2] In this way, central state power has been strengthened by devolving power to trusted but still independent allies. The medieval rules of feudalism thus now appear more relevant to ensuring political order than formal arrangements for decentralization. Afghan leaders at the center, to reinsure their own power, have conceded roles on the periphery to traditional actors. No outsider seeking to influence the outcome of the present civil war can afford to ignore the complex algebra of these internal relationships.

Indeed, throughout the developing world the relationship between formal power at the center and traditional sources of power in outlying regions varies from discreet alliance (as in Afghanistan) through uncomfortable indifference to clear opposition. In Nigeria, for example, the central government made a major mistake when it chose a new Sultan of Sokoto in November

1988 without the support of the local kingmakers: the result was heavy rioting in the north and a major challenge to the military federal government. Few African governments can act without taking into account the positions and local influence of traditional chiefs. Sometimes central governments are able to disturb the traditions of country populations in the interests of national security or out of modernizing zeal. Brazil's Calha Norte policy in the late 1980s was directed towards moving entire Indian settlements away from borders with Colombia and Peru in order to prevent illegal trade. The deforestation of the Amazon, which was carried out for economic reasons but which has also displaced some tribes, has been attenuated because of the concern of environmentalists.

If it is true that modernist forces can sometimes overwhelm traditional social and political orders, the opposite problem is also encountered. Superficially modern societies in the developing world are sometimes challenged at the center by traditional groups who seek a deceleration of history, a return to a past that they understand better, a reversal of the achievements of modernity. They aim to relegate the modern techniques of political order and social control to the background, giving preeminence instead to ancient ideologies or beliefs as more effective tools of organization. Disaffected by the fruits of modern society, these groups, if they come to power, often advocate a degree of isolationism from global affairs.

The rise of Iran's theocracy in the revolution of 1979 is perhaps the classic example of this phenomenon. The desire to establish a political order based on the tenets of early Islam became quickly subject, however, to the exigencies of modern life and specifically the war with Iraq. Gradually the interests of the revolution had to give way to the interests of the state. Managing a war economy sometimes meant compromising the revolutionary spirit, both in terms of social justice and the desire for economic independence.[3] Eventually the need to blend religious piety and secular pragmatism came to be reflected in Iran's political institutions: most of the clergy both in and outside parliament are concerned to keep the elements of the Imam's legacy but also to allow the administration to work toward that degree of integration in the world economy consistent with the needs of the state. As yet there is no challenge to the primacy of theocratic rule, but the concessions made to pragmatists are illustrative of the way different types of political and social order can coexist even in revolutionary developing states.[4] Again, the record of outside actors in attempting to pick the radicals from the moderates in Iran's political order is an indicator of the difficulties that foreign states have in dealing with developing societies pulled between modern and feudal conceptions of civil society.

If, as for Charles Peguy, *"Tout commence par la mystique et finit par la politique,"* the intermingling of the two in so many parts of the world poses challenges to the practice of foreign policy by the developed states. Where opposition groups with retrogressive political agendas operate against the central power they also severely limit the modernizing programs of governments and their capacities to deal with the outside world. Peru's Maoist Sendero Luminoso movement plays on native Indian distrust of Lima's white elite, and having controlled large parts of the countryside during the past decade, has frustrated any conceivable plans for rural economic development. Its interaction with narcotraffickers has not only raised the intensity of conflict but also made combating the drug problem awkward. Certainly the United States must be cautious in Peru (as in other areas, such as Myanmar, formerly Burma) that its efforts to arrest international drug traffickers do not involve it in civil wars or ethnic rivalries. India's involvement in the conflict between Sinhalese and Tamils in Sri Lanka between 1987 and 1990 helped to revivify the Janata Vimuthi Peramuna (JVP) movement, which espouses an ultra-Sinhalese nationalism. While the leadership of the JVP has since been crushed, its appeal in the south cannot be discounted, particularly if programs for greater social justice are stymied by the imperatives of the continued conflict with the Tamils.

These illustrations are meant merely to indicate that managing modern aspirations and economic challenges just when traditional, historically rooted demands are made on the state remains one of the most recurrent dilemmas in the vastly different areas of the developing world. When the problems of the modern world are grafted on to the legacies of more primordial disputes, solutions offered for one category of issues may have dangerous repercussions on the other. State management is thus made awkward by the elemental tension between the imperatives of the modern world and the attractiveness, for many, of traditional society. The management of domestic stability in these circumstances depends on ensuring that the advances of modernization do not destroy the social fabric and that the demands of tradition are not so retrogressive that the state is disenfranchised from an ever more interdependent modern world.

This problem is compounded by the fact that the pluralism of privately held political opinion, religious belief, and social practice in the developing world is rarely equaled by the opportunity to have these represented publicly at the political center. Regimes in the developing world that have intentionally confused their own security with that of the state are now faced with growing demands for liberalization.

THE CHALLENGES OF DEMOCRACY
AND THE MANAGEMENT OF STATE POWER

One of the effects of the East European revolution of 1989 that has been most commented on throughout the Third World—but most spectacularly in Africa—has been the rise in local pressure for democratization. This has produced a need for leaders in the developing world to pay heed to the international trend in favor of full participation in domestic politics, and it has often had unpredictable effects on domestic order. The early months of 1990 saw uprisings in Gabon, Côte d'Ivoire, Benin, and numerous other francophone states where personal rule implicitly and sometimes explicitly supported by the various presidents of the French Fifth Republic was no longer considered a satisfactory means of government. The traditional and often entirely sound argument of many African leaders that the proliferation of political parties would be coextensive with the existence of ethnic groups and that therefore democracy could lead to disintegration will no longer be able to deter democratic movements in Africa, particularly if the participants believe that they have the tide of history with them. With international attention focused on this trend, regimes such as those of Daniel Arap Moi in Kenya and Sese Seko Mobuto in Zaire, long favored by Western governments, will not necessarily be able to rely on moral support from the outside to buttress their authority. The World Bank Report on sub-Saharan Africa of November 1989 openly called for greater pluralism and more honest government, arguing that "because countervailing power has been lacking, state officials in many countries have served their own interests without fear of being called into account."[5]

Further to the north, the states of the Maghreb are grappling differently with the democratic impulse. In Algeria, Chadli Bendjedid has encouraged a process of economic and political reform from above, but the victories in municipal elections in 1990 of the Front Islamique du Salut (FIS) over the ruling Front de Libération Nationale (FLN) will have worried those concerned by an Islamic revival. Tunisia has taken a more secular view of the democratic process, prohibiting the main Islamic group, Nahda, from forming a legal political party.

Although there have been some demands in the Arab Middle East for greater democracy, the desire for pluralism has been usually met by the argument that traditional structures offer adequate avenues for debate. In Kuwait, for example, demonstrators throughout the first half of 1990 called for the reopening of the National Assembly, closed in 1986 at the height of the Iran-Iraq war. Officials defending the refusal to restore of parliamentary democracy in the country have argued that parliament only reproduced political and religious divisions and that Kuwait's *diwaniya* system, whereby officials held open house on certain days of the week at which petitioners could air complaints, was a sufficient substitute for Western style democracy.[6] Iraq's invasion of Kuwait made this debate moot, but reaction to it raised two further questions. What will be the long-term effect of the large and primarily U.S. military deployment to the feudal states of the Gulf on the capacity of their leaders to hang on to autocratic and hereditary principles of leadership? Will the broad tension between "rich and poor Arab," which Saddam Hussein tried to exploit in the early weeks of the crisis, eventually result in more "people power" in the Middle East? Even in that region, while the problem may be defined differently than elsewhere, the demand for more pluralism of political participation will become more vociferous.

Yet it must be underscored that however awe-inspiring the events of 1989 in Europe might have been, to apply a domino theory to the kinetics of democracy has limited justification in observable fact. The wish that this be otherwise may be the father of much analysis in the case of Cuba. Many in the United States and elsewhere began to predict Fidel Castro's demise after the fall of Nicolae Ceausescu in Romania. But despite the economic pressures Fidel Castro confronts owing to the fall of socialism in Europe, his own grip on power remains impressive. A "palace coup d'état" may be in the offing, but it must be recalled that the Cuban revolution was national, not imposed from outside, and however irrational his logic or fabricated his conspiracy theories, it appears that Castro can still turn foreign hostility to the revolution to his advantage by appealing to a sense of national independence. Although there has been some debate on economic reforms in preparation for the fourth party congress in 1991, there is little chance that the more important proposals for decentralization of the economy can be met when economic circumstances dictate central control. Liberalism and pluralism seem as far away as does a strong and organized internal opposition.

The existence of parties and the fact of elections elsewhere in Central America have been more encouraging but the task of consolidation is enormous. Violeta Chamorro's National Opposition Union (UNO) government coalition has been, since her electoral victory in February 1990, a victim of the Sandinista promise to "rule from below." Two weeks of strikes in July 1990 brought the country to the edge of another civil war. The capacity to rule of the elected government of President Alfredo Cristiani in El Salvador remains conditioned by the interests of the military and their capacity to govern "from alongside," as well as by the power of the Farabundo Marti National Liberation Front (FMLN) to disturb both village and urban life. Peace negotiations in El Salvador must therefore result in the establishment of a new social contract if they are to be successful.

An implied social contract is, indeed, often a precondition for democracy. The tragedy in so many parts of the developing world is that the practices of leaders with narrow bases of support are rarely such as to create an atmosphere of ordered and peaceful dissent. Even where formal democratic practices exist, the capacity of those outside power to frustrate sometimes entirelythe normal activity of elected governments makes of democracy a more than usually ineffective means of government. The power of provincial leaders in Pakistan, especially in the Punjab where the opposition Islami Jamhoori Ittehad (IJI) is especially strong, to obstruct policies developed by Prime Minister Benazir Bhutto was extremely high. The military was able to exert its effective veto over Pakistani politics when, on August 6, 1990, President Ghulam Ishaq Khan dismissed the Bhutto government, charging that it was corrupt and inefficient in its rule. The army's desire to have more policing powers in Sind and its general disapproval of the regime were, however, perhaps more important reasons for this action. The holding of elections following this constitutional coup d'état would not change the fact that the ritual of democracy may be more respected in Pakistan than its practice in the day-to-day life of the country.[7] Sometimes elections are held and the results are not even notionally respected by those who hold both official and coercive power. Following the election held in Myanmar in May 1990, the ruling military junta refused to hand over power. The leader of the victorious National League for Democracy, Aung San Suu Kyi, two months after the election was able to celebrate only completion of a full year under house arrest.

The need felt by many Third World leaders to defend institutional, sectarian, or ethnic interests makes difficult the creation of an atmosphere conducive to peaceful competitive politics. The frequent identification of ruling political parties with clans or sects, as in the cases of the Baathist regimes in Syria and Iraq, inhibits a development of loyalty to the state that is separable from loyalty to an ethnic group. There remain many presidential palaces in the developing world where the remark of former

President Habib Bourguiba of Tunisia—"What state? I am the state"—would be held in cynical high regard. The "weakness" of new states will for some time still be used as an excuse not to allow internal discussions that might "damage" national cohesion. The disorganizing effect of democratic practices will be the ultimate line of defense of the autocratic scoundrel. If the 1990s will see a greater spread of the democratic ideal, it remains the case that in most developing societies the establishment of political institutions and struggles for power will often take place simultaneously—and therefore awkwardly. Unfortunately, the opportunities will be rare, even for the best motivated of outside powers, to help build a national consensus for a peaceful yet competitive political process in the Third World without becoming embroiled in domestic rivalries.

NATIONAL COHESION
AND THE PRESSURES OF REGIONALISM

The high degree of autocratic control in developing states has often been justified—especially in the cases of those that emerged out of the post–World War II process of decolonization—by the need to "build nations." Nation-building, which has concentrated on forging a single identity and sense of purpose to present to the outside world, has not always been compatible with the aims of regional alliances or organizations. The fissiparous tendencies within many developing states and the new greater capacity of regional powers (given the likely unwillingness of the superpowers to involve themselves in Third World conflict that remains at low intensity) are impediments to regional cooperation. While, therefore, North America and the European Community (EC) are both engaged in and promoting the idea and the practice of a new form of bloc politics—regional economic and political integration—many regions in the world are still ill-prepared to engage in a new process of pactomania. Although many leaders in the developing world pay lip service to the idea of regional cooperation, largely in opposition to the perceived or actual interventionist policies of the great powers, the record of such cooperation is mediocre.

The high incidence of ethnic conflict, especially in Africa and Asia, means that the forces of secessionism still appear greater than those for integration. The ideology of national self-determination remains attractive and can find easy support among citizens of provinces or remote areas who are victims of uneven state development or of the success of a particular ethnic group with a firm grip on the central organs of power. The international relations of parochialism are also such that the strength of ethnic groups, either holding or dissenting from central power, can often rely on aid and succor from neighboring states.

Sometimes such groups are virtually created and almost entirely sustained by external powers, as in the cases of Iranian support for Hezbollah activists in Lebanon, or South Africa's links with Renamo in Mozambique. In other cases the links are less direct, and the objects of support are more evidently autonomous as in the examples provided by Ethiopian support for the Sudan People's Liberation Army (SPLA) in Sudan and for the Somali National Movement (SNM) in Somalia, or the putative assistance provided by Pakistan to Sikh extremists in India, or Indian help (often denied) to Sind separatists in Pakistan or to Chakmas in the Chittagong Hill Tracts in Bangladesh. These links, which tend to be more subtle than overt and heavy military assistance (such as China's aid to the Khmer Rouge in Cambodia), are no less complicating for regional security since they touch at the core of central state control over the population. Leaders in the Third World whose nation-building tasks are incomplete are bound to feel particularly threatened by such activity.

The potential nature of regional conflict in the future suggests that it may be easy for countries with narrow agendas to involve themselves in the disputes of neighboring states. Organized rebellion against state authorities by ethnic groups, secessionist movements, or drug lords acting in collaboration or through terrorists shows no signs of subsiding. Numerous states are bound openly to exploit the existence of rebel entities to advance their own external ambitions. Because direct military involvement by the superpowers is now less regularly anticipated, many leaders fear the "Lebanonization" of regional conflict. In early

1990 this fear came to be expressed most notably by leaders in the Horn of Africa because of the rise in Israeli support for Haile-Mariam Mengistu's Ethiopia (in order to help preserve the territorial integrity of the state and in return for greater emigration of Falashas) and the apparently greater interest of Arab states in supporting Eritrean secessionist groups. Whether such assistance, military and other, actually could materially affect the battles on the ground was less important than the political fear that the region was falling prey to regional influences at a time of superpower indifference to local events.

Against this continued trend of intraregional tension and prospective Lebanonization of conflict in some areas, it is important to gauge the countervailing desire for regional cooperation. The now long and basically successful history of the Association of Southeast Asian Nations (ASEAN) is often held up as an example, although the glue of a common Indochina policy may soon begin to wear thin. Few other regions display the potential for continuing amicable relations necessary to achieve the same level of consultation. The South Asian Association for Regional Cooperation (SAARC) explicitly excludes bilateral issues from its meetings. Indo-Pakistani tensions over Kashmir or Indian policy in Sri Lanka may be treated in "corridor meetings," but cannot receive general and official attention. Continental-sized groupings, such as the Organization of African Unity (OAU) or the Organization of American States (OAS) have rarely been able (for very different reasons) to mediate in subregional conflicts. Smaller groups may have a greater chance for limited success. Although, for example, the South African Development Coordination Conference (SADCC) has achieved some levels of economic integration among the member states in Southern Africa, interstate tension (as between Zimbabwe and Mozambique) can still be high, and the relevance of SADCC to the achievement of the Southwest Africa accords of 1988 was nil. The attempt by the Economic Community of West African States (ECOWAS) to provide a five-nation peacemaking force in Liberia in August 1990 only resulted in greater confusion, as more divisions became apparent among the rebel groups, and the neutrality of the peacekeepers questioned. A cease-fire was supposedly arrived at on September 22 after U.S. diplomatic intervention and was promptly put into doubt—proof that the subtleties of intense ethnic conflict can easily escape the management both of superpowers and local regional organizations.

During the 1980s and especially in 1989, the greatest surge of regional groupings took place in the Arab world, but none has had a preeminent role in managing regional stability. The Gulf Cooperation Council (GCC) did not craft the policy that led to the deployment of Western navies to the Gulf—Kuwait did—and was certainly divided about its consequences. The existence of the organization did not help to facilitate Western deployments: the United States and Western European states negotiated access rights on a bilateral basis. In August 1990 it took some time for the GCC states to agree on a policy to deal with Iraq's agression against a member state, and although all eventually took a common line it remains doubtful whether the GCC could operate efficiently as the principal local security organization. Any outside attempt to collaborate in the creation of a post-crisis stable balance of power (an extremely delicate business) would have to take into account a broader range of countries than those represented in the GCC. The creation in 1989 of the Arab Cooperation Council (ACC: Egypt, Jordan, Iraq, and Yemen) comprising states left out by other arrangements raised the hopes of some that a new organization could help better shape inter-Arab politics. This was all changed in August 1990, and although Jordan, Iraq, and Yemen may still be said to have a loose relationship with each other, the organization is all but dead. Most such arrangements in the increasingly disunited Arab world have only meant to serve narrow and sometimes fleeting politcal agendas of state leaders rather than to set up permanent security structures. The establishment in 1989 of the Union du Maghreb Arabe (UMA: Algeria, Morocco, Mauritania, Tunisia, and Libya) was made possible by Algerian-Moroccan rapprochement and may have a greater chance of survival. Through its goal of political and economic integration for the region it reduced the importance of the Polisario struggle for the western Sahara in regional relations. Its existence raises the political costs of major disputes between the member states because so much capital has been invested in the ideology of integration. Although this (like other regional alliances) may impose constraints on the activities of radical powers (Libya), it will not be able to prevent radical activity defined as necessary to the state.

Given this general record, one may be justified, therefore, in being cautiously pessimistic about the prospects in the 1990s of greater integration of the Central American economies and of those of Latin America as a whole, as proposed by Secretary of State James A. Baker III and President Bush in June 1990. Were the situation in Nicaragua to improve, and peace talks in El Salvador and Guatemala to bear fruit, greater integration of the Central American economies might be politically feasible. Yet most Central American states remain very concerned to protect limited export markets, and the transition to creating more complementary economies in the region will be difficult. Before June 1990, almost no official thought had gone into the prospects for integration in the capital cities of the region. Equally, the history of economic integration in South America is pretty sorry. While Argentina and Brazil continue to sign further trade agreements between themselves to which Uruguay has partially attached itself, each of these countries puts up barriers to trade whenever it feels the need. The experiences of the failed Andean Pact have left psychological traces. A former Uruguayan minister of industry and minister of foreign affairs opened a recent article on Latin American integration with the stark sentence: "I judge Latin American integration impossible."[8] Regional organizations still have a measure of attractiveness throughout the developing world, but the imperatives of national development, both political and economic, remain such as to override most projects for integration.

THE POLITICS OF INDEPENDENCE
AND EXTERNAL ASSISTANCE

The most ambitious Third World attempt at bloc politics, global nonalignment, is now being rendered almost irrelevant. This is so because of the reduced polarization of East-West affairs, which makes policies of political equidistance between the two superpowers more meaningless than ever, and because of the dramatic diversity of the so-called nonaligned states. Yet most Third World states remain jealous of their independence, and their leaders are sensitive to the need to balance good relations with the states or institutions that may give them financial and other assistance with the requirements of national independence and sovereignty. No state can remain permanently isolated (though some like Iran, Cuba, South Africa, and others try or may be forced to adopt near-autarkic policies) from the normal current of international economic activity. Few are likely to accept the degree of dependence chosen by the states of francophone Africa who belong to the franc zone and are reliant on France for economic, financial, and military assistance. Yet attempts by some of the poor states to protect themselves from an international economic order that moves too fast for them by instituting exchange controls, passing protectionist legislation, and placing restrictions on the free movement of persons may often harm prospects for needed investment or technical know-how. Such reactions to perceived vulnerability and penetrability so often lead to further isolation and deprivation.

This psychology of economic and financial protection in the name of national independence is being further tested because of the widespread fear that Western economic aid will be shifted from the South to the East. Throughout the latter part of 1989 and the first half of 1990, leaders from every region of the developing world showed themselves concerned by this as yet not established trend. Clearly, some U.S. assistance to Caribbean states has been reduced and some bilateral European aid to countries in the South has stagnated. U.S. aid to countries such as Panama and Nicaragua will probably go up, while EC aid to the Lomé group of countries showed a real increase in November 1989, and the EC in early 1990 promised increases to the Maghreb states. The aid environment is, however, much more competitive for those developing countries above the poverty threshold whose economies bear some similarity to those in Eastern Europe. These countries are now having to pass much more attractive investment legislation if they are to retain some prospect of foreign private investment. The poorer countries, more dependent on public aid, will in the current climate have to pass higher tests of good government and public accountability in order to receive economic aid. Even without the events of 1989, a buildup both of aid fatigue and aid cynicism within Western donor states would have made this necessary. Because of the Eastern European revolutions, the specificity of aid to the developing world has been lost. There are just too many *demandeurs,* and the interests of realpolitik, which in part govern assistance to the East, are greater than perceptions of North-South interdependence. All this will require domestic political and economic changes in the developing world in response to external pressure from donor states and institutions that a few years ago would have been dismissed as unwelcome interference.

This familiar tension between sovereignty and aid reliance is now compounded by the challenges to national economic decision-making arising from international concern over environmental exploitation and resource use. This exists at two levels: North-South and regional. On the North-South level, concern for environmental protection has produced tensions since moves by developing states to increase income (often to pay external debts) by rapid industrialization or resource exploitation has inspired the ire of northern states now more ostensibly concerned about global environmental issues. The most obvious case of this is Brazil's deforestation of the Amazon, which aside from disturbing Indian populations is also said to contribute to the greenhouse effect. Specific proposals of "debt for nature swaps" notwithstanding, there is still considerable progress to be made in delineating adequate codes of conduct on the environment that do not so impinge on the national sovereignty of developing states that they make economic advances impossible to achieve or inspire emotional rejection of all environmental safeguards.

More significant for regional security is the tension over use of resources within specific regions. Access to the Kuwaiti oil fields and to the money this would bring inspired Saddam Hussein's actions against the al-Sabah ruling family, but in the long term other resources are equally important. Water use in the Middle East raises one of the more acute examples of the relationship between national economic strategy and international stability. Certainly the pressure to exploit agricultural lands, particularly in the face of accelerating population growth, means that water is bound to become a more obvious element in regional relations. Since sources of water cross boundaries, there can be few water exploitation policies whose effects are neutral on neighbors. For example, construction of the Ataturk dam in the Turkish section of the Euphrates River affects the downstream exploitation of water by the Iraqis and the Syrians. Closure of the dam for thirty days in January 1990 created a crisis between Turkey and the other two states. Tripartite negotiations over this problem have rarely been satisfactory. Israel has diverted water from the Litani River that crosses southern Lebanon, thus reducing the amount of water available to Lebanese farmers. Israeli dependence on water from the Golan Heights and the West Bank remains high. While the water tables in the West Bank are declining and the Palestinian population increasing, Israeli authorities have allowed Palestinians in the territories to consume only at 1967 levels. Egypt depends on the Nile for some 95 percent of its water resources, but water flow to Egypt is dependent on consumption in Uganda, Sudan and Ethiopia. In the last eighteen months, Egyptian interest in regional cooperation in the Nile Valley has increased as Egypt has come to realize potential vulnerability. If Egypt were to insist on a strategy of food self-sufficiency, its water problem would be aggravated and its relations with Ethiopia, whose cooperation on water management issues has been inconsistent, would decline.[9]

Analogous international rivalries have been exacerbated by issues concerning resources (primarily forest use) in South and Southeast Asia. The fact that in many parts of the developing world economic futures are determined by the successful management of natural resources points to the significance of sound environmental policies for strategic stability. The natural or induced decay or destruction of the resources on which economic stability rests, or around which international attention focuses, can therefore intensify existing conflict and create the conditions for new rivalries.

THE MILITARY IMPERATIVE AND NONMILITARY THREATS TO SECURITY

The fact that in July 1990 Iraq chose to deploy troops on its frontier with Kuwait in protest at Kuwait's breach of OPEC production quotas, and the fact that Arab states later met to agree on a higher oil price to defuse the crisis, point to the obvious coercive value of military power to ensure fair use and distribution of resources. Iraq's later attack on Kuwait demonstrated yet again that the military choice is still live and that imbalances of power offer temptations to unsavory leaders who believe that might makes right. Although the sources of instability are rooted in the history of state structures, the exacerbating effect of economic and environmental factors, and the complexity of regional relationships, they are naturally aggravated by the persistence of the military solution as the ultimate option of state leaders and their internal or external opponents. Even the poorest states in the developing world have, through their arms acquisition programs, entered the modern world with vigor. Ethiopia, by some measures the poorest country in Africa, has the continent's largest standing army with over 300,000 men under arms. Three of the other poorest African countries, Sudan, Chad, and Mozambique have nevertheless sought to maintain the ability to conduct armed conflict. In these and other poor countries of the Third World affected by civil conflict, war has become politics by other means; government has become the management of conflict; opposition has meant insurgency; and guerilla activities have become a life-style.

In some of the world's poorest areas of conflict combatants have been insulated, often by the generosity of the international community, from the consequences of their actions. Throughout much of the recent fighting in Ethiopia, for example, the West has provided considerable food aid to alleviate great famines. Such aid has been used by the combatants in their conflicts with each other; convoys have been attacked by rebel groups; and the government for a time resisted allowing the use of the port of Massawa, in rebel hands in 1990, from being used by donors to deliver supplies. Throughout the Horn of Africa, refugee populations have been created by conflict, and the refugee camps established by the United Nations High Commissioner for Refugees are in many areas the main source of rudimentary housing as well as of food and water. Particularly in Somalia, refugee status is actively sought by internally displaced people. Refugee camps there (as in many other places), being areas of minimal infrastructure, have been the object of military attacks by opposition groups. The fact that combatants in many poor regions of the world do not, at least in terms of famine relief or refugee assistance, have to face the consequences of war is not an argument for slowing or cutting humanitarian aid to these areas, but it is a partial explanation for why military action remains an option in poor, embattled areas.

Richer states have sought to make great leaps forwards in their ability to produce and export arms for reasons of prestige, regional rivalry, and external markets. Brazil's medium-technology arms industry has made that country a leading actor in the South-South arms trade. More states appear close to crossing the nuclear threshold. They are doing so in South Asia, the Middle East, and Latin America in circumstances in which it is not clear that robust mutual deterrence structures that would make nuclear inventories stabilizing factors can be developed simultaneously with the rise in possession. The proliferation of chemical weapons and their actual use during the Iran-Iraq war points to how hard it is to bring new types of weapons within deterrence frameworks. Iraq's threat in 1990 to use chemical weapons if attacked by Israel borrows from the language of deterrence effectively deployed in Europe over the last forty years, but in the special context of the Middle East it is reasonable to be skeptical about the stabilizing effects of sophisticated weaponry. (In the autumn of 1990, people rightly wondered both in the United States and Europe whether the sale of further combat aircraft to Saudi Arabia might not in the long term be regretted. Especially in the Middle East, attempts by outside powers to construct and maintain balances of power, given the shifting bilateral and wider alliances of the region, hold great risks of leading to grief). The general spread of ballistic and cruise missile delivery systems indicates a growing capacity for over the horizon combat that may heighten regional perceptions of threat and raise the possibilities of preemption no matter what particular balance of power is eventually achieved in the area.

This general interstate proliferation of armaments and their delivery systems, which complicates both the prospects for arms control and for conflict management, is coupled to an active diffusion of intrastate armaments diffusion that heightens the internal opportunities for armed conflict. The sophisticated small-arms trade is such that guerrilla groups throughout the world are able to garner for themselves quite impressive inventories. The permeability of borders means that states close to conflict zones will find that arms circulate uncomfortably freely: the war in Afghanistan has meant that in Pakistan arms are easily available to various groups. In such situations the state loses one of its usual major attributes: monopoly control over armed force. The capacity of those who oppose state policies to translate this into armed opposition is becoming more pronounced. Where semifeudal political structures are married to the diffuse possession of arms, the chances of conflict is all the higher. This factor only increases the need that state leaders perceive for outside assistance and arms suppliers, just as it raises the level of tensions that can produce conflict.

Despite the growing understanding of, and emphasis on, the nonmilitary aspects of international security, states in the developing world in the 1990s are bound to be concerned still by the military component of power and influence. The opportunities will be rare for states to emulate Panama's action in early 1990: disband their armed forces and concentrate only on the awesome challenge of economic and social reconstruction. Expenditure on armaments will remain higher than justified by the level of national resources, and the incidence of conflict will remain greater than beleaguered peoples should be asked to tolerate. Regional powers will still seek the establishment or the maintenance of a regional security order that is consistent with long-held ambitions and the requirements of domestic security.

Except in the case of a very major conflagration, the great powers are unlikely to be perturbed by most regional conflict that takes place in the 1990s. The disengagement of the superpowers from most regional conflict and the elimination of their rivalry as an ordering principle of international relations mean that the global significance of local conflict in the Third World is much diminished. The local salience of traditional disputes may have increased, but their international importance is more difficult to measure. The condemnation of the international community of Iraq's attack on Kuwait may well serve to deter some from taking analogous action. By and large it will be rare that the outside world, and particularly the United States, is confronted with a case where the defense of international law and the interests of realpolitik coincide so happily. Civil wars throughout the world will not offer easy opportunities to invoke international law as a spur to action from outside, whereas much international conflict will not offer as clear evidence of the breach of law as was the case in the Gulf in 1990. Much regional conflict will remain at a sufficiently low intensity (from the perspective of outsiders, although not of the participants) to ensure, however sadly, the relative indifference of the international community. Few newspapers in the summer and early autumn of 1990 filled their front pages with the many continuing military conflicts in Third World areas outside the Persian Gulf.

CONCLUSION:
THE INCOHERENCE OF THIRD WORLD POLITICS AND INSECURITY

The fact that there is no coherent threat within or from the Third World limits the possibilities for establishing a grand strategy to deal with the instability of the developing states. Economic and technical assistance from North America, developed Europe, Japan, and Australasia is in demand from both the East and the South. Some of the principles that have (or should have) guided development assistance to the South are now relevant to the East. The developed powers will continue for reasons of humanitarian concern, and sometimes for reasons of realpolitik, to support allies and friends in the developing world, just as they encourage their new friends on the European continent. Diplomatic efforts will be made to resolve conflict, and military aid will be proffered to long-standing allies, and to others in instances where the transfer of military equipment or the granting of a precise guarantee is seen to have a powerful stabilizing effect. The reasons to do this will be more ad hoc than in the days where anticommunism provided an overarching rationale for much of Western military and diplomatic activity.

The tremendous reservoir of military power that exists in the United States, which planners will no doubt wish to make more rapidly deployable in the coming years, means that the United States will be capable of intervening abroad. Some countries may seek effectively to rent U.S. power (as Kuwait did when it asked for reflagging of its ships, or as Saudi Arabia did in August 1990) but the complexity of Third World insecurity is such that it is hard to imagine many instances where U.S. interests would be sufficiently at stake to sacrifice U.S. lives. One wonders whether an ambitious attempt to enforce international law, known to be honored more in the breach than in the observance, could have the sustained support of the U.S. people. Becoming the United Nations's policeman is unlikely to be an attractive option for U.S. presidents. Acceptance of the natural anarchy of international affairs may be unsatisfying, but it is easier, and therefore in the long term more tempting, than to give a blanket commitment to uphold the rule of law in all areas.

Given the ambiguities of Third World security, we must be cautious about falling prey to a "rent a threat" psychosis. Whatever the challenges to Western interests sometimes made by leaders of Muslim states, there is no Islamic threat against which one can easily deploy military resources. Fighting the drug problem, illegal migration, or nuclear, ballistic, and chemical proliferation are all appropriate ends of foreign policy, but they cannot form the foundations of that policy. In the absence of a general threat against which a coherent defense policy can be constructed, it may also be ill-advised to fashion too grand a mission or design that would govern foreign policy. The defense of international law is one such case, but so too is the promotion of democracy. The consolidation of democracy is a goal that, for example, the United States rightly gives itself in Europe and in Central America, but as the principal theme of its foreign policy throughout the world it would be unsustainable, not only for lack of resources, but because there will always be compelling reasons of realpolitik to put to one side considerations of the political structure of foreign states. This is precisely what happened when the United States and many other Western democratic states rightly decided to deploy force in defense of Saudi Arabia and to seek the eventual restoration of the Kuwaiti royal family to its throne.

That said, North Americans, as well as the people of Western Europe, now have a great opportunity to return to first principles (or to develop them) in their policies towards the Middle East, Africa, Asia, and Latin America. Development assistance, which will come to be seen more and more as an integral part of security policy, can be more directly aimed to ensure that democratic processes are respected where they exist and nurtured where they are nascent. The end of the Cold War, however, does not mean that a new Wilsonian order is upon us. Internal and international relations in the developing world are entering into a period of greater anarchy. While they muddle through in their bilateral relations with these states, the instinctive reaction of the world's large and developed powers should be more to stand by and watch rather than to become overly engaged in promoting specific regional security regimes. The United States or European states will not be able, especially in areas like the Middle East, to reshape and hold balances of power, without getting dangerously enmeshed in ever changing domestic and international politics. Regional security "systems" can help to attenuate conflict that is already structured (the East-West confrontation in Europe during the Cold War), but their attempted construction by outside powers in areas where political alliances shift regularly is both difficult and dangerous. In these circumstances the onus to create the local conditions for development and security will be, rightly and more than ever before, on the regions' leaders themselves. That will be a good thing.

NOTES

1. Speech recorded in the official daily newspaper *Haqiqat-i Engelab-i Sawr*, December 21, 1985, cited by Olivier Roy in *The Lessons of the Afghan War*, Adelphi Paper (London: Brassey's for International Institue for Strategic Studies [IISS], 1991, forthcoming).
2. Hamish Macdonald, "Back to Feudalism," *Far Eastern Economic Review*, 145 (July 13, 1989).
3. See David Menashri, "Iran: Doctrine and Reality," in Efraim Karsh, ed. *The Iran-Iraq War: Impact and Implications* (London: Macmillan; Tel Aviv: Jaffee Center for Strategic Studies, 1989), pp. 42–57.
4. Salamat Ali, "Hand of God," *Far Eastern Economic Review*, 149 (July 5, 1990), pp. 24–25.
5. See *Strategic Survey 1989–1990* (London: Brassey's for IISS, 1990), p. 63.
6. Victor Mallet, "Kuwaitis Step Up Demand for Democracy," *Financial Times* (London), January 16, 1990.
7. See Mahnaz Ispahani, *Pakistan: Dimensions of Insecurity*, Adelphi Paper No. 246 (London: Brassey's for IISS, 1989), for a still relevant discussion of Pakistan's security dilemmas.
8. Santiago Rompani, "La Integración Imposible: America Latina," *Revista Occidental* (Instituto de Investigaciones Culturales Latinoamericanas, Mexico) Vol. 7, No. 1 (1990), p. 11.
9. Tony Allen, "Water in the Arab Middle East: The Nile, Changing Expectations and Priorities," *Arab Affairs*, No. 8 (Winter 1988–89), pp. 50–51.

_____ **Appendix 7**

NEW SOURCES OF INSECURITY IN THE 1990s:
MANAGING THE INTERNATIONAL
ECONOMICS AGENDA

Theodore H. Moran

I

The list of international economic problems that may trouble policy-makers in the 1990s is long and diverse. What are the principal areas of concern for national security strategists, and how can the security objectives raised in these economic issues be achieved?

This paper surveys seven topics from the international economics agenda, which will inspire debate within the national security community. The first three (Encouraging Stability and Economic Reform in the Soviet Union; Maintaining a Cooperative U.S.–Japanese Relationship; Avoiding Vulnerabilities from the Globalization of America's Defense Industrial Base) pertain primarily to relations among the developed countries. The second four (Reducing Dependence on Oil from the Persian Gulf; Slowing Commercial Dispersion of a Post–Ballistic Missile Generation of Lethal Technologies in the Third World; Moderating the Impact on the Third World from Prolongation of the Debt Crisis; Dealing with Narcotics and Terrorism) cluster around a North-South axis. Clearly the list is not exhaustive; it could be lengthened without difficulty.

Several subjects that could be highlighted in purely economic terms, from the outcome of the multilateral trade negotiations, to the competitiveness of American industry, to the future of the U.S. budget deficit, weave their way in and out of the entire list. They surface here whenever they have particular salience for the national security community.

The objective in this paper is to provide a summary of the economic arguments that surround each of these seven contentious issues. The study offers a larger conclusion as well: one need not agree with every policy recommendation to see that in case after case the obstacle to achieving a satisfactory outcome springs not from some huge cost for an appropriate response but from the difficulty in mobilizing public support to make the rather small changes and forfeitures required for success. As a result, U.S. national security policy in the 1990s faces a challenge of a different order than during the Cold War period: not great sacrifices against clear and present dangers, but small sacrifices against dim and distant dangers. The array of threats to American well-being on today's horizon is no less real than in earlier periods and in some cases may turn out to be even more troublesome. Meeting these threats will require a new kind of leadership, leadership in the management of the mundane.

II

Before turning to this broader theme about economic policy and the evolving strategic concerns of the United States, it is important to look closely at each issue on its own terms.

Encouraging Stability and Economic Reform in the Soviet Union
Does the United States have an interest in joining with other countries to provide large-scale financial support to the Soviet Union as the country struggles to transform its economy?

The deterioration of the economy in the Soviet Union has been so precipitous that it has become fashionable for experts to vie with one another in exposing new weaknesses. In April 1990 the Central Intelligence Agency (CIA) calculated the Soviet gross national product (GNP) to be no more than half that of the United States.[1] Viktor Belking, a prominent economist from the Soviet

Academy of Sciences, promptly took advantage of *glasnost* to pronounce the CIA revisions too optimistic, asserting Soviet output was at most little more than one-quarter of the American GNP.[2] The combination of shortages, inflation (hitherto unheard of), and regional blockages has made it difficult to assess even the current rate of decline with any accuracy.

The question of whether the major capitalist powers should provide assistance to help stabilize, reform, and reconstruct the Soviet economy has taken on fiercely partisan overtones in the United States.[3] One side hopes such assistance might strengthen the effort to lead the Soviet Union in directions beneficial to the West. The other side fears such assistance might prop up a decaying authoritarian state and provide succor to its military establishment, which otherwise would disintegrate and disappear as a threat.

There are three economic arguments in favor of external assistance. There is one economic argument against it. Thus far the one against has carried the day.

The three economic arguments In favor of external assistance are: first, to supply the working capital, bridge financing, support for convertibility, and infrastructure development that are needed before domestic markets and foreign investment can begin to work on their own; second, to take advantage of economies of scale in a coordinated effort to address multiple problems simultaneously; third, to capture a unique opportunity to provide incentives to see that reforms stay on track. The objective would be to help buffer the transition in an ongoing semi-democratic context since the pain (higher prices, harder work, less job security, more unemployment) comes *before* the gain (greater investment, higher productivity, larger output).

The economic argument against external assistance is that the Soviet leadership has simply not yet made the firm decision in favor of transforming the economy to a market-based system. After all, the Soviet Union is not like the other countries of Eastern Europe: it has a low level of foreign debt ($48 billion); it has large gold reserves ($30 billion); it has vast resources available for development (American oil companies, for example, report a large inventory of already discovered fields lying idle for lack of capital and technology). In short the Soviet Union has the where-withal to undertake determined action on its own, yet the steps toward price reform, property leasing/property ownership, the expansion of private enterprise, and the loosening of labor markets have been, at least until the 500-Day Plan, halting and indecisive.[4] State ministries continue to exercise monopolistic power as buyers and sellers of goods. A plan to make the ruble convertible has yet to appear. In such a context, foreign assistance might well substitute for making tough domestic choices.

To be sure, the temporizing approach on the part of the Soviet authorities is quite understandable. Even the most sincere re-formers face the dilemma of whether to bet everything on em-barking down a risky and uncharted path, without a genuine mandate from the people to do so, and with dwindling popular support for the leadership itself.

In this context the question of offering a long-term program of external assistance as a catalyst for fundamental reforms is all the more fateful. On the one hand, the major industrial powers can simply watch internal dynamics play out in the Soviet Union with a high probability of further economic deterioration and no natural point of new equilibrium in sight. On the other hand, the major industrial powers could undertake a dramatic initiative when the moment was right, to lend vigor and direction to invariably worried reformers.[5]

The stakes are high. In economic terms a reinvigorization of the Soviet economy along market lines would add to European (and world) growth incalculably more than the resuscitation of Poland, for example, or Czechoslovakia, for which the industrial powers are willing to spend generous sums. Stagnation and decline in the Soviet economy, in contrast, will constitute a large drag on European prospects. Most ominous, of course, in po-litical terms, is the prospect that failure to integrate the Soviet Union into the Western economic order may mean that, instead of progress and further democratization, there is chaos, disinte-gration, and ultimately the return to a resentful and authoritarian Russian regime (still in control of awesome military assets). There could then indeed be serious concern that "decaying superpowers do not go quietly into the night."[6]

The evolution of the Soviet Union into a stable market-based confederation of republics with growing economic links to the industrial democracies would be a feat worthy of comparison with the original Marshall Plan. Like the revival of Europe after the Second World War, it will depend primarily on courageous decisions taken internally under highly uncertain circumstances. A successful outcome will almost certainly require external assistance of Marshall Plan dimensions as well, for support and reassurance. Some of the assistance may be wasted or used inefficiently; if the effort is carried out piecemeal, like the German credits for consumer goods, the likelihood of a dissipated and counterproductive impact is high.[7] For fundamental reform to work, there will have to be major program of economic conversion and reconstruction lasting over an extended period of years, preferably in the form of loans under International Monetary Fund (IMF)–World Bank auspices. Ultimately, of course, the effort may fail. But historians, looking back at the decade of the 1990s, will be astounded if the opportunity is allowed to pass by with no attempt to seize it.

Some kinds of small-scale aid might be particularly effective, e.g., support for infrastructure projects at the municipal or republic level, as Arnold Horelick has suggested, to lend credibility to local efforts at reform, thereby avoiding the criticism that foreign aid encourages foot-dragging. Technical assistance would also help. These will provide scant relief if the underlying economy is simply disintegrating. On the other hand, the original Marshall Plan would cost no more than $84 billion in 1990 dollars, only one-fifth of which would be borne by the United States (in proportion to its IMF–World Bank share) or approximately one-tenth the net present cost of the S&L bailout. One major element of an economic reconversion package, a large stabilization loan to backstop the convertibility of the ruble, does not need to involve the actual expenditure of foreign funds at all if the shift to convertibility is successful. Once convertibility is achieved the expansion of foreign investment and trade will be much easier; without it, the expectation that foreign investment and trade will lead the process of restoring stability and growth to the Soviet economy is implausible.[8]

For the idea of assisting the reconversion of the Soviet economy to be adopted, however, American leaders will have to persuade the public why such resources are better devoted to the Soviet Union than to competing causes (worthy causes) at home. That will be no easy task.

Maintaining a Cooperative U.S.–Japanese Relationship

With national security interests as well as economic interests in mind, how should the United States approach the U.S.–Japanese relationship (tougher or softer, more hard-line or more accommodationist) in the 1990s?

The growth in Japan's share of global GNP, from 5 percent in 1950 to 16 percent in 1990, represents the most rapid peace time shift in relative economic status in the history of the world. Such explosive movement on the part of a single nation would cause substantial dislocation to other nations, even if the expansion were entirely due to fair, legitimate practices such as longer work hours, higher productivity, and more attention to quality. Helping to fuel the resentment at having to adjust, of course, is the fact that Japanese success is due in part to unfair, illegitimate practices, in particular, a history of protecting the local market from imports and promoting certain sectors for export-led growth. Overall Japan has a much smaller import penetration ratio in manufacturing than any other Organization for Economic Cooperation and Development (OECD) country (one-third to one-tenth as large), and of those goods it does import almost 60 percent come from its own firms (in contrast to 9 percent of U.S. imports from U.S. firms).[9]

The persistence of a large bilateral trade deficit with Japan has led to proposals that the United States shift to a tougher posture, demanding reciprocity in access between the two markets and threatening exclusion of Japanese products to the extent equal access is not reached. The argument on behalf of this approach extends beyond mere Japan bashing; the contention is that only a "results oriented" approach will reduce the trade imbalance with a partner for which the abstract exhortation to "open markets" has no meaning.[10]

From an economic point of view, the difficulty with this approach is that all of the Japanese unfair trade practices taken together block no more than $8–15 billion in lost sales whereas the recurrent bilateral trade deficit runs to $40–50 billion.[11] The fundamental cause of the disequilibrium lies in the disparity between savings and consumption in the two countries; that is, the United States consumes more than it produces and does not save enough to build the additional productive capacity to make up for the difference, leading to a trade deficit to supply excess American consumption, and inflows of foreign capital to make up for insufficient American savings. In this unbalanced setting even the most aggressive (and, let one hypothesize, successful) market-opening demands on the part of the United States will leave the largest part of the problem untouched, unless there is a simultaneous change in underlying U.S. behavior toward savings and consumption (including public consumption as embodied in the federal deficit).[12] Threatening Japan with dire consequences if the bilateral trade balance does not improve simply cannot produce the desired results in the absence of a fundamental commitment to address America's own macroeconomic misalignment at the same time.

From a political point of view, the problem with the hard-line stance is that it is likely to fuel further internal resentment in Japan without producing relief. The combination of a growing domestic anti-Americanism and a changing geostrategic environment in which the need for the U.S. nuclear umbrella is disappearing renders it no longer implausible that the United States might push Japan "too far," so as to fracture the U.S.–Japanese alliance, especially if the finger pointing is regularly used to divert attention from America's share of responsibility for the problem. At the extreme, maverick positions like those of Ishihara Shintaro and Morita Akio, who argue that Japan should play a more forceful role in the international arena by "saying no' to America,"[13] or others who urge the exploration of fundamentally new political-economic relationships for Japan, could become more mainstream in Japanese politics.

Should one conclude, therefore, that a more benign stance is appropriate for U.S. policy-makers, accepting a slower pace of liberalization in Japanese markets and greater toleration for American macroeconomic disparities in the consumption/savings ratio? Those who argue in the affirmative note that changes in Japanese consumer behavior combined with the evolving demography of the Japanese population will ultimately reequilibrate the U.S.–Japanese economic relationship without the need for radical alterations in either country's policies.[14] In the long run, the greater proportion of older Japanese retirees (who consume more) in relation to younger workers (who save more), accompanied by changes in spending habits on the part of individuals, will move the Japanese economy naturally toward greater consumption and less savings/investment.

The problem with this accommodationist approach is that the long run is likely to be too long. The demographic shift in Japan will have its major impact well after the year 2000. In the meantime the competitive position of American industry could undergo a genuinely serious weakening. The lower savings rate in the United States raises the cost of capital to American firms sufficiently to double or triple the cost of long-term investment projects in comparison with their Japanese rivals, and demands a payback period roughly twice as quick (six years for American firms versus more than ten for the Japanese with European companies in between). The higher cost of capital in fact goes a long way toward explaining the infamous short time horizons of American managers: it suggests the relatively myopic planning calculations of U.S. corporations will not change fundamentally until the cost of capital declines no matter what happens to capital gains taxes, Wall Street influences, leveraged buyouts, MBA curricula, and the like. Overall the savings/consumption imbalance in the United States constitutes a drag on American competitiveness far greater than trade barriers abroad. Meanwhile the savings/investment gap is being filled with foreign investment from abroad. Should the buildup of net dollar surpluses abroad and the corresponding conversion into dollar assets in the United States continue until demographic trends in Japan and elsewhere right the balance, the cumulative acquisition of American businesses when combined with the weakening of those which remain in American

hands could reach proportions that have real security consequences for the United States (35 percent of the capital
stock), unlike the more manageable levels of foreign investment
today (5 percent).[15]

(The same argument about improving the home-country
macroeconomic setting from which American firms can compete
with their rivals abroad holds for Europe 1992 as well as for
Japan. For a more detailed analysis of vulnerabilities of the
defense industrial base in America, see the next section.)

The national security community therefore faces the task of
preventing the political process from tilting too far in either
direction, toward Japan bashing at one extreme or toward toleration of ongoing economic imbalances at the other. Instead, the
goal of preserving a close U.S.–Japanese political relationship
requires a delicate balance of maintaining well-justified pressure
against Japan's unfair trade practices while addressing (rather
than avoiding) American responsibility for the fundamental
economic misalignment.

Avoiding Vulnerabilities from the Globalization of America's Defense Industrial Base

*Does the globalization of the defense industrial base in the United
States pose an authentic threat to U.S. security in an era in which
traditional preoccupations about wartime mobilization and the blockage of sea lanes are disappearing?*

The question of how to manage the extraordinary economic
success of Japan (above) introduces a further dimension of
concern for national security analysts, which is not limited to
Japan itself: namely, how to deal with a world in which technological prowess and production sites for goods and services vital
for the U.S. economy are spread more broadly across the globe
than in the past.[16]

The Department of Defense has reported that the lead in one-
quarter of the technologies most essential to American industry
is held by non–U.S. firms, and a growing proportion of the
products and components needed for defense come from abroad
(a proportion whose exact dimensions could not even be measured by the DoD).[17]

One the one hand, international flows of products, technologies, and capital carry great benefits. They bring superior performance, innovation, and lower prices for military as well as commercial purchasers. This is the aspect of globalization that traditional economic analysis tends to emphasize, celebrating the benefits of comparative advantage and dismissing concerns about the nationality of supplier firms or the location of production sites.

On the other hand, globalization does pose real threats, threats which could become more prominent, not less, as the Cold War recedes. A survey of post–World War II experience suggests that external domination of technology, goods, and services may well lead to persistent attempts at meddling, manipulation, and harassment in the recipients' sovereign affairs even in peacetime relations among allies.[18] Such interference has ranged from denial of computer technology to inhibit Charles de Gaulle's *force de frappe*, to insistence on permission to reexport products, which incorporate foreign inputs to designated areas (mainland China, Cuba, Arab states), to retroactive cancellation of licensing agreements (the Soviet gas pipeline case). Since the United States has frequently enjoyed the position of "manipulator" in the past, it has largely ignored the prospect of being the "manipulee," until now. The possibility of having the strings of globalization pulled in the future by Japan's Socialists, or Britain's Labour, or Germany's Greens is unsettling. Foreign dependence for key technologies or crucial components may have an unexpectedly high political price in an era in which Cold War solidarity could give way to partisan gestures on international issues.[19] Hence there is a legitimate concern about American vulnerability as local industries crucial to defense are "wiped out," or high-tech firms are acquired by foreigners.

One response has been to urge the United States to turn in a neo-mercantilistic direction itself, protecting its own "industrial base" (as America has already done with steel, machine tools, even textiles), devising an industrial policy to support its "own" national champions (Sematech, the Semiconductor Agreement, a civilian Defense Advanced Research Projects Agency [DARPA]), blocking foreign takeovers (Fairchild, Perkin Elmer), and requiring the U.S. government to "buy American" (ball bearings, machine tools).

The neo-mercantilistic response saddles American users of steel or machine tools or semiconductors with high cost inputs, and reduces their competitiveness even further vis-à-vis foreign rivals (a 25 percent cost disadvantage for steel users, a 50 percent cost disadvantage for semiconductor users who produce high-tech products). Moreover, there is no evidence the U.S. government can pick "winners" for public support appropriately, or ensure that political forces do not divert such support to "losers" instead.

How should the United States cope with this dilemma? What can be done to maximize the benefits of globalization (efficiency, competition, innovation) and minimize the costs (foreign interference, loss of autonomy)?

In all of the cases of external interference, there has been a genuine threat from foreign dependence only when there is a concentration of external suppliers of technology, products, or inputs. When sources of supply have been dispersed internationally, there has been no ability to control, to delay, or to deny, and hence no real peacetime threat. As a rule of thumb, when there are more than four foreign companies or four foreign nations supplying more than fifty percent of the world market, they lack the ability to collude effectively even if they wish to exploit or manipulate recipients. This provides a useful guide for designing U.S. policies to cope with globalization in a period in which the blockage of sea-lanes is vanishing. For American industries that are being "wiped out" by imports, those in which the sources of external supply are concentrated *do* represent a source of concern and should be eligible for legitimate "national security" trade protection; those in which the sources of external supply are deconcentrated *do not*. By the concentration test, semiconductor equipment manufacturers would qualify for national security protection, textiles and footwear manufacturers would not. (Soldiers do wear uniforms and march in boots, as proponents of protection for textiles and footwear point out, but the sources of supply are widely dispersed worldwide and short-term requirements can be easily stockpiled.) Similarly, within an industry, subcategories of high performance machine tools might be concentrated enough to justify protection, but measures to restrict imports of standardized cutters and grinders, which have multiple suppliers, would not be justified. This would provide for legitimate American security interests without incurring the costs of blanket protectionism.[20]

For American firms that were targets for foreign acquisition, the degree of concentration in the world industry again provides the relevant screening device. If there are multiple external suppliers, the acquisition should be allowed to proceed by the CFIUS (the Committee on Foreign Investment in the United States, given new status by the Exon-Florio Amendment to the 1988 trade legislation) even though the target firm might be the last American entrant. If there are concentrated external suppliers, the acquisition should be blocked by CFIUS and the U.S. parent granted national security protection if need be (e.g., Perkin Elmer's advanced lithography unit for semiconductor fabrication, sought by Nikon in an industry with very few producers).

This approach identifies the threat from dependence on foreign companies or dependence on foreign production sites as a problem of concentration, and limits public policy concern to those situations in which there is a potential for external control, allowing trade and investment flows to proceed unhindered in all cases where suppliers are dispersed. The security objective of maximizing efficiency and innovation in vital national industries while avoiding foreign dependence requires channeling popular protectionist and neo-mercantilist instincts into those narrow areas in which foreign domination actually poses a genuine threat.

Reducing Dependence On Oil from the Persian Gulf
How can the United States utilize the reaction to the confrontation with Iraq to avoid even more severe energy shortages in the future?

The Iraqi invasion of Kuwait has reawakened public consciousness to the extent of American dependence on imported oil. The restoration of stability in the Gulf will provide only temporary relief, however, to the looming prospect of energy crises in the 1990s. In the absence of policy changes the United States is likely to be importing between 54 percent and 62 percent of the oil it consumes by the end of the 1990s, with the foreign sources growing to more than two-thirds of U.S. consumption after the year 2000.[21] The previous historical high for import dependence was 47 percent in 1977; the figure for 1973 when the first oil crisis struck was 35 percent.

The price projections that accompany this growing dependence on imported oil vary widely, by more than 60 percent, due to uncertainties about Organization of Petroleum Exporting Countries (OPEC) cohesion and OPEC strategy. (Imprudent producer strategy in the 1980s nearly destroyed the cartel.) What is less uncertain is that the production volumes demanded from OPEC will rise substantially (from 22 to 39 percent greater than today by the year 2000), with increasing concentration in the Persian Gulf plus Libya. The expansion of output from Saudi Arabia, the United Arab Emirates, and Venezuela in response to the blockade of Iraq and Kuwait in fact has revealed the narrow availability of excess capacity. By the mid-to-late 1990s the number of major OPEC exporters will have shrunk, with Gabon, Ecuador, Algeria, and even Indonesia and Nigeria consuming domestically much of what they produce. Since 1985, 90 percent of the increases in world oil production have come from the Persian Gulf, a trend that will continue in the 1990s as non-OPEC countries plateau.

Adding to the energy vulnerability of the United States in the 1990s is the dilemma faced by electrical utilities as they seek to build the next generation of power facilities. In the 1970s and 1980s electrical utility capacity was in oversupply, leading to low rates of new construction. In the early 1990s electricity demand is overtaking production capacity at the very moment when there is strong opposition to the two principal sources of base load output, coal and nuclear power. As a result, utilities are choosing to install combined-cycle and turbine units, which rely on natural gas or fuel oil. In 1989, the use of imported oil as a utility fuel rose by more than thirty percent. This adds to the demand for petroleum used by the transportation sector.

As the Iraq-Kuwait crisis revealed, the United States and other industrial democracies are, in one respect, better off than they were during the oil crises of 1973 or 1979. Under the International Energy Agency agreement, the United States now has oil stored in the Strategic Petroleum Reserve (SPR) nearly sufficient to equal ninety days' net oil imports (current); Japan and Germany also have substantial reserves. Over time the SPR can be expanded in the United States and abroad, and rules for dispersion and sharing strengthened.

In general, however, the prospects for energy vulnerability are growing ever more worrisome. As the next section points out, the expansion of indigenous military capabilities for semi-precise theater bombardment could have enormous consequences in the demonstratedly volatile environment of the Persian Gulf. A renewed outbreak of violence among the states of the Gulf, perhaps combined with domestic tensions within the Gulf states themselves, could come to have a genuinely devastating impact on the international economy.

In this context, any policy recommendation for reducing energy vulnerability would have to combine conservation with the promotion of domestic sources of supply (especially for electricity). For conservation, the most efficient approach is to continue to raise energy taxes, which are still far lower in the United States than elsewhere (averaging 32¢ per gallon of gasoline versus $1.20 to $3.00 per gallon in Europe and Japan).[22] Energy taxes are appealing in revenue terms; each 10¢ increase in gasoline taxes, for example, generates approximately $6 billion in government receipts. For environmental reasons (global warming, acid rain), some analysts recommend a more general carbon tax and a turn away from coal. For promotion of domestic sources of supply, solar energy has long-term appeal, but nuclear power offers the only realistic alternative to coal for the next generation of utilities.

Both options have strong domestic opposition. A gasoline tax discriminates against farmers, truckers, and other heavy users. Any energy tax weighs disproportionately on the poor, although much of the regressive incidence could be offset by appropriate social policies. Nuclear power raises concerns about reactor safety and waste disposal.

Nevertheless difficult choices about substantially higher energy taxes and the resumption of nuclear plant construction are unavoidable if the United States is to decelerate the rate of growth of imported oil to a more moderate pace from the current headlong rush.

Slowing Commercial Dispersion of a Post–Ballistic Missile Generation of Lethal Technologies in the Third World

Are there further generations of military technology, following on the wave of ballistic missile proliferation with chemical/nuclear warheads that the world has witnessed in the Persian Gulf, which might intensify the severity of regional crises in the Third World?

The answer is not encouraging. In the not too distant future, the unimpeded spread of dual-use technologies could lead to a new delivery-system "package" in some ways even more worrisome than ballistic missiles.[23] The package consists of two parts: first, relatively inexpensive drone airplanes, constructed with low-observable simple composite materials (e.g., fiberglass) built around increasingly efficient turbofan engines, which are currently available from American, European, Indian, and Brazilian sources; second, a growing availability of in-flight navigational updating from multiple commercial sources (U.S., Soviet, French, Chinese, Japanese, Brazilian, and Israeli satellites with Sony or Motorola or Hughes communication downlinks).

Combined, this package creates a "poor man's cruise missile," which, by the mid-to-late 1990s will compete with ballistic missiles as delivery vehicles, providing a burgeoning number of Third World countries with an ability for quasi-precise theater bombardment (30 meter CEP over 500–1,000 km), without the considerable cost of maintaining a fleet of high performance airplanes and pilots. Deployable in large numbers, with semi-stealthy flight characteristics, these vehicles will be capable of carrying chemical or ultrahigh-explosive fuel-aerosol warheads. (They will not, of course, have the terrain-hugging conformal flight patterns of advanced cruise missiles.)

The presence of these delivery vehicles will exacerbate the problem of supplier competition outlined in the earlier

Aspen studies, making control over ballistic missile technology even more difficult.[24] Altogether, the evolution of technological capabilities will magnify the destructiveness of regional military conflicts when they occur; raise the probability of occurrence during periods of crisis, given the advantages to each side of preempting the other and the severe risks of waiting to see whether the other side will itself preempt; and make intervention by major powers much more costly and risky.

In the Middle East and the Persian Gulf, the barrage capabilities from this technological evolution take on particularly frightening dimensions. The decade of the 1990s may see areas of the Middle East (Israel, Syria, Iraq, Iran, Jordan, and staging areas in Lebanon) become the first post–Cold War site for a quasi-nuclear balance of terror, with Arab chemical and ultrahigh-explosive area weapons (gasoline airburst) countering Israeli nuclear bombs. Like the disquieting postures of the United States and the Soviets in the 1950s, the relative primitiveness of the retaliatory systems could deteriorate quickly in a crisis, leading to counter-city attacks. Adding to the instability, there could also be a race on the part of outside powers to provide increasingly sophisticated anti-air systems and technologies, a race with unfavorable proliferation consequences of its own.

The policy alternatives for managing this technological evolution have powerful domestic constituencies arrayed against them. On the one hand, the United States and the other industrial powers could reintroduce export controls on sensitive dual-use technologies (far more comprehensive than the nuclear constraint regime), arousing the ire of the international business community, which is just celebrating the relaxation of COCOM restrictions. On the other hand, the United States and the other industrial powers could accept a dwindling ability to control exports and turn to building theater-deterrent structures (with common surveillance and nonpreemptible forces) to provide neo-MAD (mutual assured destruction) stability as cities in a region become exposed to weapons of mass destruction. While beneficial to all sides, this would hardly be popular with pro-Israeli electorates.

Moderating the Impact on the Third World from Prolongation of the Debt Crisis

Is the Brady Plan dealing adequately with the LDC debt problem, or will the national security community want to back more forceful measures?

With the exception of East Asia, the Third World is just ending a "lost decade" in which the attempt to pay off foreign loans with a net capital outflow of $20 billion per year from South to North has reduced per capita living standards thus far by more than ten percent in real terms below 1979 levels, producing a social setback already greater than the Great Depression of the 1930s.[25]

Any analysis of the causes of the debt crisis bestows an abundance of blame on all parties. Public and private borrowers sought, and commercial banks provided, funding for many dubious projects in the late 1970s. Then, the dramatic rise in U.S. interest rates from 9 percent to 19 percent (1978–1981), followed by recession in the developed countries and the consequent collapse of commodity prices, left both less developed countries (LDC) borrowers and the bank creditors unexpectedly overextended. The interest expense to Argentina, Brazil, and Mexico, for example, tripled while the terms of trade dropped by almost 10 percent.

A preoccupation with past responsibility begs the question of what may happen if most of these countries head into a second "lost decade" without much better prospects. Reacting to the onset of the debt crisis, the Baker Plan placed initial priority on maintaining the viability of the international financial system by ensuring the health of the commercial banks themselves. The Brady Plan has for the first time permitted discussion of the concept of debt relief for the LDC borrowers. The Brady Plan combines a U.S. Treasury bond guarantee for the principal of new discounted bonds plus IMF–World Bank guarantees for interest payments, in return for domestic policy reforms in the debtor countries. It has been expanded in 1990 to include the possibility of relief on debt owed to governments as well as commercial banks ($12 billion versus $200 billion in the case of U.S. official debt toward Latin America).

For the American national security community the case of Mexico has perhaps greatest salience. The United States welcomed the inauguration of President Carlos Salinas de Gotari, whose administration had more coherence and ideological commitment to market forces than at anytime in the past quarter century. Mexico, consequently, became the showcase for the Brady Plan. But at the end of long negotiations relying on voluntary participation by the banks, the magnitude of the relief in fact turned out to be quite small (approximately 35 percent in comparison with discounts on Mexican loans in the secondary market of 50–70 percent prior to the Brady Plan).[26] The outcome raises doubts about the utility of allocating scarce public resources to a program that fails to reduce the debt burden sufficiently to "jump start" the economy.

One alternative might be to press for greater debt relief under IMF auspices in return for sensible domestic policies without permitting commercial bank cooperation to be merely voluntary. But, to a certain extent, this option has been overtaken by the guarantee features of the Brady Plan, at least in the Mexican case. The new U.S. Treasury–backed bonds embodying the 35 percent reduction are designed explicitly for broad resale by the commercial banks, rendering impractical subsequent renegotiation with widely dispersed creditors. Likewise the stream of interest payments supported with IMF set-asides cannot be reduced without simply transferring the burden of payment onto the International Monetary Fund and the World Bank. The modest outcome of the Brady Plan in the Mexican case may thus be permanently locked in. Looking to the future, for Mexico to regain its economic momentum requires more favorable economic conditions stretching throughout the 1990s than have yet been achieved (for Latin America to "grow out" of the debt crisis, the IMF estimates baseline economic expansion must average 5.5 percent per year through the late 1990s in place of the current 2.0 percent).[27] Adding to the growing pessimism is evidence that the potential boost, which could come with the repatriation of "flight capital," is not likely to appear simply with the introduction of favorable policy changes (since many are by now already in place), but only with the appearance of growth-induced profits themselves, creating Catch-22 for the prospects of sustained economic growth.

Magnifying the importance of the outcome, Mexico is undergoing a significant political transformation, which could result in a robust pluralism, a divisive polarization, renewed authoritarianism, and even internal upheaval. The evolution of the political drama inside Mexico will have a large impact on migration as well as trade and investment across the border. (See also the next section on narcotics and terrorism.)

For other countries like Brazil and Argentina (there are thirty-six remaining countries eligible for the Brady Plan), postponement of debt repayment is taking place de facto, if only because their dire straits do not permit a Brady Plan negotiation of Mexican dimensions. The outcome is turning out to be the worst of all worlds, however–a slow-motion slide toward bankruptcy without the "new start" that actual bankruptcy proceedings afford.[28]

The very "success" of the Brady Plan, providing strong guarantees but only small debt relief, shifts the burden for turning around the LDC economies to the other side of the equation, trying to solve the debt problem via the expansion of trade. Here the outcome rides to a great extent on the results of the Uruguay Round of multilateral trade negotiations. The key market-opening initiatives for the Third World, with special importance for Mexico, Central America, and the Caribbean as well as the rest of Latin America, involving textiles and apparel, leather goods, footwear, ceramics, sugar, fruits and vegetables, and other agricultural products, are highly sensitive. They may be politically palatable for the developed countries only in a context that simultaneously includes breakthroughs on the issues of most benefit to the developed countries, like services, intellectual property, and unfair trade practices. In short, the Uruguay Round will have to be a major triumph to touch those areas of most importance to the Third World.

(An alternative to a successful multilateral outcome in the Uruguay Round might be the vigorous pursuit of a free trade agreement with Mexico. To have an equivalent economic benefit for Mexico, the price paid by the United States in politically sensitive labor-intensive industries would have to be significantly greater in a bilateral arrangement than in a multilateral one since there would be many fewer compensating gains than with liberalization on a global basis.[29] Higher oil prices will boost Mexico's growth prospects, but slower economic expansion [or recession] elsewhere will lower demand for Mexican exports and stiffen resistance to trade liberalization. Extending the free trade idea to all of Latin America, as the Bush Administration has proposed, would attenuate the benefit for Mexico, and still be more costly to the United States and less beneficial to the recipients than the multilateral approach.)

This analysis suggests that national policy-makers will not be able to relax their geopolitical concern about the economic and political fate of the Third World, especially to the south of the border, as Cold War U.S.–Soviet rivalries diminish. Instead they will have to develop new visions of mutually beneficial economic engagement. persuasive enough to overcome short-sighted opposition from workers, bankers, and taxpayers.

Dealing with Narcotics and Terrorism

Will national security considerations demand a radical (economic) solution to the problem of narcotics and terrorism?

Favorable outcomes on several of the issues examined earlier could significantly reduce the prospects for international terrorism: prosperity and stability in the Soviet republics, Eastern Europe, and Latin America, for example, would remove many of the causes and much of the support system for violence-prone groups in large portions of the world. Unfavorable outcomes, in contrast, could lead to the proliferation of disaffected subnational communities, and generate new connections among terrorists around the globe. In this latter setting, narcotics traffic may become the successor to the Cold War in providing resources to sustain worldwide terrorist activity.

To deal with the growing dimensions of the drug trade, George Shultz and Milton Friedman have articulated the starting point of most economists when faced with cartel power, namely, to propose decriminalization as a means to eliminate the basis by which the cartel extracts oligopoly rents.[31] An approach thattreats narcotics use fundamentally as a medical problem, Shultz and Friedman have argued, would undermine the ability of producers and traffickers to reap such high profits and eliminate the incentive for pushers to "get kids addicted so that they can create a market for themselves."

Analysis subsequent to the recommendation for decriminalization has suggested that the consequences, especially in the case of crack cocaine, are more complicated than the proponents of decriminalization first envisioned.[32] The outcome might be not merely a semipermanent underclass of addicts, but a form of addiction that leads to particularly destructive paranoid behavior (in the case of crack cocaine) unless a methadone-like substitute for the latter can be developed.

On the other hand, the profitability of the current system is so great that even dramatically improved success in supply-side enforcement (interdiction of production and distribution) will only marginally offset the incentive for generating new sources. The prospect of providing alternative economic opportunities to woo Peruvian, Colombian, Bolivian, and (all) other peasants away from coca production appears dim when one considers that drugs have come to be the largest cash crop of California's rich, fertile, and irrigated agricultural regions where alternative opportunities are abundant. It is not implausible, therefore, that narcotics traffic could proceed in its growth to nation-state-threatening dimensions, unless the current system of oligopoly pricing is eliminated.

To prevent this from happening, political leaders may have to develop a national security rationale on the sensitive question of drug policy to tilt the debate in the direction of decriminalization.

III

This paper has surveyed topics from the field of international economics that will gain increasing prominence on the national security agenda as the Cold War recedes. Each carries its own policy alternatives, and preferred outcomes. In working through the policy alternatives and preferred outcomes, certain economic themes appear and reappear at multiple points of keen importance to national security strategists.

Continued improvement in the *budget deficit*, for example, is desirable in economic terms because it will help restore the balance between savings and consumption and lower the cost of capital in the United States. This objective emerges for the national security community as a requirement to improve the competitive position of American companies and strengthen the defense industrial base in a period of globalization. It is also a *sine qua non* for re-equilibrating the U.S.–Japanese relationship and maintaining transpacific as well as transatlantic political ties with post-1992 Europe as international economic competition intensifies.

The success of the *Uruguay Round of trade negotiations* follows an equally intricate journey onto the national security docket. Not only is a favorable outcome important to improve efficiency and expand the range of comparative advantage, as economists are wont to argue, but General Agreement on Tariffs and Trade (GATT) accomplishments play a central role in ensuring the conditions needed for the political stability of countries still struggling with the debt crisis, like Mexico and Brazil, as well as other parts of Central and South America and Africa. Success in multilateral trade agreements will likewise ease the pressure for more insulated neo-mercantilistic blocs in Europe, Asia, and North America and help build the economic "substructure" for the "superstructure" of ongoing political coordination among the industrial democracies.

Better *macroeconomic performance* on the part of the United States appears here not only as an economic objective but also as a growing strategic concern in order to maintain a position of leadership in national security affairs worldwide. On the expenditure side, new resources are needed to pursue the option of offering assistance to Eastern Europe and the Soviet Union, as well as providing economic and military aid to allies in the Third World beleaguered by enemies nearby (the Middle East and Persian Gulf) or within their own borders (the narcotic producing districts in Latin America). On the revenue side, the analysis of the relationship between the cost of capital and the competitiveness of American business suggests that any future attempts to seek new resources by raising the corporate tax rate would be counterproductive. The requirement to balance savings and consumption carries a bias toward rewarding savings and taxingconsumption. The need to hold down the growth in energy usage in particular points to further increases in the gasoline tax. (There may be other candidates for new revenues as well, like a value-added or general consumption tax.)

In *regional terms*, the economics agenda gives national security strategists much to be absorbed about in relations with the major powers, the Soviet Union, Europe, and Japan. It also suggests, however, that the Third World will be the source of renewed preoccupation for the national security community for reasons that have nothing to do with U.S.–Soviet competition. The selection of international economic policies that ignore Third World growth and stability would bode ill for the longer-term security environment.

Searching for solutions across all the topics from the economics agenda, there is a final conclusion for national security strategists that is greater than the sum of the parts: the traditional distinction between high politics (vital interests affecting national security) and low politics (petty questions of economic dispute and rivalry among states) may be disappearing. Looking toward the post–Cold War world, *low politics is becoming high politics*.

The difficulty with this blurring of the traditional distinction is that high politics has usually been assumed to entail the wherewithal to build a domestic consensus on appropriate policies in the face of threat to the nation, whereas low politics has always been much more likely to be mired in domestic struggles for short-term partisan advantage. In the security environment of the future, the dangers are likely to be more diffuse, the connections between them and the policies needed to respond to them more murky, and the need for sacrifice in order to advance national interests more opaque than in the period of bipolar antagonism.

The ultimate question for the United States in the post–Cold War era, therefore, may be one of *governance*: how to achieve the consensus and the continuity of domestic policy in the realm of low politics that are now required for America to continue as a great power into the twenty-first century.

NOTES

1. The Central Intelligence Agency and the Defense Intelligence Agency, "The Soviet Economy Stumbles Badly in 1989," a paper presented to the Technology and National Security Subcommittee of the Joint Economic Committee of the Congress, April 20, 1990.
2. The estimate that Viktor Belking gave was 28 percent. "Soviet Economists Say Their Economy is Worse Than U.S. Has Estimated," *New York Times*, April 24, 1990.
3. See, for example, the controversy surrounding the "Z" article. "Z", "To the Stalin Mausoleum," *Daedalus*, Vol. 119, No. 1, (Winter 1990); and William Safire, "The Z Document: 'Mr. X' in Our Time," *New York Times*, January 4, 1990.
4. For an account of how the central ministries, although reorganized under Gorbachev, have stifled the expansion of individual farms, private enterprises, and joint ventures with foreigners, see Marshall I. Goldman, "Gorbachev the Economist," *Foreign Affairs*, Vol. 69, No. 2, (Spring 1990).
5. Jan Lodal argues that fundamental reform of the Soviet economic system can come only through the shock therapy of price decontrol and privatization of industry. To enable shock therapy to be feasible in the Soviet Union, in contrast to Poland, he argues, will require installing shock absorbers first. A large long-term foreign assistance package, as envisioned here, could play a shock absorbing role. Jan M. Lodal, *Saving Perestroika: Gorbachev's Next Steps* (Washington, D.C.: The Atlantic Council, April 1990). For another set of prescriptions, see Ed A. Hewett and Richard Hornik, "Painful Prescription," *Time*, International Edition, May 7, 1990.
6. "Z", "To the Stalin Mausoleum," p. 297.
7. There may be instances, of course, when it is in the interest of the West to try to ensure short-term political stability via aid even though the money is, from an investment point of view, wasted. As Joseph S. Nye, Jr. has pointed out, there is a substantive difference between giving emergency food aid to prevent riots and offering long-term loans to facilitate eco-nomic reconstruction.
8. Trade with most favored nation (MFN) status within the General Agreement on Tariffs and Trade (GATT) framework could contribute significantly to Soviet economic growth over the very long term. In the short term, most Soviet trade will continue to be concentrated in natural resources, especially petroleum, for which MFN status is less important (MFN status would help vodka and fertilizer sales). Seventy-seven percent of Soviet exports to the United States, European Community (EC), and Japan consists of raw materials. Organization for Economic Cooperation and Development (OECD), *Statistics of Foreign Trade*, Series C (Paris: OECD, 1989).
9. Bela Belassa and Marcus Noland, *Japan in the World Economy* (Washington, D.C.: Institute for International Economics, 1988); and Robert Z. Lawrence, "How Open Is Japan?," *Brookings Review*, October 1989. For a critique of the Belassa-Noland methodology, see T.N. Srinivasan and Koichi Hamada, "The U.S.-Japan Trade Problem," draft, Yale University, New Haven, March 1990.

10 Clyde V. Prestowitz, Jr., *Trading Places: How We Allowed Japan To Take the Lead* (New York: Basic Books, 1988); Karl Van Wolferen, *The Enigma of Japanese Power* (New York: Alfred P. Knopf, 1989); James Fallows, "Containing Japan," *The Atlantic,* May 1989. The round of bilateral trade negotiations completed in the spring of 1990 addressed four of the most serious U.S. complaints, namely, Japanese procurement of satellites, supercomputers, telecommunications, and wood products. One must wait to see what concrete results ensue.

11. Complete Japanese liberalization in satellites, supercomputers, telecommunications, and wood products (note 10), for example, would result in approximately $2–3 billion in additional sales per year in the 1990s.

12. Technically macro-imbalances account for 100 percent of the trade deficit, with unfair trade practices only affecting the composition of that deficit. The correct focus for U.S. policy, of course, is equilibrium in the overall trade balance, not equality in each bilateral balance. The United States could maintain an ongoing trade deficit with Japan, and an ongoing trade surplus with Canada, for example (greatly simplified), with a Canadian trade surplus *vis-à-vis* Japan equilibrating the system. This is why a multilateral approach to trade liberalization is the only way to realize comparative advantage on a global scale.

13. Morita Akio and Ishihara Shintaro, *The Japan That Can Say"No": The Card for a New U.S.–Japan Relationship,* xerox, 1989. Morita disavowed the book after it appeared in English. For further consideration of Japanese concern about the United States as a reliable long-term partner, see Appendix 5 by Daniel I. Okimoto.

14. Cf. Charles Wolf, Jr., "Crashing Markets, Tumbling Savings: Japan in 2000," *The Wall Street Journal,* August 3, 1989.

15. Kyoji Fukao and Kazumasa Iwata, "On the International Ownership Pattern at the Turn of the Twenty-first Century," *European Economic Review,* 1989.

16. This question is part of two much larger problems (how to improve the overall productivity and innovativeness of the U.S. economy, on the one hand, and how to manage the shrinkage of specific defense-dependent industries, on the other), which require more extensive analysis than is possible here. For the debate about an "industrial policy" to bolster vital U.S. industries, see Theodore H. Moran, "The Globalization of America's Defense Industries: Managing the Threat of Foreign Dependence," *International Security,* Vol. 15, No. 1, (Summer 1990), pp. 57–99.

17. Department of Defense, (DoD), *Critical Technologies Plan,* for the Committees on Armed Services, United States Congress, May 5, 1989; DoD, *Bolstering Defense Industrial Competitiveness: Preserving Our Heritage, Securing Our Future,* Report to the Secretary of Defense by the Undersecretary of Defense (Acquisition), July 1988; and Office of Technology Assessment, *Holding the Edge: Maintaining the Defense Technology Base,* OTA-ISC-420 (Washington, D.C.: U.S. Government Printing Office [GPO], April 1989).

18. Moran, "The Globalization of America's Defense Industries."

19. In what could become an archetypical illustration of the dangers of globalization, Japan's Socialist Party forced the Kyocera company to pull back its advanced ceramic materials from being incorporated into the warhead of the Tomahawk cruise missile. Other worrisome cases involve

foreign technologies utilized in American weapons systems, which may carry restrictions, or may even be withheld, when the systems are offered to third parties, e.g., Israel, Taiwan, Korea, China, or when the systems are used for missions that generate controversy in the home nation.

20. When "national security" trade protection is granted, the most appropriate form is a tariff. A tariff is less distortionary than a quota, and the rents go to the home government instead of to the foreign firms. A voluntary restraint agreement (a common kind of quota) not only penalizes consumers but provides extra profits to external suppliers, strengthening their competitive position vis-à-vis domestic companies. The national security community should be particularly skeptical of proposals for managed trade such as those offered by Henry Kissinger and Cyrus Vance, among others: managed trade necessitates cartelization by foreign governments that then decide which of their own industries get privileged access to the U.S. market. Henry Kissinger and Cyrus Vance, "Bipartisan Objectives for Foreign Policy," *Foreign Affairs*, Vol. 65, No. 5 (Summer 1988).

21. These figures are taken from the Department of Energy's summary of base case forecasts from Ashland Oil, Conoco, Data Resources, Inc./McGraw Hill, Petroleum Industry Research Associates, and the East-West Center, as well as its own projections. Energy Information Administration, *Annual Energy Outlook: Long-Term Projections 1990* and *International Energy Outlook 1990* (Washington, D.C.: U.S. GPO, DOE/EIA-0383[90] and DOE/EIA-0484[90], 1990).

22. For those who stress reliance on market signals, the argument for an energy tax is that supply and demand among private parties create a price that does not adequately reflect the potential social costs associated with concentrated dependence on a particularly volatile region; to the market price, consequently, should be added a "national security premium." For those concerned about a "level playing field" for U.S. competitiveness, an energy tax up to $2–$3 per gallon of gasoline would simply match the burden borne by Asian and European firms.

23. Cf. Richard Cohen and Peter A. Wilson, *Superpowers in Decline: U.S. Strategy for the Transcentury Era* (New York: Taylor and Francis, 1990); J.R. Wilson, "The Teledyne Ryan Aeronautical Family of RPVs," *International Defense Review*, Vol. 23 (May 1989).

24. Aspen Strategy Group, *New Threats: Responding to the Proliferation of Nuclear, Chemical and Ballistic Missile Capabilities* (Lanham, Md.: University Press of America and Aspen Strategy Group, 1990).

25. *Economic Report of the President* (Washington, D.C.: U.S. GPO, 1990), Table 7-1,   p. 236.

26. The exact magnitude of debt relief is difficult to calculate since under the Brady Plan the banks could select a range of choices, including new discounted bonds with commercial rates of interest, or new bonds at par with reduced interest, or new loans at commercial rates of interest.

27. International Monetary Fund, *World Economic Outlook*, May 1990. These are the same projections that Richard N. Cooper uses in Appendix 2 The difference in our assessments springs from my pessimism that the average 5.5 percent growth rate will not be achieved.

28. For an argument in favor of a Chapter 11 approach, see Benjamin J. Cohen, "A Global Chapter 11," *Foreign Policy*, No. 75, (Summer 1989). The Brady

Plan negotiations in Mexico have largely eliminated this option there. For a less radical approach, see Economic Commission for Latin America and the Caribbean, *Latin America and the Caribbean: Options to Reduce the Debt Burden* (Santiago, Chile: United Nations Economic Commission for Latin America and the Caribbean, 1990).

29. Cf. Jeffrey J. Schott and Gary C. Hufbauer, "The Realities of a North American Economic Alliance," draft, April 1990.

30. There has been a substantial loss of U.S. exports and jobs as a result of depressed conditions in Latin America. At the beginning of the 1980s the developing countries were purchasing more than 40 percent of U.S. exports, a share greater than Japan and Europe combined. By 1987 a loss of $78 billion in exports had cost almost two million American jobs. John W. Sewell, Stuart K. Tucker, and contributors, *Growth, Exports & Jobs in a Changing World Economy: Agenda 1988* (Washington, D.C.: Overseas Development Council, 1988), Tables A-9 and B-8, pp. 216, 234.

31. Milton Friedman, "An Open Letter to Bill Bennett," *Wall Street Journal*, September 7, 1989; and George P. Shultz, "Shultz on Drug Legalization," *Wall Street Journal*, October 27, 1989.

32. William J. Bennett, "A Response to Milton Friedman," *Wall Street Journal*, September 19, 1989; A.M. Rosenthal, "The Case for Slavery," *New York Times*, September 26, 1989; and "Legalizing Drugs: Failures Spur Debate," *New York Times*, November 27, 1989.

Appendix 8

THE GOALS AND INSTRUMENTS OF AMERICAN FOREIGN POLICY UNDER THE IMPETUS OF REVOLUTIONARY CHANGE

John D. Steinbruner

The events of 1989 provided the political equivalent of a phase change in nature—a sudden altering of state as continuous changes in underlying parameters reach critical thresholds. The political revolutions in Eastern Europe were particularly decisive. They both documented and consolidated changes in the conditions of military power, in the operations of the international economy, and in the internal political dynamics of contemporary societies, all of which had been gradually developing over several decades. The crystallization of a new configuration of international politics was sudden and astonishing, but the preparations had been lengthy and extensive.

Among the many consequences of the dramatic shift that occurred is the ability to understand more clearly the underlying trends that produced it and the policy implications that can be expected to emerge from it. With the benefit of that instruction, U.S. foreign policy should, in principle, be in a better position to align with emerging events that appear to have, on the whole, quite fortuitous implications. To do so, however, requires the very considerable effort of adjusting prevailing perspectives, operating principles, and fundamental objectives.

The major substantive changes are reasonably apparent in broad outline. The alliance confrontation in central Europe that has provided the foundation for international security generally is now dissolving. It will almost certainly have to be replaced by more cooperative arrangements for regulating military power. In addition, the stark, self-imposed isolation of the centrally planned economies is breaking down under the relentless pressure of international market operations. The world as a whole is presented the very demanding task of integrating across this traditional divide. These major shifts in international security and economic conditions are reinforced, moreover, by domestic politics. Political consent and the expanded participation it requires have become indispensable for operating any large society at acceptable levels of efficiency. This underlying imperative is releasing long-suppressed nationalist sentiments, creating considerable tension between the expression of separatist identities and the formation of cooperating economic and political communities.

These interacting conditions are forcing profound changes of policy on all major governments but the nature of the changes required differs substantially among them and few of the specific consequences have yet been worked out. It is a moment of redefinition when the actions taken could structure events for very long periods to come. There is great scope for constructive statesmanship as well as for tragic misjudgment.

In analyzing the goals and instruments of U.S. foreign policy under these circumstances it is necessary to be strategically selective. It is reasonable to assume that virtually all the objectives and all the instruments of policy will ultimately be affected, but it is not reasonable to attempt a completely comprehensive assessment. Even under these sweeping circumstances, some limited set of issues will undoubtedly emerge to provide an organizing focus of attention and to lead the way for more general redefinition. An attempt to understand what is happening necessarily involves an attempt to identify the specific formative issues.

The pattern of recent events provides some very strong clues for reaching these judgements. As the conditions of security in Europe alter what has been the central point of engagement between the opposing military establishments, clearly the military instruments of American policy will be forced to undergo substantial revision, and in the process, central security objectives are likely to be refined as well. German unification will almost certainly be a major catalyst for these revisions and the transformation of NATO a very likely organizing focus. The principles of cooperative security, which have been initiated politically within Germany and amplified in sharp revisions of Soviet security policies will predictably be the central theme of this transformation. These principles enable a sharp reduction in the size of U.S. military forces and in the levels of the U.S. defense budget—hence dramatic improvements in the efficiency of security policy. To support this benefit, however, there will have to be a major redirection of the U.S. intelligence process and a substantial shift in the pattern of technical investment.

In addition, the struggle to develop stable democratic governments in Eastern Europe and indeed in the Soviet Union, while simultaneously conducting a wrenching economic reform will predictably force a major reversal of the objectives and instruments of U.S. economic policy. Rather than reinforcing the isolation of these economies through a variety of negative sanctions, as it has in the past, the United States will be required by its own larger interest to encourage their internal reform and international integration through positive inducements and direct investment. That underlying issue is sharply and immediately manifested in the revision of export control policy under the current international coordinating arrangements known as COCOM.

Beyond these revisions of traditional objectives and policy instruments, new issues are clearly emerging with the definition and pursuit of greater international equity as a driving purpose. These issues appear likely to emerge from their long exile in rhetorical abstraction into the world of practical policy as the international community is forced to contend with the problem of protecting global environmental balances. The current momentum of population growth and the extension of economic activity associated with it is inexorably forcing international environmental regulation and the development of mechanisms capable of undertaking it.

The transformation of NATO, redirection of U.S. intelligence process and technical investment patterns, and the revision of COCOM are matters that have considerable potential for leading yet more extensive changes in the goals and instruments of U.S. foreign policy as does the emerging question of global environmental regulation. Together they offer a practical way to grasp the nature of the larger adjustment that must be made. The central element of that adjustment will almost certainly have to be a shift away from traditional American self-reliance and preference for unilateral action toward effective international cooperation. This adjustment is bound to be difficult in political and psychological terms for it is driven far more by the force of circumstances than by spontaneous trends in American opinion.

THE TRANSFORMATION OF NATO

The traditional objectives of U.S. security policy are so familiar they hardly need rehearsal, in fact, so familiar that there is little patience for their reiteration. Most Americans understand the United States to be committed to deterring war and to containing associated impulses for political expansion. Officially formulated policy has been designed against a calculating opponent who is assumed to be continually probing for exploitable weaknesses in U.S. capacity or resolve and to be continuously hiding aggressive intent behind deceptively reassuring diplomacy—the problem encountered and mismanaged during the 1930s. It has been a common assumption, raised virtually to the status of an axiom, that the Soviet Union is the contemporary em-bodiment of such an opponent and must be treated accordingly. The conduct of U.S.–Soviet relations has therefore been conceived according to theories of adversarial bargaining, which as-sume a continuous contest for advantage in developing and positioning military power. Any mutual accommodation, it has been assumed, must be the result of immediately applied "leverage" in the adversarial bargaining process. Denying any meaningful Soviet advantage has been the minimum essential operating objective, and securing U.S. advantage has been the unspoken preference.

U.S. Success

NATO has been the primary institutional manifestation of this policy and major embodiment of its success. Germany has been developed into a powerful industrial democracy and its reconstituted military power has been integrated into a coalition of its former Western enemies all arrayed against the Soviet Union. NATO's combination of economic and technical potential in association with U.S. allies in Asia decisively precludes any realistic Soviet aspiration to secure or sustain an overall strategic advantage. Though NATO's traditional accounting of weapons deployments attributed a ground force advantage to the opposing Warsaw Treaty Organization (WTO) Alliance, the political collapse of that alliance has revealed a very different situation. The Soviet-led coalition has not been able to develop the inherent superiority required for an invasion of Western Europe, and even with a nominal advantage in manpower and equipment any expectation of success in such an enterprise would have depended on gross mismanagement of NATO forces. In fact the mismanagement of Warsaw Pact forces and consequent defeat had all along been at least as likely and has been becoming increasingly more likely over time as NATO evolves its technical capabilities—particularly those for remote observation and deep interdiction.

It is now reasonable to conclude that the United States has won the traditionally defined contest for military position, effectively denying Soviet advantage and thereby establishing the conditions for deterrence and containment. Resistance to calculated aggression has been established beyond reasonable question. The Soviet Union has conceded that much and has radically altered its security policy in part to head off the possibility that an indefinite continuation of the traditional alliance confrontation might eventually produce a decisive U.S. advantage.

Soviet Reaction

The redefinition of Soviet security policy, which predated the political revolutions in Eastern Europe and in fact provided an enabling condition, alters the primary operational mission of Soviet forces. Whereas before they had been instructed to prepare for a rapidly decisive offensive against NATO forces in order to prevent inevitable defeat against a superior coalition in a protracted war, the new operational doctrine mandates only a defense of national territory and a restructured strategic deterrent capability sized and configured under the assumption that war is to be prevented by political means. With complete and systematic implementation of this doctrine, Soviet forces are to be withdrawn from Eastern Europe, sharply reduced, and equipped for defensive operations. They will provide in that new configuration a strong physical barrier to invasion and a credible threat of strategic retaliation but not a major threat of conventional power projection. That latter aspiration is to be relinquished as a necessary part of arrangements made to remove from Soviet forces the burdens of continuous antagonistic competition against a superior economic coalition. The traditional alliance confrontation is to be dissolved in favor of a cooperative security arrangement designed to regulate the size and operational posture of forces that might oppose the Soviet Union. Corresponding regulations on Soviet forces and dramatic increases in their transparency to the international community will be accepted as the prices to be paid for those cooperative arrangements that are to be the principal means of preventing war.[1]

This radical redesign of Soviet security policy is a rational adjustment to powerful strategic imperatives, and there is no reason to doubt its sincerity or endurance. More than that, it is a creative reaction to global economic and political trends that establishes the basis for far more effective and constructive Soviet influence on international politics than the Soviet Union was able to achieve through the several decades of alliance confrontation. In particular, the new Soviet policy enables in principle a strong and dramatically redefined relationship with the unified German state whose significance in the new international order is likely to be large.

Consequences for NATO

In coming to accept unified German membership in the NATO alliance after strong initial resistance, the Soviets implicitly acknowledged that they could not have prevented that outcome at acceptable cost using the standard negative incentives of confrontational bargaining. They would have had to apply their formal legal rights as an occupying power and would have had to suggest that Soviet forces in East Germany might act to enforce those rights thereby contradicting the entire logic of their revised policy. For that reason that option would have been exceedingly damaging and ultimately ineffective. By contrast, however, the positive inducements for the Germans that would emerge from complete implementation of the new Soviet security design offer a very effective means of producing a substantial change in the character of NATO. As Soviet forces are withdrawn, reduced, and reconfigured, German security will be dramatically improved while the intrusive presence of military operations on their crowded territory is substantially diminished. In particular, the domestically contentious presence of nuclear weapons on German territory can be gracefully eliminated. Moreover, if cooperative security arrangements form for all of Europe whose institutional manifestation is disproportionately located on German territory, then German stature in those arrangements will obviously be disproportionately strong as well. By choosing to make Germany a special focus of security and economic cooperation, the Soviets are in position to enhance German international political significance very substantially. The initial pattern for such a policy was clearly set in the German-Soviet agreement in July of 1990 clearing the way for an acceleration of the German unification process.

U.S. Adjustment

All this then sets the context for a necessary revision of NATO as an instrument of U.S. security policy and for a corresponding revision of the policy itself. Rather than indulging in querulous speculation about a possible reversal of the new Soviet policy or gleeful exploitation of what appears to be a collapse of Soviet bargaining leverage, the United States needs to develop its considerable interest in the process of implementing the security reform the Soviets have initiated. The new Soviet policy enables in principle a sharp improvement in the performance and the efficiency of United States security. Moreover, it sets terms for a new form of political competition that may be more vigorous and demanding than we yet appreciate.

As the principal embodiment of the traditional policies of deterrence and containment, NATO's military organization is likely to become a major political liability under the emerging conditions in Europe if it does not visibly alter the character of its operations to match the change in circumstances. The prevention of war will unavoidably remain the dominant security objective for all national governments, but the active pursuit of deterrence and containment in alliance coalition is not likely to be accepted indefinitely as the exclusive or even the principal focus of policy. As the implications of the change in Soviet policy are absorbed, the threat of deliberately calculated aggression manifested in observable preparations for an invasion of Western Europe will predictably recede as a a potential cause of war sufficiently plausible to legitimize NATO's current doctrines and deployments. Moreover, though it is less certain that this traditional definition of threat will be replaced by any comparably well-focused conception, there is a strong candidate with highly revisionist implications for NATO's traditional posture.

Because of their global reach and capacity for extremely rapid destruction, strategic nuclear forces cannot be disengaged to the extent that is possible for conventional weapons. Even large percentage reductions of current strategic deployments signaling an intention to concede deterrent capability would leave the respective command systems susceptible to serious disruption and committed to rapid reaction to assure effective retaliation. That situation creates a significant threat of unintended war arising from an unmanageable crisis engagement. There are strong objective reasons therefore to redirect security policies for the purpose of controlling this threat while assuring the traditional, now conceded missions of deterrence and territorial defense with much greater efficiency, that is, at lower force levels and lower cost. Since that would be the major consequence of the cooperative security idea that has been incubating in German political dialogue and amplified in the official revision of Soviet policy, it is reasonable to expect that security policies in Central Europe will develop along these lines.[2]

Cooperative security implies explicit regulatory arrangements to impose force deployment ceilings and operational restrictions on national military establishments designed to keep them in a relatively defensive and minimally reactive configuration. Although the details of such a security design have yet to be examined by the Western defense ministries, it is fairly apparent that force structure redirections to approximately half of current levels with similar percentage reductions in current defense budgets are feasible in principle. To support such an outcome the idea of cooperative security also implies a systematic exchange of information among the national forces and residual alliance organizations to control their uncertainties about each other. It implies a sharp separation of nuclear and conventional force operations to improve the manageability of any crisis interaction. And it implies not merely a revision but a complete reversal of the traditional NATO doctrine of flexible response, a euphemism for the projected intention to initiate nuclear operations in response to conventional attack. The adjusted formulation of the doctrine announced after the NATO summit meeting in July 1990 was apparently designed to preserve this central feature.[3] That commitment can be defended, albeit with significant difficulty, if deterrence is assumed to be the dominant objective. It is obviously unwise, however, if crisis interactions are the major source of threat, and reassurance becomes the dominant objective.

These implications are consistent with plausible U.S. security requirements, and they probably cannot be credibly resisted even if majority sentiment in the United States should prefer to do so. Substantial resistance runs the considerable risk of being received particularly in Germany, as an attempt to preserve or to develop U.S. military hegemony. There are many choices of implementing detail available, but as a fundamental purpose, the formation of a cooperative security arrangement in Europe is rapidly becoming more than a viable option. It is virtually a political imperative—the inexorable consequence of winning, if you will, the long struggle for strategic position.

To put the matter mildly, the redirection of NATO's military structure to this new purpose requires a major feat of organizational transformation, and there are bound to be doubts about the feasibility of that project even among those who unequivocally accept the imperative. The politics of alliance coordination have made NATO to date anything but flexible about its doctrine of flexible response. Its highly autonomous military commanders have made the possession of nuclear weapons a matter of the most intense personal commitment. Its layered deployment pattern and mobilization plans have acquired in the course of many decades the deep roots of entrenched investment and bureaucratic routine. The organization is very likely to display a strong instinct for preserving its traditional commitments in judiciously attenuated forms and to be a source of detailed objection to the radical reductions of forces, the removal of nuclear weapons, the restrictions on operational training, and the extensive disclosure of information that cooperative security principles imply. None of that precludes a successful transformation a priori, but it does suggest that the impetus will have to come from outside of the organization and will have to be presented in political terms too authoritative to be rejected. If forced to adjust to preserve itself, NATO probably will. If adjustment is made a question over which NATO has authoritative control, then it is likely to take a very long time indeed and to be surrounded by a very extensive set of conditions.

It is a prudent surmise, therefore, that the necessary transformation of NATO depends on some continuation of the five-power forum convened to manage the unification of Germany. The "2 plus 4 talks" as they were colloquially styled, were restricted to the limited agenda of restoring full German sovereignty, ending occupation rights, and ratifying existing borders. That limitation was designed to restrict the role of the Soviet Union, and it reflects the traditional U.S. and NATO attitude that the Soviet Union is the putative enemy against whom Western security is being organized. The essence of the required transformation, however, is to allow the Soviet Union to escape the unmanageable burden of maintaining a competitive military organization against the full array of industrial democracies and to admit it as a cooperating partner in the management of international security. The conditions of admission are quite important, of course, and they will probably require as much as a decade or more to work out in appropriate detail. The five-power forum is the natural working group for doing so. Moreover, even the original agenda cannot be truly completed without continued coordination. Not all of the arrangements for managing military forces that have evolved since World War II can responsibly be terminated without replacement.[4]

As a result of providing effective partnership for the Soviet Union, an extension of the five-power forum would also provide a natural complement for the Conference on Security and Cooperation in Europe (CSCE) process, and the two together might create the external impetus for a transformation of NATO. The legitimacy and utility of the CSCE derives from its inclusive membership, but that is also a defect in terms of coherently organized operations. Refined policy coordination is not likely to be possible for its 34 members acting as an institutional body. CSCE is a mechanism for ratifying policy decisions rather than for formulating or implementing them. Conversely, coordinated policy decisions emerging from five-power discussions could not be implemented until they were sustained by broader agreement. With the five-power forum providing inner political coordination and CSCE the ratifying body, it would be in principle feasible to evolve NATO into the institutional machinery that a robust cooperative security arrangement would require.

INTELLIGENCE AND TECHNOLOGY

One of the driving elements of the cooperative security arrangements that appear to be forming in Europe is the promise of sharply improved efficiency in the management of security. Part of this improvement is to result from the physical reduction of conventional attack capability. With weapons deployments equalized, reduced, and disengaged, warning times will be longer, and the immediate readiness of defending forces can be reduced, saving both investment and operating expenditures.

Were that the sole effect, however, the improvement is likely to be marginal. Historical experience with strategic warning would not inspire enough confidence to support a major change in posture. To have a more decisive effect, therefore, cooperative security arrangements must enable truly fundamental reductions of uncertainty about strategic intentions, enabling the military establishments to shift their methods for managing risk away from reliance on immediate readiness. That in turn would enable a revision in the management of supporting technology, a revision that is independently required by the dramatic changes that have accrued over recent decades in the process of developing technology. Much of the potential appeal of cooperative security arrangements derives from the opportunity to overcome traditional deficiencies of intelligence assessment and thereby to support a technical development effort less dominated by immediate weapons projects.

The Shifting Sourcesand Uses of Information

Since the early 1960s the United States intelligence agencies have relied heavily on the development of sophisticated technologies for remote sensing and electronic intercept. Although details have been carefully protected, it is apparent from the public record that these technologies have been remarkably successful in their direct purposes. The basic locations at which military activities are conducted have been identified. Major weapons deployments have been counted, and their technical characteristics have been estimated with reasonable precision. Daily operations are routinely observed and characteristic patterns have been recognized. In terms of immediate physical manifestation and routine behavior, the opposing military establishments have come to know each other very well indeed. The ignorance of immediate capability, which created sensational political scandals in the 1950s, has been conquered and is extremely unlikely to recur.

At least for the U.S. and allied governments, however, this success based on remote technical observation has had some important limits. Western intelligence analysis has not systematically understood the inner deliberations of the Soviet military planning system. It evidently has not been able to observe directly the way Soviet decision-makers formulate their problems to themselves, nor has it generally provided definitive evidence on the planning and operational decisions of Soviet officials as they are made. Natural tests of this capability were posed during the crisis over Cuba in 1962, the intervention in Czechoslovakia in 1968, the Middle East war in 1973, the intervention in Afghanistan in 1979, and in a number of other lesser instances. In these cases the United States was able to observe background preparations and thus was alerted in a general way but was not able to determine the exact character of Soviet decisions with sufficient refinement or in sufficient time to have a substantial effect on its own reactions. The success of technical collection has not precluded strategic surprise, and uncertainty therefore remains a driving consideration in defense planning.

The fundamental reasons for this limitation are not difficult to understand despite the obscurity of classification that surrounds the topic. The concentration on technical collection systems has produced a vast flow of discrete information and of interpretive results both of which focus on observable events and on issues amenable to technical analysis. Connecting this information to strategic intention requires a process of inductive inference that is notoriously difficult to constrain. Since authoritative Soviet policy deliberations are not directly observed and since Soviet public statements are dismissed as misleading propaganda, Western assumptions have had a decisive influence on the inferences made. These assumptions have been systematically biased by the logic and emotion of the adversarial relationship. Overall military capabilities and belligerent intentions have been exaggerated. Practical problems have been overlooked. Legitimate fears have been discounted. Uncertainty and interpretive error are the endemic by-products of a confrontational security posture causing significant inefficiency and misdirection of defense expenditures.

In shifting the primary security objective from deterrence to reassurance and in codifying a presumption that war is to be prevented by political means, the cooperative security principles emerging in Europe enable, in fact require, systematic exchange of information about the planning and operational practices of deployed forces. The inspection activities associated with the intermediate-range nuclear forces (INF) treaty provide a limited example of what this might involve, but under a fully developed arrangement the scope would clearly be much broader and the purpose less exclusively focused on the verification of treaty limitations. Cooperative security arrangements would have to establish an extensive, legally sanctioned exchange of information involving direct inspection of deployment sites and production facilities in order to document defensive capability and offensive restraint. This continuous detailed exposure of the respective military establishments to the internal operations of their counterparts, supplemented, of course, by the continuation of remote technical observation appears to be becoming feasible. It does have the possibility of providing strategic assessments detailed and reliable enough to support a fundamental shift in posture and corresponding improvement in efficiency.

This development promises to be a revolution for the U.S. intelligence agencies. Direct access to Soviet planning and operational practices would compensate for the most glaring traditional weaknesses, and it is an opportunity that can hardly be rejected. Systematic development of the opportunity would shift the internal balance of activity, however, in ways that would be institutionally uncomfortable. Legalized inspection is a labor-intensive enterprise that would absorb a large number of people and would produce large amounts of information. It would yield in principle a much better account of planning and operational decisions. Reliable strategic understanding would not emerge directly from this information, however, and would require a commensurately expanded interpretive effort.

Since even the most extensive and intensive cooperative arrangements will stop well short of having note takers attend critical Soviet planning meetings or those of other foreign governments, the information acquired would have to be combined with information independently gathered. Overall performance would be determined more by the ability to select critical information from an exceedingly large volume and to integrate across different categories and sources. That implies a redirection of emphasis from clandestine acquisition of information to systematic use of legal sources as well as a shift generally from collection to analytic integration.

Fortunately this realignment, motivated by considerations of strategic stability and overall security efficiency, is consistent with trends in tactical requirements as well. It is evident that the massive use of military force in lengthy, large-scale relatively predictable operations is becoming less likely, precisely because it has been so powerfully deterred and so effectively contained. The occasions for the application of military power that are likely to arise as a practical matter will be smaller in scale and less predictable in character and location. The ability to deal with them will require the classic attributes of military power in some measure—firepower, mobility, adequate training, etc., but the outcomes will be primarily determined by the use of information. To operate military forces successfully will require very precise information about the time, location, specific purpose to be accomplished, and the immediate identity of the opponents. Any significant error or vagueness on these matters is likely to produce perverse consequences no matter how well-equipped, brave, and willful the forces in question may be. Since situations cannot be predicted with the extreme precision required for successful operations, adaptive analytic integration will almost certainly dominate the brute force collection of raw information, and the ability to sustain international collaboration is likely to be a significant comparative advantage in producing it.

The redirection of the U.S. intelligence process implied by these charges of circumstance is perhaps not as radical as the transformation required of NATO, but it clearly involves far more than simple marginal adjustments. The apparently impending opening of overt sources of information is likely to be accompanied by increasing restriction on traditional covert sources for both political and technical reasons. The unavoidable diffusion of sophisticated telecommunications systems to all of the traditional WTO members will undermine the massive investment made in penetrating their current antiquated systems, and it is unlikely that covert penetration will be allowed to keep pace in the emerging political environment. The politics of alliance confrontation enabled covert penetration to be pursued with complete disregard for legal regulation. The emerging politics of cooperative security are unlikely to be so permissive even for former adversaries, and they certainly will not be so permissive on the new subjects of economic competition.

In their predictable efforts to resist these secular trends in order to protect their traditional sources and methods, the U.S. intelligence agencies will be prone to underutilizing the emerging opportunity for the systematic development of overt information. In addition they will be at least as reluctant to adjust the internal balance of commitment to enhance analytical integration with greater priority than technical collection. As with NATO, strong impetus will probably have to come from some sources outside of the existing intelligence agencies in order to motivate an internal adjustment of the magnitude required. Unlike the NATO case, there is no natural candidate to perform this function other than the familiar and usually forlorn appeal for presidential leadership.

The Technical Connection

If it is difficult to identify a viable existing mechanism for redirecting the intelligence process, one can at least note a powerful reinforcing motive in the long accumulating pressures for redesigning national technical investment. The current arrangements for organizing and financing technical support for the United States military programs were initiated in the 1950s when the sense of political confrontation was particularly acute, when uncertainties about the Soviet weapons development efforts were the greatest they have ever been, and when the United States enjoyed a substantial advantage in virtually all the basic technologies. Technical investment in areas associated with major weapons components—airframes, jet engines, rocket engines, inertial guidance systems, optical sensors, communications, etc.—was heavily associated with U.S. weapons projects and was managed to support an active competition in weapons deployments. The United States was straining to deploy military forces that enjoyed a substantial qualitative authority over those of the Soviet Union. The practice of concurrent development and production and the drive for successive improvements in critical technical parameters regardless of the cost involved were ingrained into the weapons procurement process to support this strategic competition and were justified in terms of grave uncertainty about the possible evolution of the Soviet threat. A cascade of troublesome consequences—large increases in the cost of mainline weapons, design errors propagated deep into the weapons production runs, an overlay of stupendous bureaucratic procedure, and periodic scandal—was tolerated in deference to the bottom line: most of the major weapons eventually came to approximate their demanding technical aspirations, worked distinctly better than their Soviet counterparts and were deployed on the whole sooner. The technical investment pattern achieved its main purpose: effective victory in the competition for strategic position.

The original environment has now dramatically altered, and the organizational pattern that evolved within it is now an endangered species for compelling reasons. After four decades of intense investment, marginal technical advantage is much more difficult to achieve and the cost of doing so looms as a decisive consideration. The connections between the familiar parameters of technical performance, standard military missions, and broader security outcomes have also become much more complicated and interactive, demanding a level of analytic integration that clearly exceeds the capacity of the U.S. defense planning system, as dramatically documented in the B-2 bomber program.[5]

The strategic context, moreover, is rapidly shifting as are the basic circumstances of technical development. With the primary issues of strategic military position essentially settled and with deployments headed for increasingly explicit regulation, relative economic performance looms as a driving political objective. Technical investment will increasingly be judged in terms of its contribution to this purpose. The primary impetus for the development of basic technologies has already shifted away from military programs into commercial markets whose competitive pressures and rapidly evolving product cycles are leaving even the most advanced weapons programs increasingly far from the technical frontier, particularly in the critical area of microelectronics. In this emerging environment the narrowly and traditionally defined success of major U.S. weapons projects will not be able to cover for the notorious inefficiencies of procurement systems. A major realignment of technical investment is likely to be triggered as declines in the defense budget force an unavoidable crisis in the traditional system.

There is as yet no specific design for this realignment that would command the broad consensus required to undertake it, but a few of the guiding principles have been identified. A sharp conceptual and organizational distinction will have to be made between technical support for military programs and technical support for broader economic performance. The latter will be a national objective of increasingly compelling priority, but the justifying logic, the organizational design, and the necessary financing will all have to be created anew with virtually no precedent either to shape or to obstruct the process. By contrast, technical support for military programs will have to be extracted from its deep historical entrenchment in the weapons procurement process. That will require a wrenching financial reallocation within the defense budget and presumably major surgery within the existing industrial structure. The personnel teams that actually embody U.S. technical capability must be given conceptual and financial independence from immediate weapons procurement programs enabling them to broaden their scope and increase their design flexibility. The practical discipline required to structure their efforts must be provided by prototype projects rather than immediate, large-scale production runs. This, in principle, would allow more rapid design evolution and more effective incorporation of leading technology while giving the planning system the time and information required to achieve a better integration of technical capability with broadly defined security requirements.

The management of uncertainty will probably be one of the elements necessary to enable this adjustment. The fear of technical surprise or of some unpredictable Soviet threat has helped to rivet U.S. technical investment to immediate weapons projects. Although that fear has not been the sole determinant and its relaxation will not be the sole solution, the greater confidence in strategic assessment expected to emerge from a more coopera- tive intelligence process would materially assist the required realignment. If one is instructing the principal carriers of techni- cal expertise to broaden perspective and to examine distant horizons, it is useful to reassure them at the same time that they will not be upended by some hazard in their immediate path.

ECONOMIC ENGAGEMENT AND TECHNOLOGY TRADE

Just as alliance confrontation was reinforced during the Cold War period by economic isolation, so will the formation of co- operative security arrangements be reinforced by economic inte- gration. The fundamental shift in policy taking place clearly has both military and economic dimensions, and the relative priority of economic interest is clearly increasing. Incorporating this con- nection in the objectives and instruments of American foreign policy is likely to be difficult because of the traditional separation of security and economic matters in the conceptions of most people and in the institutional machinery of government. The handling of technical investment, however, forges a strong natu- ral link between security and economic considerations and that is a main reason why that subject appears likely to be a major cat- alyst for the reformulation of objectives and policy instruments.

The basic nature of the impending changes is already appar- ent. Both the moral and the practical appeal of economic reform in the communist countries is fundamentally irresistible. A dominant inclination will almost certainly develop in the United States to dismantle the apparatus of economic sanction that was created during the Cold War period and to promote economic reform in some active fashion. That inclination will not be easy to implement, however. There are no generally agreed designs for an effective reform sequence and presumably a great deal of experience will have to be accumulated before any settled judgment is likely. Moreover, investment resources are scarce, and it is not likely to be feasible to flood conceptual problems with plentiful supplies of money. Manageable, practical mechanisms of engagement are bound to be unusually valuable in this situation, and that also is something that the issue of handling technology provides.

Beginning in 1949, as a natural extension of alliance confrontation and the competition for strategic position, the United States organized a trade embargo against the Soviet Union and its allies, covering not only weapons products but also the primary products and technologies that contributed to weapons development. The objective was to retard Soviet military development, and in an expansive pursuit of that purpose, controls were imposed on an extensive list of items whose military significance was indirect and highly uncertain. Informal but explicit and continuous coordinating arrangements were formed among U.S. allies to secure cooperation with the embargo. The coordinating group known as COCOM has long operated out of the U.S. Embassy in Paris. It has induced U.S. allies to adopt restrictive trade legislation and enforcement procedures that are nominally comparable, although as a practical matter U.S. policy has usually been more restrictive.

In their original incarnation these export controls on advanced technology deemed to be militarily significant were reasonably effective. A relatively high proportion of the products and technologies involved were in fact predominantly associated with weapons programs, and there was no inclination on the Western side to sell weapons to the Warsaw Pact. The members of the WTO were themselves practicing highly protectionist trade policies and systematically denying any direct investment in their economies, thereby precluding any meaningful, positive, economic incentives that might be brought to bear against the embargo. Their extensive efforts to acquire Western technology relied heavily on covert, illegal means—espionage and conspiratorial trade diversion. Although partially effective these methods were inherently inefficient.

The practical effectiveness of the trade embargo has declined over time, however, as market conditions have evolved. The technologies most significant for military application—most notably in information processing and secondarily in materials science—are now developing in internalized markets driven primarily by commercial purposes. For even the most advanced U.S. weapons programs the fundamental technology being applied is lagging increasingly behind that available in the leading commercial products. That fact has reversed the security implications of technology trade. Denying market access is increasingly infeasible. Moreover, effective applications to weapons programs are increasingly less determined by simple market access, either for the Soviet Union or for the United States. Extensive controls on items that have predominant commercial application have become irritants whose justifying purpose is increasingly less credible, and the international consensus required to sustain them is breaking down.

This market trend is reinforced by the shift in Soviet and Eastern European policy. In attempting to connect their economies to world markets, these countries are at least trying to open up opportunity for trade and investment. Although their internal reform efforts have not yet reached the stage where that opportunity is likely to be attractive enough to harness spontaneous market forces, the opportunity is in principle quite significant precisely because of the horrendous historical inefficiency of these economies. Elemental improvements could produce a large return. Moreover, the Soviets, in particular, are attempting to divert some portion of their more advanced technical assets from weapons applications to commercial purposes. They are actively seeking international joint ventures to supply investment capital, to upgrade their own technology, and to provide marketing expertise that is almost entirely absent in the Soviet system. Implicitly this is a shift in emphasis from acquiring Western technology for military purposes through illegal espionage to acquiring it for commercial purposes through contractual cooperation. For most of the world, particularly in Western Europe, that effort will be received in political terms as constructive and desirable whatever its economic prospects turn out to be. It will legitimize Soviet claims for international market access and will undermine the traditional policy of discriminating against them. Since the removal or circumvention of export restrictions is a necessary condition for the successful operation of joint ventures, Western export policy has acquired a *de facto* role in Soviet defense conversion.

These changes in market conditions and in prevailing policy have been sharply focused by the process of German unification, and that has already produced a significant adjustment in the export control arrangements. As a consequence of economic union, the enlarged German state has acquired responsibility both for modernizing dilapidated East German industries and for honoring their existing supply contracts with the Soviet Union. At the COCOM meeting in June of 1990, the United States prudently conceded that the prevailing list of export controls could not be applied to the disappearing East German state and agreed to an interim set of restrictions, pending complete unification, on a minimal number of items that have the most direct relevance for weapons applications. It was acknowledged as well that Poland, Czechoslovakia, and Hungary had ceased to be plausible military opponents, and more liberal export licensing was allowed for these countries comparable and in some instances somewhat more favorable to special allowances previously defined for China. In addition, thirty categories were eliminated from the general COCOM list of restricted items (approximately one-third of the total), including particularly computers, telecommunications and machine tools where background commercial interest and political pressure on licensing decisions had been particularly strong. Provisions were made for reviewing all the items remaining under control by the end of the year and for reconstituting the entire control list focusing on eight categories of "strategically critical" products and technologies. These actions were the result of a major policy review within the United States government mandated by President Bush in January of 1990 as well as spirited bargaining among COCOM members, who, in effect, had threatened to withdraw from the coordinating arrangements if the highly restrictive U.S. policy was not relaxed.

These adjustments to changing technical and political conditions are explicitly designed to preserve the traditional policy of retarding Soviet military development by categorically denying access to relevant technology. The licensing exceptions allowed for Poland, Czechoslovakia, and Hungary are contingent on their implementation of legislation and administration enforcement arrangements that would prevent reexport of the licensed items to the Soviet Union. The current official U.S. inclination is to preserve as extensive a set of export controls as can command the consensus among the major industrial countries that is necessary to make the controls effective. (Increasing congressional impatience with the effects of export controls on U.S. commercial competitiveness has made it apparent that restrictions imposed unilaterally by the United States will not be sustained in the impending renewal of trade legislation.)

This retrenchment in the instruments of export control in order to preserve the traditional embargo on technical trade to the Soviet Union is not likely to be the end of the story, and in fact a fundamental revision of both the objective and the machinery is the more probable eventual outcome. Categorical denial to the Soviet Union of market access to advanced technology is no longer feasible as a practical matter and no longer desirable either, if support for economic reform is accepted as a serious objective. It is more realistic and more appropriate to regulate technical export to the Soviet Union through end-use specification than through categorical denial, and the Soviets have generally indicated they would cooperate with such measures.

Reliance on end-use specifications involves documentation and verification of sensitive technology, such as supercomputers, to assure that it is in fact used for accepted commercial purposes rather than for military programs. That shift in the instruments of regulation would offer positive inducements and material support for conversion of elements of the Soviet defense industry and might also encourage a new security objective of obviously increasing importance—that is, cooperation in the control of direct weapons exports. The process of international technical diffusion that is making the denial of Soviet access infeasible is also evolving the general proliferation of weapons technology. The single most important step that might be taken to control the dangers inherent in this trend is to forge effective cooperation between the United States, the Soviet Union, and their respective allies in regulating direct weapons exports. It is fair to surmise that this form of cooperation is more likely to be achieved if the basic technical embargo is ended for commercial activities. Moreover, even the traditional objective of constraining Soviet military development would probably be more effectively served by substituting end-use regulation for absolute denial as the policy instrument. There is ample evi-dence now that civilian technology is not readily applied to military programs even within the same company let alone within a country experiencing increasingly diverse forms of political identity. Inducing the Soviet Union to distinguish between commercial and military application and to enforce the distinction to some demonstrable satisfaction would not be a trivial accomplishment.

The discussion of such a revision in the instruments of export control has already centered disproportionately on telecommunications equipment, and that is likely to be the test case for the broader issues involved. In its most recent actions COCOM allowed fiber optic and microwave transmission technology to be exported to Czechoslovakia, Poland, and Hungary up to data rates of 156 megabits per second (as compared to the current U.S. standard of 565 MBPS). Moreover, switching systems were included that have the common channel signaling feature that makes intelligible electronic interception far more difficult to achieve. This technology has been denied to the Soviet Union at the particular insistence of the Western intelligence agencies whose concerns are not difficult to infer. Since the action will not in fact prevent the Soviet Union from obtaining both higher data rate transmissions and common channel signaling, the issue is bound to be contested by Western companies that are aware of the decisive effects that initial position can have in the development of a market with natural monopoly features. That discussion will in turn raise general consciousness of the fact that a great deal of physical infrastructure investment in telecommunications and transportation will be necessary to connect the Soviet Union and Eastern Europe physically with the rest of the world.

It seems likely that the great wheels which forge the instruments and objectives of American foreign policy will be driven by these smaller gears and that at the end of the process the U.S. economic posture towards the Soviet Union will have changed its sign, from predominantly negative to positive and will have become very assertively engaged. That, at any rate, will be necessary to complete the great transformation that was triggered in 1989.

BEYOND NATIONAL POLICY

The shifts in security and in economic posture that have occurred have surely ended the Cold War era, but they cannot by themselves define the character of the new one. In absolute terms the military power of the United States has never been greater, nor has the national economy ever been more capable. Even so, the scope for unilateral action has diminished, and higher standards of behavior have emerged to discipline many of the habits of the past. The conquering of territory, the projection of physical intimidation, and the imposition of economic hardship have not entirely disappeared as instruments of policy—as the Persian Gulf crisis demonstrates—but the time when they could dominate international politics appears to have irretrievably passed. Capability has dispersed too widely and principles of legitimacy taken hold too thoroughly to allow classic forms of hegemony to hold sway on an international scale or even to allow the traditional maneuvers of power politics among nation-states to dominate events. The most significant events emerge from massively dispersed, spontaneously evolving human interactions not directly determined by any of the traditional instruments of national policy. It is clearly too soon to declare that the nation state itself is receding as the primary form of political organization that produces policy objectives and devises the means to serve them. But it is not too soon to acknowledge the press of circumstances that clearly exceed the scope of any single country or even of an alliance that is not global in character.

The major corporations are no longer national entities. That fact has frequently been mentioned and sometimes studied, but it is doubtful that its full implications for the pattern of economic activity have completely emerged. These entities have not yet fully absorbed the technical revolution that is occurring in the processing and transmission of information but they eventually will. Managing economic activity will be driven to an international scale even more than it currently is. The momentum of world population growth and its multiple environmental consequences will soon present extremely urgent and divisive problems of resource management, including that of containing the size of the world population below extreme natural limits. For all the uncertainty about their validity, current models of atmospheric dynamics present a very sharp warning. It is now widely noted that all these models predict significant global warming. It is less noted that setting worst-case assumptions on these models is capable of driving the results into domains where the equilibrium composition of atmosphere might be altered. Most people will not want to wait for a definitive test of that proposition before attempting to impose controls, and that implies a massive conversion of energy sources using technologies that are not yet developed. One does not need an exhaustive study to determine that there is a serious mismatch between the inherent demands of these problems for international coordination and the capacity of prevailing instruments to produce it.

That implies that we must look beyond the dramatic and highly constructive revisions of national policy now underway to define the emerging new era in terms of policy instruments not yet created. We will have to develop rules of equity and principles of legal procedure that can command consent across the cultural diversity and the contentious emotions of current nation states. That above all is the urgent requirement of the future.

NOTES

1. These developments are reviewed in more detail in Raymons L. Garthoff, *Deterrence and the Revolution in Soviet Military Doctrine*, (Washington, D.C.: Brookings, 1990); Michael K. MccGwire, *Perestroika and Soviet National Security*; and John D. Steinbruner, "Revolution in Foreign Policy," in H. Aaron, ed., *Setting National Priorities* (Washington, D.C.: Brookings; 1990).
2. The logic of cooperative security and its basic implications for the U.S. defense budget are outlined in Steinbruner, "Revolution in Foreign Policy."
3. "London Declaration on a Transformed North Atlantic Alliance," NATO Press Communiqué S-1 (90) 36, July 1990.
4. Paul B. Stares, *Allied Rights and Legal Constraints on German Military Power*, Washington, D.C.: Brookings Occasional Paper, October 1990.

5. The development of the B-2 is a very impressive technical feat but the mission specification used to justify the effort could not pass even the most routine scrutiny. It does not extend strategic target coverage in any way that could possibly justify the expense incurred. Given the long established commitment to destruction of the highly vulnerable Soviet air defense system before any bomber arrives to penetrate, the B-2's stealth features do not appear to be required for the advertised mission and are probably in excess of what is necessary to penetrate the current Soviet system even if it is undamaged. Moreover, the presence of stealth aircraft in large numbers could cause truly serious instability under crisis circumstances in which the opponent is attempting to avoid war and requires reassurance that it is not in fact in progress. The U.S. planning system has clearly made no attempt to integrate even these considerations, and they are not the limit of what might be involved.

Appendix 9

BEYOND ALLIANCES: GLOBAL SECURITY THROUGH FOCUSED PARTNERSHIPS

Alice M. Rivlin, David C. Jones, and Edward C. Meyer

Since the end of World War II, the strategic landscape has been dominated by the bipolar power structure that coalesced out of the postwar competition between the United States and the Soviet Union. For two generations, U.S. national security policy has been focused on a singular, highly visible threat (Soviet expansionism, backed by massive conventional force superiority and an awesome nuclear arsenal) and a single overarching strategy (containment). Whatever the current state of Soviet intentions, doctrine, and rationality, U.S. security policy must continue to take into account the fact that the Soviet Union is the *only* nation capable of physically destroying the United States.

On balance, however, we believe that the Cold War is, if not over, at least in a period of protracted armistice. Both superpowers are finding that the most potent threats to their long term security are more *internal* than *external*. The major difference is that, in the Soviet case, the internal perils lie in an inherently flawed system while for the United States they are self-inflicted. Both superpowers need to deal with broader and more fundamental threats to their long-term security that flow from confrontation with each other.

Nonetheless, we believe that total *elimination* of nuclear weapons is neither theoretically attainable nor strategically desirable. Therefore, the key policy question is: What are the appropriate *characteristics* and *force levels* of the U.S. nuclear deterrent? These questions must be answered within the context of the three historical roles of strategic nuclear forces:

- *Deterrence of Nuclear Attack.* Deterrent strategy presumes both a rational opponent (since *no* rational policy can deter an irrational act) and a credible response to attack. If the response is credible, a rational enemy will not launch a nuclear attack because, even under the worst circumstances for the defender, thousands of retaliatory warheads would impact on an attacker's territory. Thus, whatever marginal "advantage" that theoretically might result from preempting could never be calculated as offsetting the *certainty* of major destruction and the *uncertainty* about the ultimate consequences of the exchange.

- *Maintenance of Parity.* This role is important to worldwide perceptions of equivalence. Imbalances in numbers or categories of weaponry can have significant strategic impact that, in a crisis and in arms control negotiations, can weigh heavily in an adversary's decisions.

- *Extended Deterrence.* For most of the nuclear age, the strategic forces of the United States have buttressed its numerically inferior conventional forces. Thus, the deterrent influence of the nuclear weapons of the United States has been "extended" to conventional conflict through the threat of escalation. This policy operated at the strategic level vis-à-vis the Soviets and at the theater level to deter North Korean aggression. The threat of escalation has, at a minimum, contained superpower conflicts and inhibited open military confrontation throughout tensions and crises of the sort that historically have hurled nations into war.

The foregoing logic leads the Unites States to a number of conclusions that challenge prevailing assumptions about nuclear weapons and point the way to a fresh appraisal of their role in a post–Cold War world.

First, at the dawn of the atomic age, the U.S. briefly held a monopoly on these new weapons and had a *technical*, though perhaps not fully *operational*, first-strike capability. However, this unilateral advantage quickly disappeared and, in view of the certainty of a devastating response under any circumstances, it now seems self-evident that, *regardless of the intentions, efforts, doctrine, or resources of either side, neither can achieve a* disarming *first strike capability against the other*. Not even during the most glacial days of the Cold War could one side have launched a surprise attack that would have disarmed the other side or rendered it incapable of devastating retaliation. It is this certainty of response that has enforced the strategic balance through four turbulent decades.

From the U.S. standpoint, so long as extended deterrence remains critical, the threat of escalation must remain credible. That credibility, in turn, depends upon the realistic threat of militarily significant escalation, i.e., the ability of the United States to attack the enemy's nuclear and conventional forces with high assurance of unacceptable damage. The hidden consequence of this requirement has been a fundamental schizophrenia in U.S. deterrent policy. We have seemed to be attempting simultaneously to make nuclear war both impossible and possible: *impossible* insofar as attack on the United States is concerned, but *possible* as a consequence of escalation if the Soviets attacked in Europe. History may record the fact that *both* policies worked for so long, *despite* the apparent contradiction, as one of its supreme ironies!

The changing European security environment and the ongoing negotiations on major conventional force reductions in Europe offer a potential escape from this logic disconnect. The Soviets are withdrawing forces from Eastern Europe and have begun to reduce their massive national military establishment. The non-Soviet Warsaw Pact armies no longer represent any serious threat to NATO. Even more important, the Conventional Armed Forces in Europe (CFE) process holds out the prospect for much deeper mutual reductions in conventional offensive capability. These developments not only reduce the likelihood of a NATO–Warsaw Pact war in Europe (because an aggressor would be hard pressed to mount a decisive attack on an opponent), but also present an opportunity for radically reducing the role and the quantity of nuclear forces.

This opportunity springs from the growing realization that *conventional forces can be reduced to a level at which nuclear weapons are no longer required to carry the major burden in underwriting conventional deterrence*. Recall that extended deterrence has been a Western imperative, driven by the Soviet conventional superiority. If this superiority can be erased and the offensive capabilities of all parties reduced to the point where overwhelming aggression ceases to be a realistic option, then conventional deterrence can be maintained primarily by strong defensive conventional forces the United States and would no longer need to rely so heavily on the threat of nuclear escalation. (Note that the precondition is *greatly reduced offensive forces*, not simply *equal levels* of conventional forces. High levels of conventional forces, even if evenly balanced, do not necessarily deter war.)

Reducing or eliminating the burden of extended deterrence would create possibilities for major restructuring of both sides' nuclear arsenals based on symmetrical strategic assumptions and mutual understanding of each side's security requirements. More fundamentally, it would open the door to a major reversal in *thinking* about security.

So long as the Unites States must continue to rely so heavily on extended deterrence, a credible capability for *attacking* the opponent's forces, especially its strategic capability, remains a top priority. This imperative accounts for such features as large numbers of warheads, multiple independently targeted reentry vehicle (MIRV) systems, and an emphasis on targeting mobile missiles. However, if the need for extended deterrence were substantially reduced and the principal burden on *both* side's strategic forces were deterrence of direct attack and maintenance of parity, the entire logic would reverse and *survivability* of both sides' forces would become paramount for stability and mutual security.

The consequences of such a reversal in thinking with regard to strategic doctrine, force structure and targeting would be enormous. Strategic forces could be reduced reciprocally to a symmetrical level required for deterrence of nuclear attack. This more limited role would give both superpowers an inherent interest in not threatening the survivability of the other's force structure and would shape the nature of the forces, their deployment mode, and the verification regime to assure mutual security. We believe further that, as the United States is able to reduce its reliance on extended deterrence, a complete reassessment of our national targeting policy would be appropriate.

A final conclusion from the foregoing rationale is that, if the strategic balance is more stable than we thought, if deterrence of a first strike is not extremely difficult, and if the demands of extended deterrence can be reduced through major reductions in conventional forces, then there is less urgency to pursue simultaneous modernization of all three legs of the triad.

We offer a few specific conclusions regarding strategic force structure:

- The United States should maintain a triad of strategic offensive forces backed by secure warning and command, control and communications;

- If relations between the United States and the Soviet Union continue to improve, we believe that the United States can safely negotiate reciprocal reductions to a level of about 2000–3000 warheads for both sides;

- Ideally, for maximum survivability and stability the land-based component would be a single-warhead, mobile intercontinental ballistic missile (ICBM), but silo deployment may be an acceptable alternative at reduced force levels;

- The air breathing leg of the triad (bombers and cruise missiles) should be retained for employment flexibility and to force opponents to commit resources to air defense; and

- At least one-third of U.S. warheads should be at sea on ballistic missile submarines (SSBNs) for as long as this mode remains survivable.

The defensive side of the strategic equation is more problematic. On the one hand, the principle of survivability would seem to be supported if both sides deploy a system such as the Strategic Defense Iniative (SDI). However, anything less than equality in capability would be destabilizing and to assure this parity (even assuming duplicate systems) would be difficult at best. Moreover, if one side found a way to disable the other's system while keeping its own intact, it could literally impose a space blockade and, at the low level of offensive forces postulated here, threaten anything, from destroying the adversary's surveillance and communications assets to a potentially disarming first strike. Neither side could be expected to accept this kind of vulnerability, and the most likely counter—proliferation of offensive warheads—is precisely the result we wish to avoid.

Therefore, we are not prepared to endorse deployment of SDI. However, we recommend that research and development continue in order to preserve U.S. options for future deployment if the strategic situation so dictates and to gain valuable knowledge about derivative applications (e.g., tactical ballistic missile defense). The pros and cons of deployment should continue to be studied within the framework of the anti-ballistic missile (ABM) Treaty or negotiated changes to it, and with particular emphasis on mutual security and progress toward reciprocal reduction of offensive weapons.

During 1990, two epochal changes have converged to offer world leaders a "clean slate"—the first genuinely new opportunity for strategic reconfiguration since 1945. With these changes there are new opportunities for promoting peace and constructive change in the world.

We have already outlined one such change: the reduction of the Soviet military threat. The second major change attaches to the concept of national security itself. Americans have traditionally regarded security in military terms—absence of attack—and identified hostile foreign powers as the main threat to their national survival. However, the shrinking of the world and the global reach of threats now require security to be defined in broader economic, social, and political terms.

NEW CONCEPTS OF SECURITY

A secure nation needs a viable economic system producing the goods and services required for an improving standard of living. A secure nation's economic development must be sustainable. It cannot be bought at the price of despoiling the land and fouling air and water. Nor is a nation secure if its people are oppressed, deprived of human rights, and without an effective voice in their government. Above all, security requires cooperation among nations and must be mutual to be sustained. No nation, however strong or prosperous, can any longer feel secure in isolation.

In the years ahead, the United States will face a wide variety of serious threats to its security and that of other nations:

- Danger of military conflict will remain for the foreseeable future;

- Interruption of oil supplies dramatized in the Middle East crisis of 1990;

- Proliferating high-technology military power, including chemical and nuclear weapons and the means to deliver them;

- Third World poverty and the instability it engenders;

- Rising ethnic, racial, nationality, and religious tensions, feeding instability and global terrorism;

- Global environmental degradation; and

- Defective U.S. economic policy, especially budget deficits, trade imbalance, and dependence on foreign capital.

With the recession of the Soviet threat, those threats that rise to the top of the list are not primarily addressable through an alliance system. Preventing wars in an age of proliferating nuclear weaponry, maintaining international economic stability and growth, and safeguarding the global environment are not zero-sum games for which alliances are suited. Rather, they require positive cooperation among nations that recognize that all will benefit from successful multilateral efforts. Hence, we believe a fresh approach and new institutions are necessary.

The new national strategy of the United States should be to take the lead in creating working partnerships with other nations to develop pragmatic solutions to the specific problems that undermine the security of all. We call this strategy "focused partnerships."

The word "partnerships" dramatizes a reversal in the traditional defensive mind-set that uses alliances as instruments to curtail or oppose the power of one or more adversaries. Instead, we favor proactive international efforts to reduce threats, settle disputes before they turn violent, and promote cooperative solutions to common problems.

The term "focused" emphasizes that this concept neither implies world government nor depends on referring all problems to global institutions. Rather, the operating framework would be an overlapping network of multinational relationships, tailored to respective regions and/or issues, with substantial ceded power for well-defined purposes.

Focused partnerships are not conceived as instruments to eliminate the world's political or economic conflicts; rather, their goal is to contain, mediate, and manage them, hopefully short of armed conflict, but continuing to do so even in the event of war. We believe this constructive approach promotes democratic values, mutual security, and negotiated solutions to problems, is workable internationally, and is consistent with the American value system.

A key feature of an approach based on mutual security rather than confrontation is that the Americans can engage the Soviets in a cooperative effort to solve problems of concern to both, such as European security, nuclear proliferation, environment, terrorism, etc. (The recent joint statements and coordinated actions following the Iraqi invasion of Kuwait typify the potential for productive cooperation.) The United States should also attempt to reach explicit agreement with other nations, including the

Soviet Union, on the principle that people should decide their own destiny through democratic means. An important by-product of abandoning the confrontational norm between the United States and the Soviet Union is thatU.S. policy toward autocratic regimes around the world can focus on their human rights performance, not on whether an authoritarian leader is a "bad" left wing tyrant or a "tolerable" right wing dictator.

The concept of focused partnerships is flexible and pragmatic. The first principle is that the nature of the issue on which the partners are focusing determines the proper level of organization and membership. The United States would take the lead in some and play a supporting role in others.

Some focused partnerships will be small and others large. For example, the threat of international financial instability can be controlled by cooperation among a small group of financially powerful nations, such as the Group of Five or the Group of Seven (G5 or G7). Control of some kinds of contagious diseases, by contrast, requires the cooperation of every country in the world.

In some cases, the appropriate grouping is regional. Acid rain, river pollution, and many military security issues fall in this category. In other cases, regional groupings would be totally ineffective. Global warming, ocean pollution, international trade issues, and control of nuclear weapons cannot be handled on a purely regional basis.

In some cases, formal organizations with rules, voting procedures, and international staffs will be required. In others, quite informal diplomatic communication may be able to produce the necessary joint actions. Moreover, while some new international organizations undoubtedly will be required, many existing ones are natural instruments of effective focused partnerships or can become so. For example, now that the United Nations Security Council is no longer paralyzed by U.S.–Soviet competition, the UN could become a major instrument for containing and resolving conflicts around the world.

The success of focused partnerships will usually depend on partial surrender of sovereignty and enforcement of rules (as is the case today, for example, under the terms of arms control agreements and the Nuclear Nonproliferation Treaty). The partners will also have to create new mechanisms for resolving conflicts among themselves as the premium for enhanced security.

Enforcing these rules and resolving conflicts will be difficult at best, and impossible if unanimity of a very large number of nations is always required. In many instances, the great powers are going to have to take the lead and cooperate among themselves to get other nations to follow. No such regime will work (as the UN, in many respects, did not) as long as the major powers are not cooperating. However, if they do (especially if the United States and the Soviet Union continue to cooperate in new ways), the potential for reducing threats is unprecedented.

EUROPEAN TEST CASE— MAKING FOCUSED PARTNERSHIPS WORK

Europe is the region where it is most urgent to test the concepts and principles of a focused partnership strategy. For over forty years, it has been the area of greatest potential East-West conflict and therefore the focal point of U.S. containment strategy and force planning. We recommend a dual approach: first, undertaking a new focused partnership for cooperative security and second, maintaining the cohesion of the NATO alliance.

We envision three essential characteristics of the new focused partnership for cooperative security:

- *The scope must be pan-European.* All nations with a stake in the security of Europe must be involved, including the Unites States, the Soviet Union, Canada, and all the nations, large and small, of Eastern and Western Europe. This is not to say that each nation would have an equal role in the arrangement and its various functions, but each would have a seat at the table and a voice in the organization's policies. We envision the Conference on Security and Cooperation in Europe (CSCE) as the appropriate legitimizing organ, providing a political umbrella for the range of security functions carried out at different organizational levels, as it does today with the Confidence and Security Building Measures (CSBM) negotiations and the negotiations on Conventional Armed Forces in Europe.

- *Institutions must be created for carrying out the key operational security functions,* i.e., arms control, monitoring and data exchange, and crisis consultation. These functions will be the heart of the new security arrangement. Initially, even though the Warsaw Pact is moribund, the operational body should consist of the *nations* that now comprise the NATO and Warsaw Pact alliances. It is these nations whose forces and planning are central to European security today and that will have to be integrated into a single cooperative structure for the arrangement to work successfully.

- *The most powerful nations must exercise a leading role on behalf of cooperative security.* The recent "Two Plus Four" negotiations that resulted in the reunification of Germany were a model for big power cooperation in resolving difficult and divisive issues. Continuing the close communication and coordination among the five nations would help to guarantee the future stability of Europe. We call this concept "Five Plus."

The "Five" would be the United States, the Soviet Union, the United Kingdom, France, and Germany. The "Plus" denotes both the possible *expansion* of the core group (for example, on some issues, Italy would play a key role along with the Five) and the necessary sensitivity of the larger powers to the security concerns of all the nations of Europe. The Five would probably operate most effectively by exerting leadership informally within the mutual security framework.

The critical issues affecting overall European military stability (such as establishing and verifying conventional forces levels and deployments, resolving nuclear forces issues, etc.) principally involve these five nations. Their combined resources and influence could also exert powerful leverage for containing, mediating, and/or resolving subregional issues involving other countries, e.g., border disputes, human rights abuses, economic development, and environmental measures.

The second path in the dual approach is to maintain NATO as a defensive alliance, serving both as a hedge against a resurgent Soviet military threat and as the Allies' principal negotiating bloc for managing the transition to a pan-European structure. Later, to the degree the military threat continues to decline and the cooperative security framework becomes sturdier and more capable of ensuring European security, NATO could gradually recede in importance.

We foresee important roles for both NATO and the Pan-European Security Organization in reducing the risks of conflict in Europe through arms control, mutual verification, and confidence-building measures. The initial move to reduce U.S. and Soviet forces to the 225,000/195,000 ceilings is a good first step, but should be seen as a way point for much deeper reductions, possibly as low as 75,000–100,000. Once the current CFE negotiations have been concluded, some other multilateral structure will be necessary within which the parties can continue these negotiations and can verify negotiated and unilateral reductions. We see the Pan-European Security Organization taking over this role. NATO should continue to serve as the vehicle to coordinate the negotiating strategies and verification regimes of the Western allies as the negotiations proceed.

Over the next few years, we believe the residual U.S. military presence should concentrate on combat support and force multiplier capabilities. Examples include space support (intelligence, communications, etc.), command and control, and reinforcement forces. However, for military and political reasons, we also favor retaining some forward deployed air and ground combat forces, including perhaps an Army division as part of an international Army Corps. Some dual capable aircraft (i.e., those configured to deliver either conventional or nuclear weapons) would remain. However, at greatly reduced force levels, *all* theater nuclear weapon could be withdrawn. We would retain the capability to reintroduce such weapons if circumstances were to dictate this course.

As this much reduced level of forward deployed forces is reached, we recommend shifting to a system of rotational (rather than permanently stationed) units in Europe. Rotating units for three to six months at a time would be significantly cheaper since we could forgo the present costly family support infrastructure. Even more important, the quality of training and the cohesiveness of the units would be improved by deploying and training together in a focused, stable environment. The rotation would be spread across the entire U.S.-based force structure, thereby limiting the frequency of absence, minimizing family separations, and sharing the benefits and burdens of training overseas. Even assuming a high tempo of unit training while deployed, the *total* impact on the host nation (e.g., tank traffic, aircraft overflights, etc.) would be far less than at present since the size of the deployed force would be so much smaller.

As the military threat continues to diminish, NATO should play a larger political role. In this regard, we applaud the NATO proposal to offer observer status to the nations of Eastern Europe. This initiative can deepen the political contacts among former adversaries and would let all nations see that NATO represents no threat to anyone's security.

Soviet and German Concerns

Although this framework includes all nations of Europe and is intended to meet the security needs of all, two central and, in some respects, competing issues have to be addressed in order for a European mutual security structure to succeed: Soviet security and Germany's role in the new arrangement.

We believe that any framework that fails to take into account the security concerns of the Soviet Union is inherently flawed and unstable and carries within it the seeds of future conflict. The Western powers must acknowledge the legitimacy of Soviet security interests and ensure that the resultant structure provides reasonable safeguards against external threats. Although this explicit concern for Soviet security has not figured prominently in U.S. policy since the end of World War II, it is inherent in cooperative security.

Our proposal differs markedly from other efforts to satisfy Soviet security concerns in that earlier formulas demanded little or nothing in return. In contrast, the focused partnerships strategy would make the Soviets accountable for being part of the solution (i.e., eliminate their offensive threat) and for working constructively toward mutual security as the price for their own security guarantees.

The second key issue is the role of a unified Germany. It would be difficult to overstate the depths of Soviet concern with the prospect of a resurgent German state. The memory of more than 20 million war dead is deeply embedded in the Soviets' psyche and in their security policy. (Recall that the Warsaw Pact was not created in 1949, as a response to the formation of NATO, but in 1955, when the Federal Republic of Germany was established and the Bundeswehr began to rearm and join the NATO integrated command structure.)

Thus, the central question is how a unified Germany can enjoy the stature of a sovereign nation without being seen as a threat to its neighbors. The accord recently initialled in Moscow takes constructive steps toward satisfying the security concerns of both the Soviets and the other nations of Europe. For example, Germany will limit its armed forces to 370,000, NATO's military forces will not be expanded into what is now East German territory, a united Germany will renounce the possession of nuclear, chemical, and biological weapons (as both the FRG and the GDR had already done separately), and Soviet troops will be allowed to remain in Eastern Germany for a four-year transitional period. On the other hand, Germany will be a full member of NATO.

OTHER OPPORTUNITIES
FOR FOCUSED PARTNERSHIPS

A variety of regional and functional problems should be approached cooperatively within the focused partnerships framework.

Security in the Middle East/Southwest Asia

Looking at the bitter hostilities that currently divide the nations of this region, it would be easy to conclude that no basis exists for *any* mutual security regime. Nevertheless, we believe that the issues dividing the nations of the region, while deeply felt and difficult, are not so intractable as to defy eventual resolution. Despite this climate of bitterness (or more precisely, *because* of it) we believe the seeds of a mutual security apparatus employing the principles of focused partnerships *must* be sown at once. The presence of nuclear and chemical weapons (and their means of delivery) and of sophisticated conventional capability throughout this region poses the chilling prospect of escalating conflict and argues even more urgently for decisive action to contain the threat of war.

The actions of many nations and institutions to contain the aggression of Saddam Hussein suggest ways in which a focused partnership can contribute to mutual security in the region. In addition, it highlights criteria to consider in determining the extent and form of the involvement of the United States in distant regions when its interests are threatened.

The United Nations

The United Nations, freed from its Cold War straitjacket, took swift and forceful action to condemn the Iraqi invasion and impose meaningful sanctions. This achievement is of striking importance, as this is the first time that the Security Council has faced clear-cut aggression since the end of the Cold War, and it reacted with speed and firm resolve under the mandate of the UN Charter. If this body is to realize its original charge of stopping international aggression, it must continue to outline steps for its member nations to turn back the Iraqi aggression. In turn, its members must keep their actions within the bounds delineated by the Security Council.

Basis for United States Involvement

Its behavior in the Persian Gulf crisis illustrates that the United States sees the Iraqi aggression not only as a threat to U.S. access to cheap gasoline, but as a challenge to the norms of international behavior. Rather than acting unilaterally and using the UN Security Council actions to legitimate actions that it would have taken anyway, the actions of the United States have remained carefully within the bounds of international law. When U.S. actions to enforce the naval embargo early in the crisis were criticized for violating international law, the United States responded with vigorous diplomatic efforts in the Security Council. These efforts were rewarded with a resolution sanctioning the use of warships to enforce the embargo.

The deployment of U.S. forces in Saudi Arabia also falls squarely within the confines of international law, as they are there at the request of the Saudis, along with a multinational force from various Arab and European countries.

Arab League

The move by this multinational Arab body to condemn the Iraqi invasion refuted Saddam's claim that he moved against Kuwait in the name of Arab unity. Insistence by this organization that nations in the region have legitimate sovereign rights indicates a basis on which a peaceful settlement of political disputes throughout the region could be achieved.

U.S.–Soviet Cooperation

The concerted and coordinated action by the superpowers is unprecedented and serves the interests of both nations. The joint statement issued by President Bush and President Gorbachev in Helsinki that "no peaceful international order is possible if larger states can devour their smaller neighbors," signals an acceptance of terms on which the two former rivals can jointly exercise international leadership.

Along with the simple condemnation of aggression, the Soviets have traditional strategic interests in opposing the Iraqi invasion. Although the Soviets do not share with the Americans an overarching priority on maintaining unimpeded access to Persian Gulf oil, they recognize the potential for conflict should this economic lifeline be threatened and the fact that such a conflict could expand in an unpredictable manner. The prospect of nuclear or chemical conflict literally in its back yard is even more threatening for the Soviets than for the United States. Moreover, they are concerned about their restive Muslim republics and the increasing porousness of their southern border, which raise the prospect that these republics might secede and align themselves with the growing Muslim fundamentalist movement.

Presence of Formidable Conventional Armaments Plus Weapons of Mass Destruction

Saddam Hussein is manifestly willing to use force to achieve his ambitions and has demonstrated the capability and the willingness to use chemical weapons against his enemies. The quick response of the United States demonstrated its resolve and provided the time to mobilize and deploy an international force to the region to block further aggression.

Deployment of U.S. Military Forces to Distant Bases/Waters

Operation Desert Shield has underscored both the type of military capability that will be needed in the post–Cold War world (see Appendix 7) and the difficulty inherent in projecting force quickly to distant trouble spots. The bases that the United States needed were made available by threatened hosts, the probable model for base access in the future. The U.S. force presence, if any, after the crisis is resolved has not yet been established and will depend on the severity of the residual threat perceived by the other nations of the region. At a minimum, the United States should attempt to secure agreements for quick reentry, including pre-stocking food, water, fuel, and munitions.

Unique Contributions to Power Projection by Each Service

Joint action has worked successfully, with each service bringing to bear its distinctive capabilities. The United States must exploit this diversity and synergism rather than try to create or designate a single force projection service.

Looking beyond the current crisis, the fundamental interests of the United States will remain unchanged and dictate a continued influence on events in the region, irrespective of the degree of Soviet cooperation. The most critical interest of the United States is continued production and shipment of oil from the region. *In sizing the future military capability of the United States, Operation Desert Shield has demonstrated that, if Soviet force reductions continue as expected, the most demanding mission for U.S. conventional military forces would be projecting power into the Persian Gulf to protect or defend the sources of supply against seizure by an unfriendly power.* We have to be able to react quickly and in strength, preferably in concert with regional forces and other involved nations.

The second major interest of the United States is to promote a peaceful, democratic political environment in general and a stable Israel within secure borders in particular. Both these interests can best be secured within the mutual security framework out-lined herein, and the United States must urgently but patiently promote the conditions that would permit such a framework to develop and flourish.

The overriding condition for establishing this framework is progress toward fundamental solutions to the bitter hostilities and mistrust that divide the people of the region. There is reason for renewed optimism in this regard; we see fresh opportunities created by unprecedented U.S.–Soviet regional cooperation, the revival of the potency of the United Nations, and solidarity among the most influential Arab nations against the Iraqi threat, all of which might be translated into momentum toward enduring negotiated settlements.

Further to the east, the United States should build on the precedent of coordinated actions in the Middle East crisis to work with the Soviets to reduce the threat of hostilities between India and Pakistan. The Americans should reduce their military support for Pakistan as the Soviets reduce theirs for India. Both the United States and the Soviet Union should prevail on the PRC to curtail the export of high-technology weaponry to the region. It is in the interest of the United States and the Soviet Union to encourage restraint in both nuclear and conventional capability among all nations of the region. The United States and other nations should work hard, through the United Nations and other channels, to encourage peaceful settlement of the dispute over Kashmir and other points of tension.

Security in the Pacific/Northeast Asia

Conceptually, the notion of a network of focused partnerships in East Asia to moderate the assertive policies of individual states, promote mutually beneficial economic development, and facilitate security burden sharing is an attractive goal. However, the vast distances, long-standing national and cultural rivalries, and the absence of an existing multinational infrastructure upon which to build make regional cooperation a difficult challenge. In the area of security, for example, mutual security, arms control, and peaceful resolution of conflicts are valid goals. However, the crosscutting tensions and threats among regional states make cooperative security difficult to achieve.

We suggest, however, three initial steps:

- Defuse the Korean conflict, the one regional situation that presents a high risk of violence on a large scale;

- Encourage efforts to establish general military stability throughout the region;

- Use diplomacy and multilateral organizations to promote economic relations throughout the region.

The driving force behind U.S. military planning in Asia and the Pacific has been the Soviet threat. With the end of the Cold War, the need for the U.S. presence can be reduced commensurate with the reduction of Soviet military presence in the area. However, we do not envision a total U.S. withdrawal; for the foreseeable future the United States will need a presence in Korea, Japan and, to a lesser extent, the Philippines. Consistent with threat reduction, the United States should aim to reduce eventually (but not necessarily eliminate) ground combat forces in favor of U.S. capabilities, such as space-based intelligence and command and control, air and naval support, reinforcement capability, etc., that complement and augment the unique needs of the country or region involved.

In the absence of a visible threat to the host, forward bases in this region, as in other parts of the world, will become increasingly difficult to support both politically and financially. *The United States should undertake a sustained initiative to tailor its basing posture to the minimum required to support rapid response in a crisis. The governing principle for negotiating base rights should be that long-term retention of reentry access is more important than extensive near-term use.*

Such an approach in the Philippines might, for example, enable the United States to lower its profile at Clark Air Base sharply (e.g., by removing the fighter wing) and to reduce its visibility and dependence at Subic Bay as much as possible. If the Soviet threat were to increase, we believe sufficient warning time would be available so that bases maintained at less than maximum capacity could be regenerated to support U.S. reinforcements and to operate at wartime levels.

Economic development is the primary goal of most states in the region. Nations are pursuing this particular goal now through bilateral trade relations, but also through existing regional organizations. The Pacific Economic Cooperation Conference (PECC) and the Association of Southeast Asian Nations (ASEAN) are good examples. It is through gradually strengthening economic cooperation that a path will be broken for broader political and security cooperation.

New Partnership with the Developing World: The Case of Latin America

It is not hard to imagine that in the twenty-first century the industrialized countries of the world, realizing how much their well-being depends on each other, finally learn to settle their differences without resort to armed conflict or mutually destructive trade wars. It is difficult, however, to be similarly optimistic about the developing world, which is likely to be the source of the most serious threats to world security in the years ahead.

Worst-case scenarios for many parts of the developing world include runaway population growth, shortsighted management of resources, stagnant or declining real income, ethnic and religious conflicts exacerbated by widespread hunger and deprivation, wars involving weapons of mass destruction, millions of refugees and escalating levels of drug trafficking and terrorism. To avoid these horrors, the industrial countries need to be farsighted enough to reach out to the developing world, to find ways to help developing countries sustain economic development, strengthen democratic institutions, and forge increasingly close links with the industrialized world.

The United States has particularly heavy stakes in the successful economic and political development of Latin America. Resumption of higher growth rates could make Latin America an important expanding market for U.S. exports, as it was in the 1960s and 1970s. Continuing the stagnation of the 1980s could mean lower prosperity for American export industries, rapidly escalating inflows of illegal drugs and immigrants, and threats to peace in which the United States feels forced to intervene.

U.S. policy toward Latin America, long preoccupied with containing communism, needs to be thoroughly reevaluated. Even in the darkest days of the Cold War, the greatest problem in the Western hemisphere was not communism, but rather the appalling political, economic, and social conditions that made Marxism attractive to desperate Latin American workers and peasants. Now that the U.S.-Soviet conflict is receding, the Unites States has the chance to focus on the real enemy. Moreover, in a significant number of countries, dictatorships of both left and right have been overthrown and newly elected leaders are struggling to manage debt-ridden economies and fulfill promises made to the electorate for a better life.

The potential for sustained economic development is high in much of Latin America, including the largest but most heavily indebted countries: Mexico, Brazil, and Argentina. Realizing this potential, however, requires several elements: reducing debt service levels to manageable proportions; resuming at least modest inflows of foreign capital and repatriating domestic capital; implementing anti-inflationary fiscal and monetary policies; moving toward more equitable distribution of income and property; making advances in education and public health; and managing natural resources with greater vision. To contribute to this process, the United States should launch a new effort to resolve the debt problem, building on the concept of the Brady

Plan, but moving decisively to reduce the debt service drain on Latin American economies and improve the chances for future growth. President Bush's June 27 speech outlined constructive first steps toward this goal.

Finally, as with regional issues, there are many global problem areas for which the focused partnership approach offers a framework for fundamental solutions. Examples include renewed efforts to deal with the proliferation of nuclear, chemical, and other high-tech weaponry and partnerships to preserve the ozone layer, combat acid rain, slow global warming, and promote sustainable economic development.

AMERICAN SECURITY STRATEGY IN THE 1990s

The Iraqi crisis and the requirements for Operation Desert Shield highlight the new challenges and unprecedented opportunities for U.S. strategy in the decade ahead:

- Politically, the end of the Cold War has resulted in a more vigorous role for the United Nations in addressing the Iraqi invasion, provided for superpower cooperation in repelling aggression, and allowed an unprecedented level of international coordination to implement economic sanctions and the introduction of military forces;

- Economically, the UnitedStates has been shown how its internal economic problems can weaken our hand abroad: our budget deficits have left it short of cash, limiting its freedom of action in the current crisis; its dependence of the Unites States on foreign oil has given Saddam Hussein the power to damage the U.S. economy; and

- Militarily, the experience of Desert Shield has already shown the United States the challenge that short warning time poses for its forces, and the need for air and sea mobility for rapid response; it has given the United States a better sense of the contributions that each service makes to power projection and how best to orchestrate them.

From this single experience, we can see examples of how U.S. strategy will have to adapt to greatly changed world conditions.

Our discussion of the concept of focused partnerships indicates that, in political terms, the United States will have to develop cooperative methods for dealing with a spectrum of international problems and threats and especially will have to work with the Soviet Union in addressing areas of mutual concern. Given our view that nonmilitary components will be of increasing importance in future security considerations, it is essential that the United States remain at the political forefront of promoting the principles of mutual security.

We believe that the center of gravity of the *political strategy of the United States* lies in the pattern of communication and verification that focused partnerships would encourage. The key to mutual security in this regime involves discouraging any potential adversary from acquiring a decisive offensive military threat. In order to enforce this precept, an extensive structure of arms limitations, inspections, notifications, and other confidence-building measures will evolve. The regional organizations would monitor the forces and activities of member nations and, though not a "balance of power" structure, could serve that function if one or more regional powers became threatening or unduly assertive.

The United States should continue to pursue arms control as an instrument of its security policy on two levels. First, the United States should strive for substantial mutual reductions in present forces through existing venues such as Strategic Arms Reduction Talks (START), CFE, etc. More broadly, the United States should engage the Soviets in a more conceptual dialogue to chart where the logic of mutual deterrence will take the United States in ten or fifteen years. These talks could lay the foundation for a more rational force posture as the relationship between nuclear forces and conventional drawdowns was put more sharply into focus.

Finally, the United Nations and its constituent agencies should play a greater role in U.S. diplomatic strategy in the 1990s than they have in the recent past. The Cold War schisms prevented the United Nations from functioning as originally envisioned, but recent events have generated substantial hope for a stronger United Nations in the future. The United Nations played a useful role in helping end the Iran-Iraq war and in resolving the conflict in Afghanistan. In the summer of 1990, the United Nations proved itself a responsive mechanism for generating rapid, coordinated, international action to counter Iraqi aggression. At the same time it worked out a promising blueprint for ending the long and bloody conflict in Cambodia. The world is coming to recognize that, when the major powers are not obstructing its action, the United Nations can be an effective instrument for resolving international conflict.

The first priority of the *economic strategy of the United States* should be to get its own house in order if it is going to remain a world leader and play an effective role in focused partnerships to increase world security. The United States should give top policy priority to moving the federal budget from deficit to surplus, increasing support for research and development, improving the effectiveness of education and training, and bringing the disadvantaged into the American mainstream. Pursuing free global markets should also be a priority.

A well-designed energy tax could make important and simultaneous contributions to several important goals. It could increase incentives to use energy efficiently, reduce atmospheric pollution, lower U.S. dependence on imported oil, and produce revenues that would help reduce the budget deficit. Such a tax should be increased gradually and predictably over a period of years. A foreseeable rise in the price of energy will give both consumers and producers incentives to make the necessary adjustments to use fuel more sparingly.

For the elements of U.S. security that are guided by military considerations, we see four overarching strategic objectives:

- Deter nuclear attack with capable, survivable strategic nuclear forces;

- Forestall conventional aggression against U.S. interests by cooperating with regional security structures and multinational peacekeeping forces;

- Establish a capability for rapid multiservice power projection to augment regional forces and to meet grave threats to U.S. interests that cannot be handled by diplomacy or regional action. The forces of the United States must be able to enforce the security of its sea lines of communication; and

- Assure adequate strategic warning through vigorous surveillance and arms control verification, and timely mobilization through dynamic reserve forces, strong research development (R&D) and a resilient industrial base.

Although these elements of military strategy bear some similarity to those of the Cold War, the goals they seek are very different. Deterring nuclear attack and conventional aggression against the U.S. can potentially be achieved at much lower levels of strategic forces. If relations between the United States and the Soviet Union continue to improve, we believe that the United States can safely negotiate reciprocal reductions to a level of about 2,000–3,000 warheads for both sides. Furthermore, U.S. power projection and maritime strategies would take on a wholly different cast once the Soviet Union is no longer the primary threat they must address.

A New Breed of Warrior in a Reconfigured
American Military

To maintain a military hedge across the spectrum of warfare—from low intensity conventional operations to the nuclear, biological, and chemical environments—U.S. military forces should develop and retain these characteristics:

- Much smaller active duty force;

- Very high levels of active duty training, exercising, supply, and readiness;

- Superior strategic and tactical mobility; and

- Much improved equipment and training of the reserve

forces to produce a highly effective mobilization/augmentation capability.

Within these guidelines, we believe that the United States can safely and prudently make force reductions of at least 25 percent over five years. Further, the constructive impact of focused partnerships can eventually permit still deeper reductions in forces and in cost.

Finally, the impact of technology and the prospects for a radically diminished Soviet threat will require all the services to reexamine critically not only their roles, but their traditional approaches toward carrying out those roles. The following list is by no means exhaustive, but is intended to illustrate the scope of the required reappraisal.

- The U.S. Army may need to rethink its entire concept of employing and countering armor in contingencies outside Europe's Central Region. Also, the periodic jostling over the issue of close air support needs to be resolved, not in terms of whether the army or the air force performs the mission, but rather whether future battlefield technologies might offer effective alternatives to multimillion dollar aircraft attacking tanks in a high-threat environment.

- If the reduction in the Soviet threat proceeds along the lines we have projected, the traditional missions of sea control and maritime force projection (including regional force presence) may be carried out by fewer ships with currently available technology. Alternatives to carrier aviation, the utility of nuclear weapons aboard surface ships, the mix of surface and submarine forces, and other related issues are questions to be studied and debated openly and dispassionately in the days ahead. In particular, most of the naval experts we consulted agreed that not every required battle group has to be a *carrier* battle group.

- The U.S. Air Force's commitment to an expensive penetrating stealth bomber will have to be backed by a clearly understood and persuasive employment concept. Also, a thorough reappraisal of future air force and navy tactical air requirements is warranted if the Soviet Air Force and Soviet Naval Aviation threats continue to decline as expected.

- The U.S. Marine Corps' long and proud tradition of amphibious warfare and its current "expeditionary" emphasis will require reappraisal in light of the expected threat and overall U.S. power projection requirements.

- All services must focus on the contributions they can make to solving the challenges of terrorism and drugs at the low end of the spectrum of warfare. Special operations forces must receive increased priority as the nature of warfare changes.

- The Department of Defense and all the services must develop a military space policy that rises above turf battles and wasteful duplication, and exploits the full potential of this medium for the nation's benefit.

However configured, the political, economic and military strategy of the United States must preserve its capability to counter surprises. In matters of national security, as in nature, there are no rewards or punishments, only consequences. If the United States are to err, it should err on the side of caution and of survival of the nation.

Appendix 10

THE 1991 DEFENSE BUDGET AND
THE 1991–1995 DEFENSE PROGRAM

Lawrence J. Korb

The d ecisions made in the annual defense budget process are among the most critical ones in the U.S. political system. For five reasons "dollars are policy" for the Department of Defense.[1]

First, the defense budget is the linchpin of U.S. defense policy. Planning is irrelevant and operations impossible if the budget process does not result in the correct mix of manpower and material. For example, during the 1980s the Department of Defense (DoD) was unwilling to purchase sufficient airlift and sealift to meet its goal of being able to move 66 million ton miles per day. On one occasion, the Pentagon leadership actually reprogrammed $600 million that Congress had authorized for fast sealift. Consequently, in August 1990 when President George Bush decided to deploy American forces to the Persian Gulf to deter Iraq from further aggression, it took DoD almost four months instead of two months to place 250,000 troops and their equipment on the ground in the Gulf.

Dollars determined policy even more notably for President Ronald Reagan's strategic defensive initiative (SDI), or Star Wars. In March 1983 Reagan announced he had decided to revolutionize U.S. strategic policy by challenging American scientists to develop an impenetrable strategic defense that would make nuclear weapons obsolete. At the time of Reagan's speech, the Defense Department had $14 billion in its fiscal 1985–1989 defense program budget allocated to research on strategic defense.[2] Despite five years of unprecedented rhetorical efforts by the president and his key national security advisers, Congress appropriated only $17 billion for SDI during 1985–1989, well below what Reagan had sought. Star Wars thus remained a research program, and U.S. strategic policy was unchanged.

Second, defense budget decisions are important because they have long-term consequences. The B-2 *Stealth* bomber, for example, received initial funding in 1978, but the first B-2 did not fly until 1989. The procurement of all 72 planes will not be completed until the late 1990s. Once built, these planes will remain in the U.S. strategic arsenal well into the twenty-first century, some fifty years after the initial funding of the project. About 150 B-52 bombers, procured in the 1950s, still remain in the strategic arsenal and are likely to do so for the rest of the decade.

Third, the size of the defense budget sends important signals to the international community. In 1977 the Carter administration and its NATO allies decided to show their resolve to the Soviet Union and its Warsaw Pact allies by increasing defense spending by three percent a year (an interesting decision, since at that time NATO was already outspending the Warsaw Pact). In 1979 the Joint Chiefs of Staff and Senator Sam Nunn (D-Ga.), chairman of the Senate Armed Services Committee conditioned their support for the SALT (strategic arms limitation talks) Treaty, then before the Senate for ratification, on President Jimmy Carter's agreement to support 5 percent increases in real defense spending. In the 1980 presidential campaign, Reagan pledged to make America number one again by increasing the defense budget by 5 percent.

Fourth, the defense budget powerfully affects the domestic economy. In 1990 defense outlays will consume about one-fourth of the federal budget and more than 5 percent of gross national product (GNP). They will represent slightly more than 14 percent of net public spending. The 3.1 million Defense Department employees constitute more than 60 percent of the total federal work force, and together with the 3.3 million defense industry employees, more than 5 percent of the total national labor force. It is not surprising, therefore, that economic factors drive defense budget decisions much as strategic factors do. For example, when Secretary Dick Cheney revealed in late 1989 that dramatic changes in Eastern Europe were causing the Defense Department to reduce its projected defense budget for 1992 through 1994 by $180 billion, many commentators focused not on the changing international environment but on whether the U.S. economy could absorb such a dramatic reduction in the projected level of defense expenditures and on how the United States would spend its peace dividend.

Fifth, defense expenditures are the largest source of realistically controllable expenditures in the federal budget. The Office of Management and Budget (OMB) estimated that the 1987 budget contained $263 billion in relatively controllable outlays, of which $175 billion, or 67 percent, were in the defense budget. Since 1987 was the first full year of the Gramm-Rudman-Hollings deficit reduction law, it was not surprising that Congress slashed the 1987 defense budget request of the Reagan administration by $30 billion or 10 percent. Indeed, Congress has cut actual defense budget authority by more than $500 billion, or almost 30 percent, since Gramm-Rudman was enacted (see Table 1). Similarly, in the budget summit agreement of September 1990, congressional and administration negotiators classified

Table 1   Department of Defense Five-Year Plans for Fiscal Years 1986–1990

Budget authority in billions of current dollars

Plan	1986	1987	1988	1989	1990	Total
Administration Request February 1985	314	354	402	439	478	1,986
Administration Request February 1986	281	312	332	354	375	1,654
Administration Request January 1987	281	282	303	323	344	1,533
Actual Authorized	281	279	284	290	291	1,425

Source: Department of Defense Annual Report, Fiscal Years 1986, 1987, 1988, 1989, 1990.

$523 billion of the 1991 budget as discretionary. About 60 percent of the discretionary programs were in the defense category, and all of the discretionary reductions made by the negotiators came from the defense budget.

THE DEFENSE DEBATE

Because of the importance and impact of the defense budget, debates over defense programs are among the fiercest within the U.S. political system. Within the Pentagon, the four armed services and the dozen or so defense agencies struggle with one another over the allocation of defense dollars, often by deriding the capabilities of their sister agencies; this is especially true when the defense budget is declining.[3] Within the administration, the secretary of defense and the director of the OMB argue about the percentage of the federal budget that should be allocated to defense, with the former focusing primarily on the threat to the United States and the latter concerned about the size of the deficit.

Furthermore, the administration and Congress debate the size and allocation of the defense budget, a debate that is exacerbated when the executive and legislative branches are controlled by different parties. Generally the debate on each budget lasts well over two years from start to finish. The original strategic guidance for the 1992 budget, for example, was issued to the armed services in October 1989. That budget will be presented to Congress in January 1991 and enacted into law in the fall of 1991.

Unfortunately, the quality of the debate surrounding the defense budget has often not matched its strategic and economic importance. Proponents of high defense spending will often point out that, even during the Reagan buildup, defense spending did not consume as high a level of GNP as it did in the 1950s and 1960s. Although true, this line of reasoning says more about the performance of the U.S. economy than about what the nation should be spending on defense. Moreover, it ignores the significant real growth of defense spending since the 1950s, 1960s, and 1970s. In 1990 defense budget authority was $291.4

billion, or 32 percent higher than the real spending of $220 billion a year in the non-war years from 1951 through 1979. Finally, when confronted by the prospect of reductions in defense spending, proponents of high defense spending will quickly point to the large cuts defense has already taken, conveniently ignoring that these were reductions from projected increases rather than from actual outlays.

The logic of defense cutters is often equally sloppy. They point to the increase in defense authority between 1987 and 1990 from $279 to $291 billion (an increase of $12 billion or 5 percent), neglecting an inflation in the defense sector of about 12 percent that reduced the buying power of defense spending by 7 percent.

Background

The debate over the size and distribution of the 1991 defense budget and the 1991–1995 five-year defense program has been more contentious than at any time since the late 1940s. Important events in 1989 destroyed the threat of Soviet military expansion, the rationale behind the defense strategy and budgets of the United States for four decades. In February 1989 the Soviets withdrew the last of their 110,000 troops from Afghanistan, ending deployments that had begun in 1979. The Soviets also announced a unilateral reduction of 500,000 people in their own armed forces. Throughout the spring, summer, and fall of 1989, the Soviet Eastern European empire collapsed suddenly and swiftly. In April Solidarity, the Polish independent trade union, was legalized, and by August Poland had a noncommunist prime minister. In October Hungary renounced Marxism and proclaimed itself a free republic. That same month the long-time, hard-line communist leader of East Germany, Erich Honecker, was arrested and in November the Berlin Wall was torn down. November also witnessed the ouster of hard-line communists in Bulgaria and Czechoslovakia. By year's end Nicolae Ceausescu of Romania, the last Stalinist-type dictator, was dead, and Bulgaria and Czechoslovakia had announced they would hold free elections in 1990. More important, all the Eastern bloc nations in one way or another made clear their wish to see the 600,000 Soviet military forces withdrawn from their territories. It became apparent that a completely unified Germany would soon emerge, that the Cold War had ended, and that the Brezhnev doctrine of intervention had given way to the "Sinatra doctrine" of letting former satellites "do it their way." It was hardly surprising that the collapse of the Soviet empire and of the threat of Soviet expansionism would elicit calls for sharp reductions in defense spending and increased spending to address pressing domestic problems.

The debate has also been intense because of the increasing size of the federal budget deficit. Only after invoking sequestration for 130 days and resorting to innumerable gimmicks (like moving the military payday) were the Congress and the Executive branch able to meet the Gramm-Rudman target of $110 billion for 1990. However, shortly after Bush released his proposed 1991 budget, the deficit was reestimated to be about $140 billion. If one excludes the $130 billion trust fund surplus, the actual deficit for 1990 would be about $270 billion.

President Bush, like his predecessors, did not inherit a blank slate for national defense. Decisions by his predecessors constrain his flexibility to change the size and distribution of the defense budget. Presidents Carter and Reagan spent more than $25 billion to develop and produce fifteen B-2 *Stealth* bombers. President Bush can either cancel the program at 15, which means paying almost $2 billion per plane, or move to produce sixty additional planes, at a cost of about $500 million for each new plane.[4]

The Context of the 1991–1995 Defense Program

The roots of the 1991 budget and the 1991–1995 defense programs reach back to the late 1940s. Since then, the defense programs have been designed primarily to deal with the Soviet threat of military expansion. Although the United States demobilized after World War II, defense spending did not fall to anywhere near the pre–World War II levels. Defense spending fell 90 percent from 1945 to 1948 but remained six times greater than in 1939.[5] Moreover, whereas in 1939 the active duty force was about 400,000 and employment in the defense industry 300,000, in 1948 the active duty force had grown to 1.5 million and defense industry employment had jumped to almost 1 million.

Figures 1, 2, and 3

Defense Spending as a Share of Federal Outlays, Fiscal Years 1950–1995

Defense Outlays as a Share of Gross National Product, Fiscal Years 1950–1995

Defense-Related Employment as a Share of the Total Labor Force, 1950–1995

Sources: Office of the Assistant Secretary of Defense (Public Affairs), "FY 1991 Department of Defense Budget Request," News Release 29-90 (January 29, 1990); and Office of the Assistant Secretary of Defense (Comptroller), *National Defense Budget Estimates for FY 1988/1989* (April 1988), pp. 120–121; and *Department of Defense Annual Report, Fiscal Year 1990*, p. 72.

The United States reinstituted military conscription and began to increase real defense spending in 1949. It took these actions as it embarked on a policy of containment, primarily in response to Soviet expansion in Eastern Europe and the triumph of the Communist Party in China. In 1950, on the eve of the Korean War, defense spending had climbed to 54 percent above the 1948 level and consumed 27 percent of the federal budget and about 4.4 percent of GNP (see Figures 1–3).

Defense spending rose markedly during the Korean War, reaching a post–World War II peak in 1952 of $395 billion (see Table 2). In that year it consumed 60 percent of the entire federal budget and 12 percent of GNP. The armed forces increased to 3.6 million people, and defense-related employment jumped to nearly 4 million. Total defense employment (active duty military, defense civil service, and defense-related industry) in 1952 accounted for almost 15 percent of the total labor force.

Table 2   Trends in Defense Budget Authority, Fiscal Years 1951–1990

Year	Authority	Year	Authority	Year	Authority	Year	Authority
1951	296	1961	218	1971	242	1981	257
1952	395	1962	251	1972	234	1982	292
1953	379	1963	254	1973	224	1983	309
1954	233	1964	243	1974	215	1984	329
1955	203	1965	233	1975	208	1985	351
1956	207	1966	279	1976	216	1986	335
1957	216	1967	305	1977	227	1987	322
1958	212	1968	309	1978	224	1988	316
1959	225	1969	298	1979	224	1989	311
1960	217	1970	269	1980	228	1990	303

Non-war year average

1954–1960	216
1961–1965	240
1973–1980	220
1981–1990	310

Sources: Office of the Assistant Secretary of Defense, "National Defense Budget Estimates for FY 1989–1990," pp. 61–66; and Lawrence J. Korb and Stephen Daggett, "The Defense Budget and Strategic Planning," in Joseph Kruzel, ed., *American Defense Annual, 1988–1989* (Lexington, Mass.: Lexington Books, 1988), p. 45; and Richard Cheney, *Annual Report to the President and Congress*, January 1990, p. 69.

After the Korean War the defense budget fell once again, despite President Dwight D. Eisenhower's recognition that the United States had to maintain a large standing military even in the absence of a shooting war and that to do so would require large and unprecedented peacetime expenditures on defense. During his administration defense spending averaged $216 billion a year, more than twice the 1946–1950 average and fifteen times more than the average in the 1930s. In the Eisenhower years defense consumed 8.5 percent of GNP and almost half the entire federal budget. The 2.7 million people on active military duty and 2.7 million people "permanently employed" in private defense-related industries, plus the 1.5 million defense civil servants, accounted for about 10 percent of the total labor force in the 1950s. It is not surprising that on leaving office, President Eisenhower warned of the power residing in what he called the military-industrial complex.[6]

President John F. Kennedy came into office convinced that defense spending under Eisenhower had been too small to support adequate conventional and special operations forces or to allow the United States to keep pace with the expansion of Soviet strategic forces. Accordingly, between 1961 and 1965 defense spending budget authority was increased to an average of about $240 billion, some 11 percent above the average level of the Eisenhower administration. Because of strong economic growth and a rising federal budget, however, defense spending fell to less than 7 percent of GNP and 40 percent of federal outlays. During the 1961–1965 period the armed forces averaged 2.7 million people, defense civil servants 1.2 million, and civilian defense employment 2.5 million—in all, about 9 percent of the national labor force.

Shortly before Kennedy died, he and his secretary of defense, Robert S. McNamara, concluded that the gaps in the Eisenhower defense posture had been filled and that real defense spending could safely decline. Indeed, the 1964 and 1965 budgets did decline slightly in real terms, but beginning in July 1965, the United States became massively involved in Vietnam, and defense spending increased rapidly. Real defense authority climbed 31 percent in the succeeding two years, peaking at about

$309 billion in 1968. Defense spending reached 10 percent of GNP and 46 percent of the federal budget. Active duty military manpower peaked at 3.5 million, civil servants at 1.4 million, and defense-related employment at 3.2 million—just over 10 percent of the total labor force.

Defense spending grew rapidly during the Vietnam War, but much less than during the Korean War. In real terms defense spending more than tripled in the Korean War and, at its height, took 57 percent of the federal budget and nearly 12 percent of GNP and accounted for 15 percent of the labor force. During the Vietnam War defense spending increased in real terms by only one-third. Moreover, at its height, spending for Vietnam never went above half the federal budget or 11 percent of GNP or accounted for more than 11 percent of the labor force.

Defense spending dropped rapidly as disillusionment set in over the conduct of the war in Vietnam and as the United States began to withdraw from Southeast Asia. Between 1968 and 1975, during the Nixon-Ford years, defense spending fell 33 percent in real terms. By the mid-1970s the defense share had fallen to below 5 percent of GNP and to less than 22 percent of the federal budget, lower than since before the Korean War. During this same period the armed forces dropped by about 1.5 million, defense civil servants by 0.4 million, and defense-related employment by about 1.5 million, the total falling to less than 5 percent of the labor force, the lowest level since before World War II.

Although everyone expected defense spending to fall after the end of the war in Vietnam, few expected the decline to be so rapid or so deep. The incremental costs of the war in Southeast Asia never accounted for more than 27 percent of the defense budget.[7] Yet before defense spending bottomed out in 1975, it was not only one-third less than 1968 but also 14 percent below the level of 1964, the last prewar year.

For several reasons this decline could not have come at a worse time for the U.S. military. First, between 1969 and 1975 Soviet military expenditures grew 80 percent measured in rubles (54 percent measured in dollars).[8] By 1976 the Soviet Union's defense budget, measured in dollars, was 50 percent higher than that of the United States. Second, the U.S. military emerged from the Vietnam War in very poor shape. To hold down the defense budget during that war, the federal government had postponed the modernization of the force structure and had drawn down worldwide stocks of ammunition. Moreover, the switch to the all-volunteer force required larger military salaries, pushing up personnel costs from 41 percent of the defense budget in 1963 to almost 52 percent by 1976.

Jimmy Carter, who had come into office in 1977 pledging to cut defense spending, held defense spending level during the first three years of his presidency. Because Soviet military spending continued to grow, the military balance deteriorated further. The American people, confronted with the Soviet invasion of Afghanistan, the seizure of American hostages in Iran, and the hollowness of their own military forces, supported increases in defense spending of 13 percent for 1981. Even so, Ronald Reagan accused Carter of being soft on defense, pledged to increase real defense spending by 5 percent a year, and won the 1980 election.

President Reagan did better than that. By the end of his first term in office, real defense spending had increased 53 percent, an average of over 12 percent a year, a higher rate than during the war in Vietnam. In fact, real defense spending in 1985 was 13 percent higher than peak spending in the Vietnam War (1968). It is no exaggeration to say that in the Reagan years the Defense Department enjoyed a wartime buildup without a war. Defense outlays rose to 27 percent of the federal budget and 6.3 percent of GNP, their highest shares since the war in Vietnam. Active duty manpower grew 8 percent and civil servants 10 percent, while defense-related employment doubled between 1976 and 1986, reaching 3.3 million, the highest level since the peak of the Korean War buildup in 1953. Nonetheless, defense employment in the Reagan years never exceeded 5.6 percent of the total labor force.

The massive military buildup of the first Reagan administration could not be sustained. Because it took place simultaneously with a big tax cut, the increases in the defense budget contributed to large and increasing federal budget deficits that in turn inspired the Gramm-Rudman-Hollings deficit reduction law.

Moreover, no overall strategy guided the buildup, and management was ineffective.[9] As a result, the American people and their elected representatives felt that much of the money spent during the buildup was wasted. Also, growth of Soviet military expenditures, which had averaged over 4 percent a year from the mid-1960s to the mid-1970s, slowed to less than 2 percent a year between 1977 and 1982, one-sixth the U.S. rate for that period.[10]

Not only did defense spending in Reagan's second term stop growing as fast as in the first, but it declined in real terms. By 1990 real defense spending was 13.6 percent below its 1985 peak. More significantly, President Reagan's $2.0 trillion projected defense program for 1986–1990 was cut sharply. The Defense Department actually received $1.4 trillion, or 28 percent less than Reagan had sought in 1985. In 1990, the share of GNP and the federal budget devoted to defense dropped to 5 percent and less than 25 percent, respectively. Active duty manpower, civil service manpower, and defense industry employment both declined slightly, as did the percentage of the national labor force dependent on defense.

Although Reagan left a sizeable defense budget to his successor, it was not large enough to pay for all the programs he had initiated. Because he and his advisers had originally refused to recognize that budget pressures would force cuts in defense spending in the late 1980s, President Reagan accommodated the yearly declines primarily by stretching out programs. Thus President Bush and Secretary of Defense Cheney inherited a $400 billion program but only a $300 billion budget. It is estimated that more than $1 trillion in programs are now in the defense pipeline and that the 1990–1994 defense program presented to Congress in January 1989 by President Reagan was underfunded by $300 to $400 billion.[11]

The 1990 Debate

President Bush inherited a five-year plan from the Reagan administration that called for $1.7 trillion in defense budget authority, $1.6 trillion in defense spending, and spending growth of about 2 percent a year (see Table 3) over 1990–1994.[12] Bush recognized that he could not spend that much on defense

Table 3   FY 1990/FY 1991 DoD Budget (Current $ Billions)

	1989	1990	1991	1992	1993	1994	Cum. '90–'94
Budget Authority							
January 1989 Budget	290.2	305.6	320.9	335.7	350.7	365.6	1,678.5
Delta	—	-10.0	-9.9	-13.7	-14.8	-15.8	-64.2
Amended Budget (April 1989)	290.2	295.6	311.0	322.0	335.9	349.8	1,614.3
Outlays							
January 1989 Budget	289.8	293.8	304.7	316.2	329.3	343.4	1,587.4
Delta	—	-4.0	-6.9	-9.4	-11.9	-13.9	-46.1
Amended Budget (April 1989)	289.8	289.8	297.9	306.8	317.4	329.5	1,541.3

Source: *Amended FY 1990/91 Department of Defense Budget,* Office of Assistant Secretary of Defense (Public Affairs), No. 174-89, April 24, 1987.

without violating his no tax pledge if he wanted to meet legislated targets for deficit reduction. He quickly trimmed the Reagan plan. By April 1989 the president and the new secretary of defense cut $64 billion in budget authority and $46 billion in outlays out of the five-year plan. As part of an agreement with Congress, the 1990 request was cut 3 percent, from $306 billion to $296 billion. This meant that real defense authority for 1990 fell almost 3 percent rather than increased by 2 percent. Although Congress appropriated the $296 billion for the Defense Department, failure to meet the Gramm-Rudman deficit reduction targets triggered sequestration on October 1, 1989. For the department, sequestration lasted 130 days, bringing budget authority for 1990 down to $291 billion and outlays to $287 billion.

While Bush and Cheney were relatively successful in achieving their goal for the size of defense budget authority and outlays, their attempts to shape defense priorities were disastrous. In modifying the Reagan budget, Secretary Cheney proposed to keep all the main Reagan strategic initiatives including such controversial programs as SDI and the B-2 *Stealth* bomber, but to cancel three major conventional programs: the U.S. Navy's F14-D aircraft, the U.S. Marine Corps V-22 tilt rotor *Osprey* aircraft, and the U.S. Army's AHIP helicopter.

Members of Congress from the areas that would be affected by the proposed cancellations challenged them vigorously. Cancellation of the F-14D would have meant that Grumman, a big Long Island corporation, would not be building any more naval aircraft for the first time in fifty years. Unfortunately, Cheney had no convincing strategic rationale for his proposed cutbacks. Instead, he fell back on cost-effectiveness analyses, admitting that if he had more money, he would fund the V-22, F-14-D, and AHIP.

Thus, rather than examining the role of the U.S. Marine Corps or naval aviation in a post-containment world, the debate focused on comparing the V-22 with the CH-53E and the F-14D with remanufactured F-14As. Eventually Congress diverted $1.1 billion from SDI, just over $0.4 billion from the B-2, and just under $0.4 billion from the *Trident* II missile (D-5) to fund the AHIP, F-14D, and V-22.

Although most analysts feel that Cheney lost in his first important budget confrontation with Congress, the real losers in the 1990 defense budget battle were the American people. The Bush administration developed no coherent plan with which to defend its priorities. Congress is institutionally incapable of developing such a rationale but is adept at protecting the interests of its constituents, and if the administration has no strategy to frame the debate on its budget, these parochial interests will normally prevail.

The 1990 battle therefore committed U.S. taxpayers to pay $1.6 billion for eighteen F-14Ds and thirty-six AHIPs that the Defense Department says the country does not need and another $0.3 billion on research and development for a V-22 that the Defense Department is still trying to cancel. True, Congress "saved" some $2.0 billion in strategic programs, but that is a short-term saving. At $3.6 billion, SDI is too big to be a research program and too small to be moving toward deployment. Cutting one B-2 *Stealth* bomber "saved" $400 million but drove up the unit cost of the planes scheduled for purchase out of 1990 funds from $1.3 billion to $1.8 billion and added about $5 billion to the total program cost. Similarly, almost $400 million was saved by cutting twenty-one *Trident* II missiles, but the unit costs of the 1990 purchases rose 12 percent, from $288 million to $347 million.

The 1991–1995 Problems

In justifying its 1991 budget and the 1991–1995 defense program, the Bush administration faces short- and long-term challenges that fall into four categories.

A rationale. The president and his advisers need to develop a convincing rationale for a significant military force tailored to an era in which the Soviet threat is sharply reduced. They should have developed this rationale in the new administration's first year. Like the Nixon administration in 1969 and the Carter administration in 1977, the Bush administration did in fact undertake a strategic review upon taking office.

This review, however, came to nothing, in large part because neither the president nor his top national security advisers provided a clear vision of how the United States should respond to the changing international environment. Bush's national security team contains no conceptual thinkers like Henry A. Kissinger or Zbigniew Brzezinski. The absence of a secretary of defense throughout the transition and the first three months of the Bush administration further hindered the strategic review by depriving the Defense Department of senior representation in the review. Without authoritative input from the department no significant changes could realistically be made to existing national security policy. Even with a full team of strategically minded planners, formulating a coherent vision in the face of changes in the international system would have been a daunting task. With a team without conceptual thinkers, the result was an inadequate strategic review that did little more than respond to fast moving events.

During the Reagan administration there was, as Senator Nunn and Representative Les Aspin (D-Wis.), chairman of the House Armed Services Committee, observed on more than one occasion, an army strategy, a navy strategy, and an air force strategy but no overall national strategy to guide the massive buildup that took place between 1980 and 1985.[13] The lack of a coherent strategy during the Reagan buildup bred waste. If the Bush administration does not develop a strategic vision, reductions in defense will be inefficiently planned, and the United States will not get the most out of whatever funds are appropriated to defense. The danger is clear and present that defense could be cut too much and too fast or in the wrong places as America "comes home" after the Cold War.

Limits. The Bush administration must reconcile its 1991–1995 defense program to the budgets it is likely to receive. Even if real defense spending authority had grown at 2 percent a year, as projected by the outgoing Reagan Administration, spending will fall more than $100 billion short of what is needed to implement the five-year program Bush inherited from Reagan. If the budget declines by 5 percent a year in real terms, as seems likely, that shortfall could approach $300 billion.[14]

Sustainability. The Bush administration must develop sustainable targets for defense spending. During the second Reagan administration, budget authority and outlay projections for the succeeding five years were radically revised every year. The 1989 budget was projected at $439 billion in early 1985, $354 billion in 1986, $323 billion in 1987, and $291 billion in 1988. In just one year the Bush administration reduced the 1990–1994 defense program three separate times, by $45 billion on February 9, 1989, by another $20 billion in April, and by yet another $180 billion in November, for a total of about $250 billion, or 15 percent.

No organization can change so much that quickly without creating chaos, especially without a bold new strategy. Outgoing Secretary of Defense Frank Carlucci knew in January 1989 that expectations of 2 percent real growth in the defense budget were unrealistic. Bush and Cheney had to know in April 1989 that the need to meet deficit reduction targets made impossible the attainment of even 1.5 percent real growth. Whatever President Bush might want, prudence requires that the Defense Department present a strategic vision to guide defense budgets in which real spending falls perhaps 5 percent a year. Congress would probably support such a gradual sustained cutback and is unlikely to spend more.

Economic transition. Even though the economy is not as dependant on defense spending as it was in the 1950s and 1960s, defense is still an important component of the overall economic situation. Therefore, the administration needs to develop a plan to help the economy adjust to reduced levels of defense spending. The defense cut can be an enormous gain, a true peace dividend, but only if the resources used for defense can be shifted smoothly to civil use. Also, careful attention to the adjustment problems generated by demobilization will improve the efficiency with which remaining defense dollars are spent. Had Secretary Cheney presented a plan to Congress to help Grumman adjust to its demise as a major defense supplier, Congress might have agreed to cancel the F-14D. Congress in effect provided its own adjustment plan: eighteen unneeded planes over the next three years at a cost of about $1.5 billion. Similarly, without an adjustment plan Cheney will not receive congressional permission to close the fifty-five bases he has designated.

The Solutions

The Bush administration has many advantages in dealing with its short- and long-term budget problems. The U.S. armed forces are well staffed and supplied because in the 1980s the Department of Defense enjoyed a wartime buildup without a war. The four services have enough modern equipment and their warehouses are full of ammunition and other supplies. The department has 10 percent more tactical aircraft and 18 percent more ships than it did in 1980.[15] In addition, the quality of personnel is at an all-time high. Over 90 percent of the new recruits have high school diplomas and score average or above average on the armed forces qualification test. Retention of qualified people is also at record high levels. Thus, even if the military threat from the Soviet Union were unchanged, defense spending could fall briefly without jeopardizing national security.

The diminishing military threat to U.S. national security is a second advantage in planning for reduced defense spending. More than half the defense budget goes to pay for the conventional defense of Western Europe. The United States has been committed to providing ten divisions, 100 tactical air squadrons, and a Marine Corps expeditionary brigade to Europe within ten days after a warning of a Warsaw Pact mobilization.[16] Whatever else the events in Eastern Europe signal, they mean that NATO will have a much longer notice, perhaps as much as two years, of any impending invasion. Because of this extra warning time, the

United States can keep a smaller force on active duty and increase its reliance on reserves as well as reduce the amount of material it must keep on hand.

Furthermore, the United States and the Soviet Union have agreed on an arms control regime that will reduce the strategic and conventional threat to the United States. At the Strategic Arms Reduction Talks (START), the two superpowers have agreed to cut countable nuclear warheads to 6,000 and delivery systems to 1,600, a reduction of about 50 percent in countable warheads and 30 percent in delivery vehicles. At the Conventional Forces in Europe (CFE) negotiations, NATO and Warsaw Pact nations have agreed to greatly reduce the number of troops, tanks, armored personnel carriers, and aircraft on each side and to move their forces away from the German and Czechoslovakian borders.[17]

Even before these agreements are signed, the Soviet Union has begun to cut its military spending and armed forces. In May 1989, the Defense Department, citing a consensus in the intelligence community, told President Bush that President Mikhail S. Gorbachev had reversed a twenty-year pattern of growth in Soviet military spending and force structure to boost the civil economy and Soviet foreign policy. The intelligence community predicts that Gorbachev will keep his public promises to cut Soviet military forces by 10 percent, total defense spending by 15 percent, and weapon outlays by 20 percent over the next two years.[18] The House Armed Services Committee reported in August 1989 that Gorbachev had already completed approximately half of the unilateral reductions of troops, combat divisions, tanks, and aircraft in Eastern Europe that he had promised in December 1988, and the Central Intelligence Agency (CIA) estimates that Soviet military spending fell in 1989 by 4 to 5 percent while weapons spending declined 6 to 7 percent.[19]

THE 1991–1995 PROGRAM

The Bush administration originally requested $295.1 billion in budget authority and $292.1 billion in outlays for national defense in 1991 (see Table 4). Although larger in nominal terms

Table 4   National Defense Topline (Current $ Billions)

	1990	1991	Fiscal Year 1992	1993	1994	1995	Total '91–'95
Budget Authority							
Current Dollars	291.4	295.1	300.0	304.4	308.0	311.8	1,519.3
Constant FY 1991 Dollars	302.9	295.1	289.2	283.4	277.7	272.1	
Real Growth	-2.7	-2.6	-2.0	-2.0	-2.0	-2.0	
Outlays							
Current Dollars	286.8	292.1	296.9	299.0	302.3	304.8	1,495.1
Constant FY 1991 Dollars	295.4	292.1	283.6	277.4	270.5	263.4	
Real Growth	-5.5	-2.2	-2.9	-2.9	-2.2	2.5	

Source: *Amended FY 1991 Department of Defense Budget Request,* Office of Assistant Secretary of Defense (Public Affairs), No. 29-90, January 29, 1990, Table 1.

than the 1990 budget, the proposed 1991 budget would result in a real decline of 2.6 percent in authority and 2.2 percent in outlays. The proposed cut in budget authority is slightly smaller than last year's cut.

For the 1991–1995 period Bush is requesting authority of $1.52 trillion and outlays of just under $1.5 trillion. If the Bush five-year plan is approved, defense authority will reach $312 billion and outlays $305 billion in 1995, an increase of 5.7 and 4.3 percent over the next five years. In real terms, however, authority will drop by 10 percent and outlays by 12 percent over the five-year plan. Compared with his predecessor's approach to defense spending, Bush's proposal is remarkable. Reagan always asked for real increases in his five-year defense plans. Even in his second administration, when the defense consensus had collapsed, and Congress was warning him that the best he could hope for in defense was zero real growth, Reagan requested real increases ranging from 2 percent to 7 percent. Moreover, with his 1991–1995 program, Bush becomes the first president since John Kennedy in 1963 to call for real reductions in the baseline defense program, the part of the budget not affected by an ongoing shooting war. For example, in 1969, 28 percent of the last defense budget request of Lyndon B. Johnson was attributed to the incremental costs of the Vietnam War. In his five and one-half years in office, Richard M. Nixon requested total budgets showing real decline, but his baseline budget request showed real increases as he reduced the incremental costs of the war by withdrawing troops. By 1973 the incremental costs of the war had dropped to 6 percent of the budget. The Bush proposal also reduces the burden of defense on U.S. economic resources. If his 1991–1995 defense plan is adopted and the economic assumptions hold up, defense outlays will drop to 4 percent of GNP, the lowest share since 1950, when it took 4.4 percent. Defense outlays will drop to 21 percent of the budget, the smallest share in fifty years, 1.5 percentage points below the 1978 low of 22.5 percent and down 6 percentage points from the Reagan administration peak of 27 percent in 1987 (see Figures 1 and 2).

For two reasons the Bush 1991 defense budget was dead on arrival. First, the economic assumptions, upon which the entire 1991 federal budget were based, proved wildly optimistic. In January 1990, the Bush budget had originally projected a FY 1991 deficit of about $100 billion, some $35 billion above the Gramm-Rudman target. By mid-year, Bush and his advisers reestimated the deficit at about $300 billion. Even though the president finally renounced his no tax pledge, there is no way to reduce a projected deficit of that size without the 1991 defense budget being reduced significantly below its projected levels—about $10 billion in outlays and $25 billion in authority.

Second, the strategic basis for the defense budget was undermined by the intelligence community. On March 1, 1990, William Webster, the director of the Central Intelligence Agency, told the House Armed Services Committee that with or without Gorbachev the Soviet Union has made a historic turn away from militarism. Webster's testimony had been foreshadowed by earlier testimony by such "hard-liners" as former defense officials, James Schlesinger and Richard Perle.[20] Webster's position was subsequently endorsed by the Joint Chiefs of Staff.[21]

Secretary of Defense Cheney, who was apparently blindsided by Webster's testimony, clearly understood the impact of Webster's testimony on the 1991 defense budget. Within days after Webster's testimony, Cheney noted that it would be easier for him to win congressional approval of the defense budget if Webster had shown more restraint.[22]

The combination of the burgeoning federal deficit and the declining Soviet threat has put the defense budget into a political free-fall. The question was not whether the defense budget would be reduced enough to reflect the diminished Soviet threat but whether it would fall so rapidly that the U.S. would no longer be able to exercise leadership in the international arena.

Throughout the first half of 1990, several attempts were made to deal with the political free-fall. In a series of four speeches in March and April, Senator Sam Nunn, chairman of the Senate Armed Services Committee, criticized the Department of Defense for *basing* its spending plans on outdated assumptions about the military threats facing the United States.[23] According to Nunn, Bush's defense budget was missing a fundamental foundation and if the Pentagon's leaders wanted to remain relevant to the budget process they needed to "fill in the blanks." Nunn himself filled in the blanks by calling for reductions in U.S. forces in Europe to between 75,000 and 100,000; elimination of from 2 to 4 carrier battle groups; adjusting downward the readiness status of various combat and support forces; retirement of older high maintenance, single purpose or tactically obsolete combat systems; buying more sealift instead of airlift; making the army and marines lighter; and elimination of several proposed new weapons—ATF, LHX, and SSN-21. Overall Nunn's strategy would reduce defense spending by about $180 billion or 13 percent below the Bush 1991–1995 defense program. This would place defense on a path of about a 4.5 percent decline per year. (In mid-July Nunn's Senate Armed Services Committee reduced the Bush proposed budget by $18 billion or 6 percent.)

In early April, two Republican senators with strong defense credentials, William Cohen of Maine and John McCain of Arizona, called for annual reductions in the defense budget twice as great as those proposed by Bush.[24] Like Nunn, Cohen and McCain argued that their effort was necessary because the administration had failed to come up with a comprehensive plan. Cohen and McCain differed from Nunn on two major systems: B-2 and SDI. The Republicans argued that B-2 should be killed and SDI spending frozen. Nunn remains a strong supporter of both programs.

In early May, General Colin Powell, the chairman of the Joint Chiefs of Staff (JCS), argued that the DoD needed to conduct a top to bottom review of weapon systems, training practices, and military strategy, which could lead to a 25 percent lower budget.[25] Powell argued that such a review could be used to reduce the armed forces by 25 percent over four or five years without endangering military security.

The House and Senate Budget Committees also proposed significant reductions in defense spending over the FY 1991–1995 period. Both bodies recommended real reductions in defense authority of about 10 percent in 1991 and more gradual reductions from 1992–1995. The House plan would cut $250 billion or 16 percent from the administration's 1991–1995 plan while the Senate plan would reduce it by slightly less. Overall the House plan would cut defense spending in real terms by 27 percent over the next five years while the Senate plan would reduce it "only" 21 percent.

By early summer it was becoming clear that defense spending would be reduced by about 25 percent over the 1991–1995 period. In late June, Secretary Cheney bowed to the inevitable and presented a plan to the Congress offering a 25 percent force reduction over the next five years. Cheney claimed that his 25 percent force reduction was for illustrative purposes only and would produce budget savings of only 10 percent over the next five years, the same amount he proposed in January. However, Senator Nunn said that Cheney in effect had given his implied consent to a 25 percent force structure reduction, and Congressman Aspin showed how that force reduction could produce a budget reduction of from 18 to 27 percent if one adjusted readiness, modernization, and research and development along with force structure. The House Budget Committee immediately seized upon the higher number as part of the deficit reduction package.[26] The budget projections made over the past year are summarized in Figure 4.

A falling defense budget without an overall strategy to guide the build down, coupled with a lack of strong civilian leadership

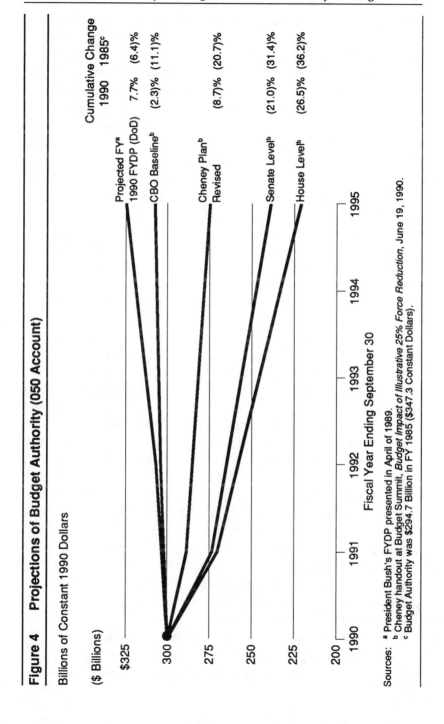

Figure 4   Projections of Budget Authority (050 Account)

Billions of Constant 1990 Dollars

Sources: [a] President Bush's FYDP presented in April of 1989.
[b] Cheney handout at Budget Summit, *Budget Impact of Illustrative 25% Force Reduction*, June 19, 1990.
[c] Budget Authority was $294.7 Billion in FY 1985 ($347.3 Constant Dollars).

in the Pentagon,[27] has led to an outbreak of interservice rivalry on a scale not seen since the late 1940s. Since late 1989, the services have apparently decided that it will be "each man for himself." The army and the marines have fought over who will have the preeminent role in contingency (small wars) operations, while the navy and air force have battled over who will have the dominant role in the power projection and strategic nuclear missions.

The battles have been fought within the halls of the Pentagon, before the Congress, and in the media, and have become increasingly bitter and reckless. The army has argued that the marines are too slow and are ineffective beyond the beaches while the marines have countered that the army has inefficient firepower to do much when it gets there.[28]

In discussing power projection forces, the air force has argued that one squadron of F-15Es or eight B-2s can match the daily ordnance capability of a carrier. The navy counters that air force planes can perform only a small fraction of the sixteen different types of power projection missions performed by the navy since World War II. Confronted by the rising unit costs of the B-2, the air force released classified data on the A-12 (ATA) with the claim that a force of B-2s can deliver 21 percent more payload at intercontinental distances for 31 percent less cost than the A-12. Moreover, the air force contends that the B-2 can take over much of the navy's maritime surveillance role.[29]

As the implications of START I for the number of ballistic missile warheads become clear, the navy and air force are both arguing for increasing their portion of ballistic missile warheads under START. At present, the U.S. arsenal consists of 5,312 sea-launched ballistic missiles (SLBMs) and 2,450 intercontinental ballistic millile (ICBM) warheads or 62 percent for the navy and 32 percent for the air force. The navy would like to see its START portion rise to 82 percent (4,032 warheads on twenty-one countable *Tridents*). The air force would reduce the navy share to 62 percent (3,024 warheads) by filling six of each *Trident's* twenty-four tubes with concrete.[30]

The political free-fall of the defense budget and the public squabbling among the services were brought to a temporary halt by the Iraqi invasion of Kuwait in August 1990. In October 1990,

Congress and the administration accepted the Nunn plan for reducing defense spending in the 1991–1995 period. As indicated above, this plan would reduce defense authority by 8 percent and outlays by 3 percent in real terms in 1991. Over the 1991–1995 period, the defense program would drop by $236 billion in authority and $182 billion in outlays.

Similarly, as each service found a significant role to play in the Gulf that corresponded to its essence, public criticism of its sister services abated. By the fall of 1990, the American deployment to the Gulf comprised heavy (armored and mechanized infantry) army divisions, marine amphibious forces, air force and Navy tactical air, and strategic air forces. Indeed, one of the primary reasons General Michael Duggan was fired as air force Chief of Staff in September 1990 was his public criticisms of the potential contributions of the other services to a military solution in the Gulf.

It is clear that even with the crisis in the Persian Gulf the defense budget will and should be reduced significantly over the next decade. For example, two former members of the JCS, David C. Jones and Edward C. Meyer, and a former head of the Congressional Budget Office, Alice M. Rivlin, argue that the United States can safely and prudently make force reductions of at least 25 percent over five years (see Appendix 9). The real question is by how much and with what impact on the military power of the United States. Too often policy-makers focus more on how much is spent rather than upon how the money is distributed.

Real cuts in defense spending of more than 10 percent over the next five years are reasonable and prudent. If the January 1990 Bush plan were approved, U.S. defense spending in 1995, in constant 1991 dollars, will be 6 percent higher than in 1981, when the Soviet Union was at the peak of its military power, and higher than the average nonwar-years defense budgets of the 1950s, 1960s, and 1970s (see Table 2). The decline that the president projected over the next five years—10.1 percent—is smaller than the actual drop of the past five years—13.6 percent. Finally, the Bush plan reneges on Secretary Cheney's own promise to reduce the 1992–1994 program by $180 billion. It shows reductions of only $140.4 billion from the 1992–1994 program projected in the spring of 1989 (see Table 5). According to a General Accounting Office audit of the Pentagon's most recent five-year plan, the Defense Department must trim $138 billion more in programs by 1994 to bring its spending in line with the Bush administration's plan.[31]

Events in Eastern Europe and the current excellent condition of the armed forces would permit holding nominal defense spending constant over the next five years without undermining national security. A nominal freeze would reduce real spending by about 25 percent over the 1991–1995 period, about twice the size of the cut proposed by the Bush administration. The resulting defense budget of about $227 billion in 1990 dollars by 1995 would match average real spending on defense from 1950 through 1980.

Table 5   FY 1991 DoD Budget Authority (Current $ Billions)

	1990	1991	1992	1993	1994	Cum. '90–'94
April 1989 Plan* (0, 1, 1, 2, 2% Real Growth)	295.6	317.5	332.4	351.0	369.4	1,665.9
Reduction	-4.2	-22.4	-32.4	-46.6	-61.4	-167.0
January 1990 Plan (-2% Real Growth	291.4	295.1	300.0	304.4	308.0	1,498.9

* Adjusted for final economic assumptions.

Source: *FY 1991 Department of Defense Budget Request,* Office of Assistant Secretary of Defense (Public Affairs), No. 29-90, January 29, 1990, Table 2.

Distribution

All the categories of the defense budget would rise slightly in nominal terms under President Bush's 1991 budget except procurement, which would fall by $4.7 billion, or 5.7 percent (see Table 6). The rest of the budget would rise $8.4 billion, or 2.8 percent. Real spending in all the major accounts would fall slightly, except for procurement, which would decline 9 percent. This pattern continues trends begun in 1986. Between 1985 and 1990 the procurement account fell 29 percent in real terms, from $121 billion in 1991 dollars to $86 billion. For the period beyond 1991, President Bush seeks to allow all the categories of the defense budget to grow at about the same rate (see Table 6).

Table 6   Budget Authority by Function and Program ($ Billions)

Budget Category								Change 1991–1995	
	1989	*1990*	*1991*	*1992*	*1993*	*1994*	*1995*	*AMT*	*%*
Military Personnel	78.5	78.5	79.1	80.5	81.8	82.8	83.9	4.8	6.1
Operations and Maintenance	86.2	86.8	90.1	91.7	93.2	94.4	95.6	5.5	6.1
Procurement	79.4	82.6	77.9	78.9	79.8	80.7	81.5	3.6	4.6
Research Development	37.5	36.8	38.0	38.6	39.2	39.7	40.1	2.1	5.5
Military Construction	5.7	5.3	5.6	5.7	5.7	5.8	5.9	0.3	5.4
Family Housing	3.3	3.2	3.5	3.5	3.6	3.6	3.7	0.2	5.7
Other	0.9	-0.7	2.3	2.3	2.3	2.4	2.4	0.1	4.3
Offsetting Receipts	-0.7	-1.1	-0.9	-1.0	-0.9	-0.9	-0.9	—	—
Allowances	—	—	-0.3	-0.3	-0.3	-0.3	-0.3	—	—
Total	290.8	291.4	295.1	300.0	304.4	308.0	311.8	16.7	5.6

Source: *Budget of the United States Government, Fiscal Year 1991*, p. 157.

The 1991–1995 plan still supports systems and forces that are Cold War relics and unsuited to the risks that the United States will confront in the postcontainment era or the impending arms control regime. If those systems were canceled and forces eliminated, real defense authority could easily be cut by 5 percent a year without jeopardizing national security.

Strategic Forces

For 1991 the Bush administration plans to spend about $17 billion on six major strategic programs: the B-2 *Stealth* bomber, the MX rail garrison and *Midgetman* mobile land-based missiles, the *Trident* II submarine and *Trident* II (D-5) missile, and the strategic defense initiative. These six systems are programmed to consume over $80 billion during 1991–1995 as the Bush administration seeks to modernize sea-launched missiles, land-launched missiles, and manned bombers (the strategic triad), as well as to develop a comprehensive defense against ballistic missiles.

Procuring all these systems at this rate does not make sense at this time. Over the last decade the United States has modernized the strategic triad and added more than 4,000 warheads to its strategic nuclear arsenal, an increase of 45 percent. The number of warheads that could survive a Soviet attack and remain deliverable has risen 17 percent.[32] More important, however, the United States and the Soviet Union are on the verge of agreeing to reduce the number of warheads and delivery systems significantly. The agreed limits at the START negotiations are 6,000 warheads and 1,600 delivery systems for each side and the sublimit is 4,900 warheads on missiles. Why would the United States spend scarce budget dollars to add to its arsenal while simultaneously signing an agreement to manage with fewer than it already has?

Secretary Cheney argues that the Soviets, while cutting their conventional forces, are still modernizing their strategic forces.[33] U.S. strategic programs must be continued, presumably as bargaining chips. The argument is absurd. If Soviet strategic modernization is a problem, the United States can conclude the START treaty expeditiously. In early February 1990 the Soviets cleared a major hurdle by accepting the American position on SDI. And at the June summit in Washington, Presidents Bush and Gorbachev cleared away the remaining obstacles on cruise missiles.[34] Although three former members of the Reagan arms control team accused the administration of a strategic sellout, most observers argued that the prospective START treaty will promote stability, predictablity, and transparency in the strategic relationship between the nuclear superpowers. If anything, the treaty favors the United States as it will allow it to have 2,300 or 26 percent more warheads than the Soviets.[35]

At this point, the administration should not only promptly conclude START I but also develop a framework for START II that will reduce the number of warheads to between 2,000 and 3,000 on each side, more than enough firepower to destroy the critical targets. Indeed, the Soviets are already pressing the Bush administration to do just that. Recent testimony of the three officers who served as chairman of the Joint Chiefs of Staff over the past twelve years indicates that Soviet forces do not now threaten our deterrent, or will they do so in the near future. These retired flag officers, one from each of the services, noted that even with the Soviet Union's modernization programs, its forces do not threaten the U.S. second-strike posture.[36] In short, the administration could slow the modernization of all three legs of the triad without risk to U.S. security.

Through 1990 the Defense Department will have received budget authority of more than $25 billion to develop and build fifteen B-2A *Stealth* bombers. Procuring the remaining sixty planes in the current plan will cost at least an additional $30 billion. The B-2 is an unnecessarily expensive way to guard against the remote possibility that other systems—land- and sea-based missiles, cruise-missile-carrying B-52s, and penetrating B-1 bombers—would be unable to launch a successful second strike. Former Secretary of Defense Frank Carlucci calls it a plane without a clearly defined mission.[37] The United States would be far better off to cancel the B-2 program and use a small part of the $50 billion saved to test (and deploy) the fifteen B-2s it has purchased and equip the B-1 with advanced cruise missiles as the remaining B-52s are phased out. (Fifteen hundred advanced cruise missiles with stealth characteristics can be bought for $7 billion.)

The Defense Department is requesting almost $3 billion to place the first twelve MX's on railroad cars and $202 million to keep research and development going on another small missile, the mobile *Midgetman*. As the three former chairmen of the Joint Chiefs noted, neither mobile missile is needed. Nevertheless, research and development on the *Midgetman* should continue pending successful conclusion of the START agreement.

To date, the U.S. Navy has received funding for seventeen *Trident* submarines. (Eight are already deployed and one is undergoing sea trials.) For 1991 it is requesting $1.5 billion for full funding of an eighteenth *Trident* and advance procurement for a nineteenth and twentieth. The seventeen *Tridents* already authorized would carry 192 warheads each for a total of 3,264, more than the entire number allowed under the projected figure for START II, and two-thirds of the number allowed under START I. Placing so many warheads on so few platforms is a risky policy, since an enemy could destroy U.S. second-strike capacity by sinking a few submarines. The *Trident* program should be terminated, and research begun on a new, smaller submarine that would be a less profitable target.

In 1991 the Defense Department seeks to purchase 52 *Trident* II or D-5 missiles for $1.7 billion. This missile is highly accurate and gives the navy the capacity to destroy hard targets such as reinforced missile silos. To date, the navy has spent about $17 billion to develop and purchase 195 D-5s, enough to equip 8 *Trident* submarines. The navy plans to spend another $18 billion to purchase enough missiles to arm twenty Tridents, eight of which are already at sea, armed with the *Trident* I or C-4 missile. It would make sense to allow the navy to purchase only the fifty-two D-5s requested in this year's budget. This would permit the Navy to arm the nine *Trident* submarines purchased but not deployed, but not to replace the C-4 missiles for the unneeded submarines requested in this year's budget. Canceling the D-5 program after 1991 would save about $18 billion in this decade.

The administration seeks $4.5 billion, or a 22 percent increase, for SDI, looking toward eventual deployment of a space-based ballistic missile defense designed to destroy a large portion of incoming missiles. The increase may appease the Reagan legacy, but it lacks any strategic rationale. The strategic defense initiative is both technically and fiscally impossible. Moreover, deploying a space-based system would violate the Antiballistic Missile (ABM) Treaty. Congress should and probably will reduce SDI to a $3-billion-a-year research program for the 1991–1995 period. Such a research program will allow the Defense Department to guard against any expected breakthroughs on the Soviet side and bring strategic defense back to the level that existed before Reagan's March 1983 speech challenging the Department to make nuclear weapons obsolete.

Conventional

A strategic vision is no more apparent in plans for conventional forces than in the budget for forces. Particularly for the navy and the air force, the administration is clinging to a Cold War mentality.

Army. The U.S. Army, which would have borne the brunt of any war in Central Europe, is wisely cutting some forces dedicated to that threat. In 1991 it will complete its purchase of 8,000 M1A1 *Abrams* Main Battle Tanks, freeing $6.2 billion over the next five years. It will eliminate two divisions in 1991 and is considering eliminating another three by 1995. Overall, its real budget authority for 1991 drops 6 percent, and its procurement account 28 percent.

The army should also consider eliminating two other expensive systems that are oriented primarily toward the central front: the *Patriot* air defense missile and the *Bradley* fighting vehicle. The 1991 budget requests $1.6 billion to buy 817 *Patriots* and 600 *Bradleys*, even though the army inventory already contains thousands of these weapons. The army should also drop its requests for $112 million (up 239 percent from 1990) for research on a new short-range nuclear missile to replace the *Lance* and for $193 million for the procurement of 377 army tactical missile systems (ATACMS). The nuclear replacement for the *Lance* is designed to be deployed in West Germany to attack East Germany and Poland. With German reunification, this contingency is remote, to say the least. Similarly, ATACMS, a surface-to-surface conventional missile with a range of about 100 miles, is designed primarily to break up the second echelon of Soviet forces launching a blitzkrieg on Western Europe. With Soviet troops heading home as former satellites ask them to leave, such an attack is another implausible scenario. Finally, the army should cancel once and for all the light-armed scout attack helicopter (LHX), which continues to experience delays (it will not be operational until 1997), rising costs (unit costs for 2,100 are $20 million), and technical problems.

Not only can the army safely eliminate five active divisions between now and 1995 (assuming the success of negotiations with the Soviets), it should also be planning to eliminate at least five more divisions by the end of the century as the U.S. military presence in Europe drops from 300,000 to about 50,000, and in Korea to 10,000. That would leave the army with a force of eight active and ten reserve divisions in the year 2000.

Navy. The U.S. Navy budget for 1991 is virtually the same as for 1990. The navy does propose to retire or deactivate twelve older ships, and it has reduced its end strength slightly, from 551 to 546 ships. However, the navy still plans to maintain fourteen carrier battle groups, a number consistent with the maritime strategy of carrying the battle toward the Soviet Union. The navy seeks $3.7 billion for five *Aegis*-equipped *Burke*-class destroyers (DDG-51),[38] designed primarily to protect the fleet from attacks by Soviet naval aviation and Soviet missile firing ships, and another $3.7 billion for two *Seawolf* submarines (SSN-21), designed to attack Soviet fleet ballistic missile submarines in their home waters (in addition to the eighteenth *Trident* submarine). Not only do these vessels lack a clear mission in the post-containment era, but they also would consume 80 percent of the navy's $9.2 billion shipbuilding budget in 1991. This allocation permits the navy to build only fourteen ships. Since navy ships last an average of about twenty-five years, this shipbuilding program would lead to a 350-ship navy, one too small even for the post-containment era.

A reasonable force goal for the navy in the mid-1990s would be approximately 500 ships centered around twelve carrier battle groups, a number that the five presidents who preceded Ronald Reagan found adequate, during more perilous times than the 1990s, to protect the sea lanes and project U.S. power. The navy could then retire five older carriers, saving $800 million per carrier on the "service-life extension" program. Such a goal would also allow the navy to cancel the SSN-21 and to cut the number of air wings from fifteen (thirteen active and two reserve) to thirteen (eleven active and two reserve), thereby relieving pressure to rush the advanced tactical aircraft (ATA) and the navy version of the advanced tactical fighter (NATF) into production. And the navy should retire both remaining battleships, because they are expensive to operate ($1 billion over 1991–1995) and inappropriate for the changing international environment.

In addition, the navy should develop a less expensive and less sophisticated frigate than the costly DDG-51s and a new small submarine to replace the *Trident*. Finally, because the changes in Eastern Europe mean that the West will have much more mobilization time to deal with an unexpected Soviet breakout, the Navy should begin developing a fast sealift program to replace current reliance on airlift. For example, fast sealift could deliver more tons to Europe (in two weeks) than airplanes can, for about 5 percent of the cost.[39] As the Persian Gulf deployment demonstrated, 95 percent of the tonnage has to move by sea. Indeed, it was the shortage of sealift that doubled the time required for deployment of the complete force to the Gulf. A C-17 can lift only one M-1 tank. An SL-7 ship can move fifty.

For the long term the navy should be aiming toward a force of nine carrier battle groups, with seven active and two reserve air wings and 400 ships. This force should be adequate to protect the sea-lanes and support flexible deployments to various areas of the world in the next century.

Air Force. The 1991 U.S. Air Force budget increases in nominal terms by $1.9 billion, or 2 percent. Its procurement budget increases by 4 percent, and no wonder. Besides the plethora of strategic programs mentioned earlier, the air force wants to purchase six C-17 cargo planes for $2.7 billion and 1,250 advanced medium-range air-to-air missiles (AMRAAMs) for $0.9 billion; continue full-scale research on the advanced tactical fighter (ATF), which eventually will cost at least $100 million each for 750 planes; and buy 186 additional F-15s and F-16s for almost $5 billion. The service leaves its conventional force structure virtually intact.

Since the C-17, AMRAAM, and ATF are oriented primarily toward a European contingency, they can easily be canceled. As discussed, with more mobilization time, fast sealift is a much better buy than the C-17, and as the Persian Gulf crisis demonstrated, the most pressing need of our current forces is for fast sealift. Thus, the program for the new cargo plane, which would cost about $42 billion for the 211 planes envisioned, should be terminated now. The AMRAAM continues to have problems in identifying enemy aircraft beyond visual range, and its costs continue to rise (at $700,000 a missile and rising, its costs are already 22 percent above the level that the secretary of defense certified to Congress as the absolute limit in 1986). Moreover, its primary mission—engaging sophisticated aircraft in a complex air battle—is far less likely to be needed than when planning for the missile began. Rather than continue to throw good money after bad, the air force should kill the AMRAAM right away. The ATF, which suffers from similar development and cost problems, should be canceled, especially since there is little need now for a long-range *Stealth* plane to fly deep behind Soviet and Warsaw Pact front lines. In its place the Air Force should develop a new combat air support plane as a follow-on to the A-10. Any high-technology missions can be handled by the two existing squadrons of stealth fighters (F-117A).

The size of the air force should decline. There is no need in the postcontainment era to maintain thirty-five tactical air wings whose primary mission is to wage high-intensity combat in Europe. Indeed, under the now outmoded NATO plans, 100 of the 116 squadrons in these thirty-five wings were to be in place in Europe within ten days after a war began. To reflect the new environment, the air force could cut five active wings, or seventeen squadrons, by 1995 and another seven wings by the end of the century.

CONCLUSION

The security interests of the United States would be adequately protected by a 1995 defense budget of $227 billion and a 2000 budget of $152 billion (in 1990 dollars), distributed as shown in Table 7. In 1995 the U.S. Army and the U.S. Marine Corps together will have twenty-seven active and reserve ground divisions, the U.S. Air Force thirty active and reserve wings, and the U.S. Navy twelve carrier battle groups with thirteen air wings and 500 ships. This force would be augmented by 6,000 nuclear weapons and have an active duty military

Table 7   Defense Authority FY 1990–2000 (1990 $ Billions)

	FY 1990		FY 1995		FY 2000		Change 1990–2000	
	AMT	%	AMT	%	AMT	%	AMT	%
Military Personnel	79	27	63	28	40	26	-39	-49
O&M	87	30	66	29	43	28	-44	-51
Procurement	83	28	56	25	37	24	-46	-53
RDT&E	37	13	36	16	28	18	-9	-24
Other*	8	2	6	2	4	3	-4	-50
Total	292	100	227	100	152	100	-140	-48

*Includes construction of family housing and offsetting receipts.

strength of 1.5 million and a civilian force of 750,000. Even this reduced force would be more than sufficient to handle the current deployment to the Gulf. By 2000, a continuation of the present trends in international relations would permit elimination of an additional four divisions, seven wings, 100 ships, 2,000 nuclear weapons, and an additional 750,000 military and civilian personnel. Real spending in all the categories except research and development would fall as the active force structure declines and emphasis shifts to protecting the U.S. technology base.

Indeed the Pentagon is already moving in that direction in the area of force structure. The Cheney plan, which, as noted above, was presented to the Executive/Legislative Budget Summit on June 19, 1990, envisions an even smaller total force structure by 1995. Cheney's illustrative plan would cut reserve as well as active force structure between now and 1995. Thus, he would be able to afford only a total of twenty-two ground divisions, twenty-five air force fighter wings, and 455 ships. A mix relying more heavily upon reserves, as illustrated above, would allow the United States to have five more ground divisions, five more tactical air wings, and forty-five more ships.

However, the Cheney force structure plan does not achieve significant budgetary reductions because it keeps readiness, modernization, and research, development, testing, and evaluation (RDT&E) at the levels associated with a higher force structure. By dropping readiness rates 25 percent below these current levels (flexible readiness), slowing modernization (living off some of the inventory built up during the 1980s), and emphasizing research as opposed to development, Cheney's 25 percent force structure cut would also result in a budget reduction of 25 percent.

As regards the military risks and obligations of the United States, the nation has clearly entered a new era. Too many civilian and military leaders of the Pentagon have not crossed the threshold psychologically or fiscally. The U.S. defense program is still basically flawed. The latest defense guidance still continues to dwell on a Soviet threat that is no longer credible.[40] In fact, DoD is still drafting alternative defense plans in case Gorbachev falters. Because the fear of a Soviet threat, in an era when the

Soviet empire and even the Soviet Union itself are crumbling, cannot keep sustaining a robust military posture, the problem is not that the defense budget will remain too high but that it will drop too fast. As Representative Les Aspin has noted, prior to the Iraqi invasion of Kuwait, the defense budget was in a political free-fall.[41] Even conservative republicans are urging massive military reductions and adopting George McGovern's 1972 campaign theme of "come home America."[42] The formidable and important challenge to the Bush administration is to explain to the American people that in the new world order, even without the specter of the "evil empire," a substantial military force remains vital to U.S. security. It must be a military appropriate for a great power dependent for its economic well-being on the smooth working of the international political system, which has always needed military power in the background. Indeed, the Iraqi invasion of Kuwait showed that military power is still vital if that system is to operate. Moreover, it also demonstrated that American military power must be in the forefront of preserving the new world order.

The coming reductions in defense spending will also require some economic adjustments at home. Overall, reducing defense spending by 25 percent by 1995 and 50 percent by 2000, and reducing it by 2 to 3 percent of GNP, will have a positive effect on the U.S. economy. Some communities will need short-term assistance to deal with base or plant closings. If a comprehensive plan is not developed, the 1991–1995 period will replay the events of 1989, when members of the military-industrial complex, scrambling for scarce defense dollars, persuaded Congress to stretch out rather than cancel programs. In addition, the downsizing of the military-industrial complex will require a policy to protect those technologies and manufacturing capacities needed for a possible mobilization. A shrinking military force will narrow the opportunities for upward mobility used by many members of the lower socioeconomic classes. Alternative educational programs need to be developed for them. In short, the Bush administration should develop a strategy to deal with the end of the Cold War rather than try to preserve the military structure that won it. Its 1991–1995 program does not do that job.

NOTES

1. This is an updated and revised version of a chapter that appeared in Henry J. Aaron, ed., *Setting National Priorities: Policy for the 1990s* (Washington, D.C.: Brookings, 1990), pp. 401–443.
2. Unless otherwise indicated, all years referring to defense budgets or to the defense program are fiscal years.
3. See, for example, the comments of U.S. Marine Generals John J. Sheehan and Charles E. Wilhelm about army contingency forces, in Michael E. Gordon with Bernard E. Trainor, "Army, Facing Cuts Reported Seeking to Reshape Itself," *New York Times*, December 12, 1989, p. 1. These interservice battles are discussed in more depth below.
4. Unit costs of individual weapon systems are calculated by dividing the total cost of researching, developing, testing, and producing the system by the number of units purchased. Since the research, development, and testing costs must be paid regardless of how many units are procured, unit costs drop throughout the production run as the up-front costs are amortized.
5. Unless otherwise indicated, all figures for defense are expressed in 1991 dollars and refer to budget authority for the Department of Defense (budget category 051).
6. The term was actually coined by C. Wright Mills.
7. Department of Defense (Comptroller), *The Economics of Defense Spending: A Look at the Realities* (Washington, D.C.: U.S. Government Printing Office [U.S. GPO], July 1972), p. 149; and Lawrence J. Korb, *The Fall and Rise of the Pentagon: American Defense Policies in the 1970s* (Westport, Conn.: Greenwood Press, 1979), p. 38.
8. Abraham S. Becker, *Sitting on Bayonets: The Soviet Defense Burden and the Slowdown of Soviet Defense Spending*, JRS-10 RAND/UCLA Center for the Study of Soviet International Behavior, December 1985, pp. 4–13.
9. See, for example, the comments of the chairmen of the House and Senate Armed Services Committees, quoted in Lawrence J. Korb, "Spending without Strategy," *International Security*, Vol. 12, No. 1 (Summer 1987), p. 169.
10. Becker, *Sitting on Bayonets*; and William W. Kaufmann, *Glasnost, Perestroika, and U.S. Defense Spending* (Washington, D.C.: Brookings, 1989), Table 2.
11. William W. Kaufmann and Lawrence J. Korb, *The 1990 Defense Budget* (Washington, D.C.: Brookings, 1989), pp. 9 and 20.
12. Although large, the final Reagan plan was considerably smaller than the $1.9 trillion in budget authority Reagan planned to request before the stock market crash of October 1987. His pre-crash projection for the 1990 budget authority was $344 billion, $38 billion (or 12 percent) above his actual request.
13. Korb, "Spending without Strategy," p. 169.
14. Kaufmann and Korb, *1990 Defense Budget*, p. 20.
15. Richard Cheney, *Annual Report to the President and the Congress* (Washington, D.C.: U.S. GPO, January 1990), p. 76.
16. Francis Carlucci, *Department of Defense Annual Report, Fiscal Year 1990* (Washington, D.C.: U.S. GPO, January 1989), p. 171; and Patrick E. Tyler and R. Jeffrey Smith, "Study Finds NATO War Plans Outdated," *Washington Post*, November 29, 1989, p. A1.

17. For an analysis of the positions of both sides in the START and CFE talks, see Kaufmann, *Glasnost, Perestroika, and U.S. Defense Spending,* Tables 20, 21, 22, 24, and 25. Because the ordnance carried by bombers is discounted, the actual number of weapons allowed under START I will be more than 6,000.

18. Patrick E. Tyler and R. Jeffrey Smith, "Bush Alerted in May to Soviet Military Cuts," *Washington Post,* December 11, 1989, p. A1.

19 "HASC Tasks," December 1989 and Council for Livable World Education Fund, *The Soviet Threat: 14 Ways It Has Declined,* January 1990, p. 1; and Reneo Lukic, "Gorbachev's Choice of Butter Over Guns," *Defense and Disarmament Alternatives,* May 1990, pp. 1–2.

20. Patrick E. Tyler, "Cheney Finds CIA Director Is No Comrade in Arms," *Washington Post,* March 6, 1990, p. A21. See also the testimony of Richard Perle, former assistant secretary of defense for international security, to the Senate Armed Services Committee on January 24, 1990 (Perle's testimony is summarized in *Defense Daily,* January 25, 1990, pp. 124–125), and that of James Schlesinger, former secretary of defense, to the same committee on January 30, 1990 (Schlesinger's testimony is summarized in R. Jeffrey Smith, "Schlesinger Urges Radical Cuts in Europe," *Washington Post,* January 31, 1990, p. A12).

21. Robert Scarborough, "Joint Chiefs 'Accept' Reform as Irreversible," *Washington Times,* March 12, 1990, p. 6.

22. Tom Wicker, "Cheney Vs. Webster," *New York Times,* March 8, 1990, p. 24.

23. "Defense Floor Speeches by U.S. Senator Sam Nunn," *Defense Budget Blanks,* March 22, 1990; *The Changed Threat Environment of the 1990s,* March 29, 1990; *A New Military Strategy,* April 19, 1990; and *Implementing a New Military Strategy: The Budget Decision,* April 20, 1990.

24. Helen Dewar, "GOP Senators Propose Doubling Bush's Defense Cuts," *Washington Post,* April 6, 1990, p. 4.

25. R. Jeffrey Smith, "Powell Says Defense Needs Massive Review," *Washington Post,* May 7, 1990, p. 1.

26. Michael R. Gordon, "Cheney Gives Plan to Reduce Forces by 25 Percent in 5 Years," *New York Times,* June 20, 1990, p. 1; Rick Maze, "Cheney's Cut Scenario Taken as Fact by Lawmakers," *Air Force Times,* July 9, 1990, p. 3; and William J. Eaton, "270 Billion, 5-Year Defense Cut Urged, *Los Angeles Times,* June 29, 1990, p. 35.

27. According to Congressman Les Aspin (D-Wis.), Secretary of Defense Cheney has become irrelevant. Senator John Warner (R-Va.), the ranking republican on the Armed Services Committee, contends Cheney is more of a bystander than a leader. The two legislators are quoted in Patrick J. Sloyan, "Pentagon Chief on Defensive," *Long Island Newsday,* April 1, 1990, p. 13.

28. Tom Donnelly, "Army Marines Butt Heads over Contingency Role," *Army Times,* March 26, 1990, p. 3; Jeffrey Record, "The Army Goes to War with the Marines," *Baltimore Sun,* February 16, 1990, p. 15; and Bruce Van Voorst, "Who Needs the Marines?" *Time,* May 21, 1990, p. 28.

29. Stephen C. LeSueur, "Air Force Plan Seeks to Cut Carriers," *Inside the Navy,* April 2, 1990, p. 8; Barbara Amouyal, "Rice Proposes A-12 Sacrifice for B-2," *Defense News,* April 9, 1990, p. 4; and "Top Secret A-12 Silhouette Leaked by Air Force," *Navy News and Undersea Technology,* June 18, 1990, p. 1.

30. Stephen C. LeSueur, *Inside the Pentagon,* April 20, 1990, p. 1.
31. Mark Thompson, "Pentagon Cuts Fall Way Short," *Fort Worth Star-Telegram,* February 27, 1990, p. 1.
32. Kaufmann and Korb, *1990 Defense Budget,* pp. 23 and 30; and Cheney, *Annual Report,* p. 80.
33. Cheney, *Annual Report,* p. 31.
34. Warren Strobel, "Soviets Drop SDI Link to Treaty," *Washington Times,* February 9, 1990, p. 1.
35. William Safire, "Taking Baker to the Cleaners," *New York Times,* May 21, 1990, p. 21; Walter Mossberg and Gerald Seib, "Agreements Reached at Summit Appear to Be More Favorable Than Critics Maintain," *Wall Street Journal,* June 8, 1990, p. 12; and Richard Burt, "START's Misguided Critics," *Washington Post,* June 10, 1990, p. C-7.
36. R. Jeffrey Smith, "2 Missiles Unnecessary, Ex-Chiefs Say," *Washington Post,* February 3, 1990, p. A5; and "Soviets Press U.S. for Deeper Reductions in Strategic Weapons," *Washington Post,* February 25, 1990, p. 14.
37. "Cut B-2, but Leave Sealift Alone, Carlucci Tells Congress," *Navy News and Undersea Technology,* February 26, 1990, p. 6.
38. *Aegis* is the code name of a sophisticated air defense system deployed on cruisers and destroyers. The system is designed to shoot down incoming missiles and airplanes that threaten a carrier task force.
39. Kaufmann and Korb, *The 1990 Defense Budget,* p. 44. Although in 1990 Congress appropriated $600 million for fast sealift, Secretary of Defense Cheney reprogrammed the funds.
40. Barbara Amouyal, "Defense Plan Gives Broad Latitude," *Defense News,* February 12, 1990, p. 1; and Patrick E. Tyler, "New Pentagon Guidance Cites Soviet Threat in Third World," *Washington Post,* February 13, 1990, p. A1.
41. His remarks are quoted in *Aerospace Daily,* December 8, 1989, p. 388.
42. See for example, Kevin Phillips, "Troops Must Come Home to Win the Economic War," *Los Angeles Times,* March 4, 1990, p. M3.